THE POVERTY OF REVOLUTION

SUSAN ECKSTEIN

The Poverty of Revolution

The State and the Urban Poor in Mexico

PRINCETON UNIVERSITY PRESS

PRINCETON, NEW JERSEY

Copyright © 1977 by Princeton University Press
Published by Princeton University Press,
Princeton, New Jersey
In the United Kingdom: Princeton University Press,
Guildford, Surrey

Library of Congress Cataloging in Publication Data
will be found on the last printed page of this book

Publication of this book has been aided by a grant from
The Andrew W. Mellon Foundation

PRINTED IN THE UNITED STATES OF AMERICA
by Princeton University Press, Princeton, New Jersey

To Ruth *and* George Eckstein,
parents and friends

CONTENTS

CONTENTS

LIST OF ILLUSTRATIONS

LIST OF TABLES

ACKNOWLEDGMENTS

I wish, above all, to thank the people who live and work in the areas I studied for their seemingly endless cooperation, concern, and interest in my work; their warmth, confidence, and friendship; and the information and experiences they shared with me during my stay in Mexico in 1967-68 and again in 1971. I particularly appreciate their willingness and desire to invite me to their homes, fiestas, and meetings, and to introduce me to their families. They not only made the study possible but they also helped sensitize me to the first-hand moments of happiness and despair of the urban poor, which my own sheltered life and readings had not. Unknowingly, they transformed me intellectually, as I point out in Appendix A.

While in Mexico I also benefited from discussions with Pablo González Casanova, Rodolfo Stavenhagen, Luis Lesur, Luis Leñero, Luis Unikel, Bernardo Giner de los Rios (Jr.), architects and social workers of El Centro Operacional de Vivienda y Poblamiento (COPEVI), and professionals and employees affiliated with various government offices. Luis Unikel and Luis Lesur were especially helpful in familiarizing me sufficiently with Mexico City to know which areas to include in my study. Luz Hernández Moreno, then a sociology student at the National University, assisted me with the questionnaire and in many other small but important ways.

I did the research in 1967-68 for my doctoral thesis. I therefore am grateful to Juan Linz, Robert Alford, Douglas Chalmers, Lambros Comitas, and Bernard Barber who served on my dissertation committee. Although Juan had left Columbia for Yale before I completed my field work and although Robert was only at Columbia as a Visiting Professor the year I completed my dissertation, both gave me encouragement, counsel, and criticism which I appreciate until this day. When I initially formulated my research project and returned from Mexico, Terence Hopkins, then at Columbia, also gave me helpful advice and encouragement.

In addition, I have benefited in writing this book especially from detailed comments on the manuscript by James Cockcroft and George Eckstein (my father), and from comments on specific chapters by Samuel Bowles, John McKinlay, Daniel Bell, Douglas Hibbs, Rosabeth Kanter, and Frances Piven. David Barkin, Wayne Cornelius, Stanley Davis, Ralph della Cava, Vernon Dibble, Mathew Edel, Peter Evans, Roslyn Feldberg, Richard Flacks, Herbert Gans, Louisa Hoberman, Eva Hunt, Christopher Jencks, Donald Keesing, Anthony Leeds, Nathaniel Leff, Sol Levine, Arthur Liebman, Seymour M. Lipset, Joan Nelson, Michael Ross, Tom Scheff, Philippe Schmitter, Peter Smith, Arthur Stinchcombe, Ellen K. Trimberger, Michael Useem, the late Ivan Vallier, Lois Wasserspring, and Maurice Zeitlin also have helpfully criticized material I included in the book. Louise Seidel has kindly typed much of the manuscript, and drafts of it, over the years, and Polly Hanford of Princeton University Press has provided me with excellent editorial assistance. To all of them I am grateful.

Financially, I received support for various phases of the study from the Sociology Department and the Institute for Latin American Studies at Columbia University, the National Defense Foreign Language fellowship program, and the National Institute of Mental Health. In addition, I wrote part of the study with the help of the Fletcher School of Law and Diplomacy of Tufts University where I was a Research Associate in 1969-70. The Sociology Department, particularly Irwin Sanders, and the Graduate Faculty of Boston University enabled me to return to Mexico in 1971 to do additional research and helped finance writing expenses. During my second period of field work the Instituto Mexicano de Estudios Sociales (IMES) provided me with excellent assistance, thanks to the Mexican office of the Ford Foundation.

I am grateful to Jane Cowan Brown for permission to use Plans I and II, which appeared originally in her "Patterns of Intra-urban Settlement in Mexico City: An Examination of the Turner Theory." Cornell University, Latin American Studies Program Dissertation Series, 40, 1972, and to Dirección General De Planificación, Mexico, for permission to use the data in Plan III. All plans were redrawn by Mr. R. L. Williams, Cartographer, Yale University Map Laboratory, New Haven.

These friends, colleagues, and institutions, in their own special ways, helped write this book. It has been a personally rewarding experience to me.

LIST OF ABBREVIATIONS

CNOP — National Confederation of "Popular" Organizations (Confederación Nacional de Organizaciones Populares)

CONASUPO — National "Popular" Subsistence Corporation (Compañía Nacional de Subsistencias Populares)

CTM — Mexican Confederation of Labor (Confederación de Trabajadores Mexicanos)

DDF — Department of the Federal District (Departamento del Distrito Federal)

FCP — Federation of Proletarian Neighborhoods (Federación de Colonias Proletarias)

FUPC — United Front for the Defense of Proletarian Residents (Frente Unico Pro-Defensa de Colonos)

IMSS — Mexican Institute of Social Security (Instituto Mexicano de Seguro Social)

ISSSTE — Social Security Institute for Government Workers (Instituto de Seguridad y Servicios Sociales de los Trabajadores al Servicio del Estado)

PAN — National Action Party (Partido de Acción Nacional)

PARM — Authentic Party of the Mexican Revolution (Partido Auténtico de la Revolución Mexicana)

PPS — "Popular" Socialist Party (Partido Popular Socialista)

PRI — Party of the Institutionalized Revolution (Partido Revolucionario Institucional)

THE POVERTY OF REVOLUTION

"*It is the Revolution, the magical word, the word that is going to change everything, that is going to bring us immense delight and a quick death.*"

Octavio Paz, *Labyrinth of Solitude*

"*A revolution is shaped on battlefields, but once it is corrupted, though battles are still won, the revolution is lost. We have all been responsible. We have allowed ourselves to be divided and controlled by the ruthless, the ambitious, and the mediocre. Those who wanted a true revolution, radical and uncompromising, are unfortunately ignorant and bloody men. And the literate element want only a half-revolution, compatible with what interests them, their only interest, getting on in the world, living well, replacing Don Porfirio's elite. There you have Mexico's drama.*"

Carlos Fuentes, *The Death of Artemio Cruz*

The state[1] in a semidependent[2] capitalist society like Mexico depends on capital to generate production and to provide resources for the administrative apparatus. State functionaries, in turn, protect interests of capital, both national and foreign, irrespective of their own class background. If they do not, capital may be reluctant to invest domestically; or it may withdraw its financial support of the government or use its influence to oust those formally in command of the regime.

A capitalist state, however, concerns itself not merely with the accumulation process—in the immediate interests of capital—but also with legitimation. In a modern polity legitimation depends on the support of all major socioeconomic groups. Since diverse socioeconomic groups do not always perceive their interests as identical, the state can most effectively deal with conflicting interests and thereby resolve both its economic and political exigencies if it operates with a modicum of autonomy of all groups.

There is no general consensus concerning the degree and bases

Note: Works cited briefly in footnotes are given in full in the Bibliography.

[1] By "state" I mean "public" as distinct from "private" organizations, institutions, and relations. Political institutions which form part of a state apparatus include government bureaucracies, the military, the executive, the judiciary, and legislature. By defining it as a specifically political set of institutions the relationship between the state, on the one hand, and society and economy, on the other hand, and the relationship between state and class power, can be treated as problematic and variant under specific historical conditions.

[2] In terms of economic production and diversification, and dependence on foreign capital and technology, Mexico, by international standards, represents a middle level of economic development. Its economy is less autonomous and more vulnerable than the economies of advanced capitalist countries, but more autonomous and less vulnerable than the economies of subsistence and export-oriented mono-crop and extractive-oriented economies. In Wallerstein's terminology, Mexico represents a "semiperipheral" country within the world capitalist system, dependent on the "core" industrial countries but in different ways than the "peripheral" countries. See Immanuel Wallerstein, "The Rise and Future Demise of the World Capitalist System," pp. 387-415.

of effective state autonomy,[3] in either highly industrialized or dependent capitalist countries. At one extreme, the state is depicted as weak, owing to domestic and international pressures. Accordingly, it is viewed as an institution subservient to dominant economic interests, either (1) because it is the "executive committee" or the protector of the "bourgeoisie,"[4] or (2) because those in command posts are recruited (a) from the same class as the economic elites whose interests they share[5] or (b) from lower socioeconomic stratum, making them dependent on the state bureaucracy and the interests it serves.[6]

Alternatively, commentators on international capitalism note that the power of the nation-state is weak to the extent that multinational corporations act independently of national governments,[7] international institutions assume functions previously performed by national governments and national capital,[8] or an international division of labor and world market dominate national markets and state structures.[9] Other commentators assess the power of the state relative to that of sociopolitical but not economic forces: They view the state as weak when other competing domestic institutions, groups, and sources of loyalty are strong, including noncapitalist ones.[10]

[3] In reference to the state, "effective" autonomy refers to actual autonomy and power, whereas "formal" autonomy refers merely to openly avowed, official autonomy and power.

[4] See Karl Marx, "The Eighteenth Brumaire of Louis Bonaparte"; Nicos Poulantzas, *Political Power and Social Class*. Poulantzas argues that under the capitalist mode of production the state must necessarily operate autonomously in order to maintain and protect the interests of the capitalist class. However, he recognizes that under exceptional conditions—when competing classes or factions within the dominant class are in equilibrium so that none of them dominate—the state is not the political organizer of the capitalist class. Like Miliband, who criticizes Poulantzas for his failure to systematically and consistently differentiate class from state power, Poulantzas confuses form with function. For Miliband's critique of Poulantzas, see Ralph Miliband, "Poulantzas and the Capitalist State."

[5] See Miliband, *The State in Capitalist Society*; C. Wright Mills, *The Power Elite*; G. William Domhoff, *Who Rules America?*

[6] Robert Michels, *Political Parties*.

[7] See C. P. Kindleberger, *American Business Abroad*, p. 207; Robin Murray, "The Internationalization of Capital and the Nation State"; Raymond Vernon, *Sovereignty at Bay: The Multinational Spread of U.S. Enterprises.*

[8] Vernon, *Sovereignty at Bay.*

[9] V. I. Lenin, *Imperialism*; Nikolai Bukharin, *Imperialism and World Economy*; Wallerstein, "Rise and Future Demise."

[10] K. Silvert, "The Costs of Anti-Nationalism."

At the other extreme, the state is depicted as capable of acting free from pressures of particular social groups with narrow interests when the political sphere is institutionalized, i.e., adaptable, complex in structure and multifunctional, internally coherent, and differentiated from social forces in terms of norms, behavior, and interests.[11] Furthermore, some scholars argue that the state *by definition* enjoys certain autonomy because of the functions it "necessarily" performs. However, these scholars do not all agree on what those functions are. Warren,[12] for example, argues that because the capitalist state performs functions for capital, it necessarily is more powerful than dominant economic interests, while Parsons and Smelser[13] argue that because the polity commands generalized power it is able to act independently of particular interests. Still other scholars view state autonomy as problematic, depending on specific historical conditions: They see the state as an independent force only when domestic and international groups are weak and subservient to the state, or when such groups are played off against each other.[14] However, even when the state is capable of initiating independent activities it may primarily act in the interests of specific domestic or foreign forces nominally independent of it, and not necessarily by choice.[15]

Despite these differing points of view, it seems likely that the

[11] Samuel Huntington, *Political Order in Changing Societies*, pp. 12-24.

[12] Bill Warren, "Imperialism and Capitalist Industrialization."

[13] Talcott Parsons and Neil Smelser, *Economy and Society*, p. 57.

[14] Marx, "The Eighteenth Brumaire"; Francisco Weffort, "State and Mass in Brasil"; Hamza Alavi, "The State in Post-Colonial Societies." While Marx recognized that the state apparatus can be independent of class control, he claimed that such rule was inherently unstable and temporary. According to Miliband, in his essay "Poulantzas," Marx and Engels by definition imply autonomy in their conception of the state for they claim that the modern state is a committee for managing the *common* affairs of the *whole* bourgeoisie and that the state *cannot* meet this need without enjoying a certain degree of autonomy. The logical implications of Miliband's assertions are that there is no state if the political apparatus does not function accordingly. Yet Marx noted, for example, that the French state at a particular point in history ruled in the interests of finance capital, not the whole of the bourgeoisie.

[15] For a study of conditions under which state bureaucrats in Japan and Turkey were able to act sufficiently independently of domestic and foreign interests to initiate a revolutionary transformation of their nations' respective political economies, see Ellen Kay Trimberger, *Bureaucratic Revolution from Above.*

state can assume independence in directing political and economic development and distribution to the extent that (1) those holding the highest posts do not have specific economic interests, for they otherwise might be concerned primarily with protecting those interests in the status quo; (2) it is financially autonomous, and in command of large resources relative to domestic and foreign forces so that it can institute programs and policies of its choosing, including ones that conflict with national and international interests; and (3) power is centralized.[16]

This book deals with relations between the Mexican state and urban poor. It shows how the state regulates lower-class city-dwellers in the basic interests of capital. Seemingly paradoxical, the official institutions which link the poor to the regime in a subordinate capacity are ones closely identified with the country's revolution. Thus, the book deals also with revolution. It is a study of poverty despite revolution, and the poverty of revolution, of revolutionary efforts to create a society in which all classes more or less equally share the nation's wealth.

The Mexican revolution began in 1910 and officially ended in 1917 with the initiation of a new Constitution.[17] Although it was not until the 1930s that major changes were instituted which effectively undermined the political and economic power base of landed oligarchs, since then the impact of the revolution appears far-reaching. Yet, official rhetoric notwithstanding, many of these developments are not direct by-products of the societal upheaval, and the revolution has not benefited all classes equally. Viewed "from below" the accomplishments of the revolution have been meager. The social and economic standing of the poor relative to the wealthy has not improved significantly. Moreover, new bases of poverty and inequality have arisen: the number of city-dwellers who are ill-housed and ill-fed has increased absolutely

[16] While the state may appear to act autonomously and coherently, Offe argues in his discussion of the state in advanced capitalist countries that the state by definition contains internal contradictions due to exigencies of the accumulation process and the internal mode of operation of the state. Claus Offe, "The Theory of the Capitalist State and the Problem of Policy Formation."

[17] The 1910-17 period actually involved no radical transformation of the social system. It was a period of civil war, not revolution. Consequently, official nomenclature does not reflect reality. For alternative interpretations of the Mexican upheaval, see the anthology edited by Stanley Ross, *Is the Mexican Revolution Dead?*

and proportionately. Despite this impoverishment, electoral participation helps legitimate the inegalitarian society and makes the poor share responsibility for the government.

Specifically, the book illustrates how the Mexican capitalist state deals with urban poor in three low-income areas of Mexico City:[18] an old center city slum, with a history predating the Spanish Conquest; a quasi-rural-looking area which now is legalized but initially was founded in 1954 by an illegal land invasion; and a large "middle-class"-looking,[19] government-financed planned community, consisting of low-cost individual houses, which opened in 1964. The areas represent three distinct types of low-income dwelling environments housing organized urban poor.[20]

[18] The terms "lower status," "low income," and "poor," unfortunately, are used very loosely in the text as they are by most scholars and the public. However, in the Appendix to Chapter Seven I present an occupation-based classification for differentiating types of employed poor (and nonpoor). Other scholars have developed alternative schemas for differentiating types of poor, e.g., poor who supposedly are culpable for their state and those who are not. Thus, Nathan Glazer and Daniel Moynihan, in *Beyond the Melting Pot*, contrast "worthy" with "unworthy" poor, and David Matza, in his "Disreputable Poor," contrasts "reputable" with "disreputable" poor. The term "lower-status" and "low-income" areas are also used loosely here. Although the areas primarily house people with low incomes and low status jobs they also house some factory workers, salaried employees, and professionals. This is increasingly the case in the government-financed housing development. Moreover, the areas house few of the very poorest inhabitants of Mexico City, persons who for the most part live on the periphery of the metropolitan area, in the State of Mexico.

[19] I use the term "middle class" to refer to the consumer-oriented life-style generally associated with salaried white-collar employees and professionals in the U.S. This stratum does not constitute a class, defined in relation to the mode of production. Since the proportion of the Mexican population included in this stratum includes—according to most estimates—the top 15-30 percent of the population, it is not a statistically defined middle socioeconomic group. For a summary of different stratification profiles of Mexico, see Claudio Stern and Joseph Kahl, "Stratification Since the Revolution," p. 18.

[20] Other kinds of low-income housing settlements found in Latin American cities include government-initiated squatter settlements; high-rise multi-unit housing developments; squatter settlements not formed by organized invasions; (still) illegal squatter settlements formed by organized invasions; and commercially developed subdivisions. For discussions of types of Latin American housing settlements see Anthony Leeds, "Housing-Settlement Types," pp. 67-99; John Turner, "Housing Priorities," pp. 354-63; and Alejandro Portes, "The Urban Slum in Chile," pp. 235-48. For a discussion of my rationale for selecting the three areas under study see Appendix A.

By comparing urban poor and their organizational life in such different settings we are able to see the limited ways in which different housing environments shape poor people's economic prospects and politics independently of class forces.

The book focuses on the way state-linked forces, legally and informally, regulate the economic and political behavior of urban poor, even though individually and collectively the poor are able to secure certain benefits from the government and improve their level of well-being somewhat. Despite (and, paradoxically, partly due to) their efforts to acquire goods and services inhabitants of the three areas are restrained in their ability to improve their socioeconomic standing relative to well-to-do urban dwellers. The structure of the economy and polity is such that those who generally labor hardest do the most demeaning work for least pay.

The country's political economy, both presently and historically, has shaped the nature of benefits extended to residents, the way they are distributed, and the effect the allocations have on the larger economic and political order. The benefits indirectly facilitate industrialization and minimize civic disorder. By legalizing squatter's land claims the government provides a quick and inexpensive solution to the housing shortage, particularly for those who cannot afford housing on the honsubsidized market. Without access to such inexpensive housing the rate of migration undoubtedly would be lower and, consequently, the supply of cheap labor less and rural tensions perhaps greater.[21] The self-help housing construction, in turn, helps increase the value of city land at little cost to the government, and it serves as a means by which the state incorporates geographically uprooted persons into the official political and administrative apparatus.

The central thesis of the book is that the "life chances" of the urban poor in the three areas and their responses to their social and economic deprivation are largely by-products of societal class and power forces.[22] Hence, the first chapter focuses on the economic and political bases of inequality in postrevolutionary Mexico. It shows that the inequalities are rooted in the way the

[21] Huntington, for example, argues (p. 299) that migration is an alternative to revolution for dissatisfied peasants.

[22] I use the term "forces" in reference to power exerted by socioeconomic groups, not to the technical equipment and organization of labor which Marx implied by the term "forces of production."

revolution was institutionalized—above all, in the dynamics of semidependent capitalism and government policies which favor capitalists and capital-intensive development.

The remainder of the book centers on political and economic life in the three areas of Mexico City. Chapter Two contains a sketch of each area's historical origin, demographic composition, housing and general physical environment, and a portrayal of each area's institutional and job-opportunity structure. It also reveals the ways in which individuals and groups within the communities are linked to national institutions, how societal forces have shaped local developments over the years, and the degree to which each area constitutes a social and cultural community, apart from the city and society in which it is embedded.

The next three chapters focus on local politics, including locally operating institutions which though nominally nonpolitical, are politically influential. Chapter Three shows that residents have little power to pressure for greater economic equity or better community services, but that their ineffectiveness is not their own fault. They have political resources, above all, the capacity to organize and establish groups which are publicly committed to protecting their interests. Their political weakness in part stems from the co-optation of their groups,[23] or leaders of their groups, by higher-ranking functionaries affiliated with national institutions, and from informal and formal constraints which shape the way residents make use of these associations. Although not apparent from the grass-roots structure and populist objectives of the groups, the groups, in effect, serve to regulate local residents.

The following chapter, Four, shows that the Catholic Church is closely intertwined with the government and "official" party— the Institutionalized Revolutionary Party (PRI, the Party)—despite the anticlerical bent of the revolution and Constitutional restrictions on the Church's secular involvements. The linkages are largely attributable to the oligarchic interests of leaders of groups associated with the Church, government, and the PRI, and the structural arrangements which induce these leaders to engage in such interinstitutional relations. Thus, not only do we

[23] Throughout the text I use the terms "group," "organization," and "association" to refer to formally organized units operating in the three areas. I specify whether these formal groups are nominally autonomous or affiliated with national or supralocal organizations or institutions.

find that political institutions legitimated in terms of the revolution serve to subordinate the interests of organized urban poor to higher social groups but that groups formally restricted by the revolution have the same effect.

Chapter Five illustrates how the very conditions which weaken residents' organizational effectiveness through civic and Church-linked groups also predispose most of them to support the PRI, even though the PRI is identified with the highly inegalitarian regime. They support the PRI largely because they gain some benefits from the government and because they are exposed to an array of influences predisposing them toward the PRI, largely indirectly and unknowingly, through nominally nonpolitical groups. The political apparatus instituted in conjunction with the consolidation of the revolution and deriving its legitimacy from the revolution, clearly does not serve as a channel through which urban poor, as seen in the three areas, can significantly improve their social and economic lot. What then are the political-economic dynamics which shape their life chances? Chapters Six and Seven focus, respectively, on local businesses and the way in which residents get access to jobs.

The first of these two chapters includes a discussion of ownership of local enterprises and how market forces and government policies account for the fact that most of the businesses are small and precarious. Many of the small local commercial and artisan businesses probably would be wiped out by capitalist competition were it not for direct and indirect government protection. Nonetheless, the most lucrative enterprises, which have an advantage locally, are owned by nonresidents of higher social and economic standing than resident businessmen. The largest local factory, in fact, since 1971 belongs to a multinational corporation, reflecting the growing foreign penetration of the domestic industrial market.

The second of the two economic chapters outlines how the range of job options for male residents has been limited because of the way in which the overall economy has been developing. It also shows that the men's socioeconomic backgrounds largely have determined their employment prospects, but that jobs tend not to be handed down from father to son. Occupational "inheritance" stems from the influence class background has on access to schooling, social contacts, and, perhaps, socialization. In contrast to class-linked forces, cultural forces and neighborhood physical environs prove to have little bearing on the men's work: To the extent that cultural factors vary with occupational status they seem to be adaptations to structurally defined situations; to the extent that the job profiles of residents differ in each area they are attributable mainly to the divergent class backgrounds of the inhabitants.

The concluding chapter discusses why and how urban poverty persists and is generally transferred from generation to generation along family lines. Here general conditions associated with poverty in Mexico are compared with those found in other Latin American capitalist countries which never experienced a social revolution, in such advanced industrial capitalist countries as the U.S. and socialist Cuba. The cross-national comparisons help highlight the universal as well as the specific characteristics of poverty, the conditions which precipitate it, and the effects it generates. It also helps highlight the impact national political economies have in shaping opportunities of urban poor. Such knowledge can serve as a useful base for developing policies to eradicate the undesirable social, economic, and political attributes generally identified with poverty.

In sum, the research and analysis suggest that the specific institutions which serve to subordinate urban poor in the three areas to the government and the interests it above all serves are historically rooted in the political economy of postrevolutionary Mexico. National institutions have influenced which groups have been established locally, their structure, their concerns, and their relations with each other and the government. However, the types of processes operating within the three areas and the effects they generate are *not* unique to Mexico. Similar ones exist in other Latin American capitalist countries with no comparable revolutionary history, particularly those at more or less the same level of economic development. Mexico's ostensibly democratic political institutions provide urban poor with no special capacity to advance their own interests.

The concluding chapter is followed by an Appendix in which I describe the various interview and observational techniques, the documentary resources used in writing the different sections of the book, and some of the ethical dilemmas I faced in doing my research. In this Appendix I also discuss how, on the basis of my field work, I shifted my theoretical orientation and accordingly altered my methodology. The reader can thereby understand the basis of my analysis. The second Appendix contains a copy of the survey administered to one hundred residents in each of the three areas.

CHAPTER ONE

The State and Society: Inequality in Postrevolutionary Mexico

The Mexican government legitimates itself on the basis of a revolution, calls itself revolutionary, and justifies social change in the name of revolution. Although the revolution with which it associates itself began as a liberal "middle-class" effort to institute free elections, the movement eventually led to the introduction of an agrarian reform that freed Indians from bondage, unequivocally established capitalism as the dominant mode of production, made suffrage universal, and created a mass-based political party. Since the civil strife subsided the economy has diversified and expanded, and the polity has stabilized within an officially democratic rubric. While the specific institutional and organizational structures prevailing since the upheaval are rooted in Mexico's unique historical development, they reflect responses to capitalist forces which had already penetrated the society prior to 1910. The changes represent deliberate policies of a capitalist state, operating in a semidependent capacity within the international capitalist system. As a result, Mexico's social and economic structure in important respects resembles that of other Latin American capitalist countries similarly situated within the world economy. The state, despite its populist roots and populist veneer, acts primarily in the interests of capital, and not merely because it is preoccupied with capital accumulation.

THE STATE AND THE ECONOMY

Mexico is heralded as a model developing country. It enjoyed for a period of time one of the highest growth rates in the world. Agriculture, which now contributes only a small share to the nation's total production,[1] is highly productive by Latin American

---

[1] Statements on general and sectoral production, national and per capita wealth, income and land distribution, and trade patterns, including comparisons between Mexico and other Latin American countries, unless other-

and Third World standards.[2] The agricultural improvements
have been sufficient both to provide raw materials for industry
and to earn foreign exchange for financing capital imports for industry. As a result, industrial as well as agricultural production
has expanded markedly. However, modern firms, which are as-
suming increased importance in terms of value added and labor
employment, make the most intensive use of capital per worker
and have the highest labor productivity. Firms with fewer than
fifteen employees are the least productive.[3] In general, production
in both agriculture and in industry is highly concentrated: According to studies in the 1960s, 3 percent of the farms produced
55 percent of all agricultural production and .82 percent of all
firms accounted for 64.3 percent of industrial production.[4]

Along with a generally favorable attitude toward private capital, the government has directly and indirectly intervened to promote economic expansion in all sectors of the economy. Since
the 1930s the state is involved in the economy to a greater extent in Mexico than in most Latin American capitalist countries which have experienced no comparable revolutionary history. Mexico ranks fourth among Latin American countries in
the relative importance of government investments among total
fixed investments. President Lázaro Cárdenas' nationalization of
foreign oil companies in 1938 was an early and dramatic example
of state participation in the economy. Since then the Mexican
state has come largely to own the electric power industry, to participate in other productive industries, and to provide infrastructure, credit, protection, and guidance for the private sector, although mainly only to large-scale businesses.[5] In the process,

---

wise indicated, are based on statistics compiled by Economic Commission
for Latin America (ECLA), *Economic Survey of Latin America, 1970.*

[2] Mathew Edel, *Food Supply,* esp. pp. 119-24, and Bela Balassa, "La
industrialización y el comercio exterior," p. 45. In fact, agricultural productivity has grown faster in Mexico than in all other Latin American countries
save Costa Rica. See United States, Department of Agriculture, *Changes in
Agriculture in 26 Developing Nations: 1948 to 1963,* p. 6.

[3] Saúl Trejo Reyes, *Industrialización y empleo en México,* p. 86.

[4] Salomon Eckstein, *El marco macroeconómico del problema agrario;*
Ricardo Cinta, "Burgesía nacional y desarrollo," Table 8.

[5] See Raymond Vernon, *The Dilemma of Mexico's Development;* Vernon
(ed.), *Public Policy and Private Enterprise in Mexico.* One agency, the
Guarantee and Development Fund for Small-Scale and Medium-Sized Industry, since 1954 provides so-called small and medium-sized enterprises

both the state and the big-business sector have been strength-ened. Recent discoveries of oil fields may further this trend.

Mexico publicly assumes a nationalistic stance, partly because the extreme predominance of foreigners in the Porfirian boom preceding the revolution made a certain degree of suspiciousness toward foreign investment part of the ideological heritage of the revolution.[6] For the emerging local capitalists, ideological pre-dilections were reinforced by the logic of self-interest. As a re-sult, fifty years after the revolution the share of net external fi-nancing to total investment was only about 7 percent in Mexico, one of the lowest ratios in all of Latin America. Postrevolutionary governments have emphasized economic nationalism through legislation designed to discourage industrial imports. Legally, Mexican industrialists enjoy preferential fiscal treatment in firms which replace imports, and protection of their industries through import licenses, import tariffs, and export subsidies. The "Mexi-canization" decree of 1944 gave the government the power to re-quire, at its discretion, majority Mexican ownership. In 1972 and 1973 the concept of Mexicanization was broadened to include control over the conditions under which foreign technology and management could be imported, and tighter legal restriction on the foreign purchases of equity in Mexican firms.

While domestic capitalism antedates the revolution, it has been expanded and strengthened since then because the government regulates foreign-controlled ventures, and because the govern-ment initiated policies conducive to national capitalism at a time when international conditions were favorable to such develop-

---

with credit. However, it offers assistance to only 694 of the 55,068 businesses employing 1-15 workers, and no financial support to the extensive number of artisan shops with less than 25,000 pesos active capital (12.50 pesos = $1.00), even though the latter are ineligible for other sources of institutional credit and have limited resources of their own. Above all, the agency's funds are limited: it extends less than 6 percent of the supply and capital equipment loans. On the Fund, see Trejo Reyes, pp. 129-36, and United Nations Industrial Development Organization, *Small-Scale Industry in Latin America*, p. 289.

[6] In fact, though, postrevolutionary governments have welcomed for-eign capital all along. As early as 1921 President Obregón stated: ". . . every effort will be made to give guarantees to all businessmen who come here with the object of making investments, and every facility will be granted them for the development of their projects." Alvaro Obregón, "What's Ahead for Business in Mexico," p. 401.

ment. The country's productive capitalism was not an automatic
by-product of the revolution. The greatest spurt to domestic enterprises came as a result of Cárdenas' (1934-40) successful nationalization efforts and his other direct interventions in the economy, both facilitated by the collapse of international capital
during the world Depression.[7] Yet not until World War II did
domestic manufacturing significantly expand, thanks to Mexico's
increased foreign exchange earnings and a rising demand for industrial goods not available abroad.

Nonetheless, the government has not always acted in the immediate interests of domestic capital. As recent economic developments have been less impressive than in the immediate
postwar years, tensions between the government and certain capitalists have become progressively more apparent. Concerned not
merely with generating growth but also with maintaining popular support and legitimacy, President Luis Echeverría (1970-76)
instituted a 22 percent wage increase in September 1974, imposed a ceiling on profits, and assumed tighter control over the
booming private investment banks.

Such political exigencies are somewhat in conflict with the economic exigencies of the state. Capital flight, affecting the government's revenue base, is an ever present constraint on the government. Entrepreneurial opposition to prolabor government
policies was manifest particularly in the industrial city of
Monterrey where the local chamber of commerce organized a
one-day illegal lockout and threatened to withhold tax payments
if strikes against their establishments occurred. Since the government has been lax in enforcing the regulations on capital, initiating only a mild tax reform and no new controls on consumer
prices, it obviously still favors business over labor.

The government partly acts against the immediate interests of
domestic capital not only by instituting prolabor policies but also
at times by favoring foreign over national capital. Transnational
industrial corporations, largely formed with U.S. capital, have
increasingly penetrated the domestic market, just as they have
penetrated other foreign markets in the post-World War II era.
The government has allowed foreign firms to maintain complete
control of many of their businesses, exempted U.S. "border industries" from ordinary export and import controls, and extended

[7] See, for example, Lorenzo Meyer, *México y los Estados Unidos en el
conflicto petrolero, 1917-1942*, p. 200.

import licenses which have protected certain foreign interests. As a result, over one-fourth of industrial production—especially in the most dynamic branches of manufacturing—is generated by multinational corporations;[8] approximately half of the 400 largest industries in Mexico are foreign-owned, predominantly by Americans;[9] there are more subsidiaries of major U.S. multinational manufacturing corporations in Mexico than in any other Latin American country; and foreign corporations increasingly are buying firms founded by Mexicans.[10] Foreign capital is concentrated in the least competitive, most productive and profitable sectors of the economy, while national capital predominates in the competitive sectors.[11]

The experience of Mexico suggests that even when a dependent country adopts a strong nationalist position, in line with a revolutionary heritage, it has difficulty maintaining the upper hand over foreign interests, if capitalism is instituted as the dominant mode of production. Although it was widely believed in the 1940s and 1950s that "import-substitution" would reduce the economy's vulnerability to and dependence on the external sector, dependence on imports actually has grown and domestic industrialization has worsened the balance of payments deficit which increasingly is financed by external sources on progressively less favorable terms.[12]

While Mexico is heavily dependent on its northern neighbor for trade, its export trade is diversified. By the late 1960s Mexico's export product accounted for only 14 percent of total national exports, a lower ratio than in any other Latin American country. Moreover, Mexico had the highest proportion of manufactured goods among its exports of any Latin American country,

[8] Bernardo Sepúlveda et al., *Las empresas transnacionales en México*.

[9] José Luis Cecèña, *El capitalismo monopolista y la economía Méxicana*; Richard Newfarmer, "Structural Sources of Multinational Corporate Power in Recipient Economies."

[10] See James Vaupel and Joan Curhan, *The World's Multinational Enterprises*. Of the 412 subsidiaries of 162 companies operating in Mexico in 1967, 143 were completely new firms, and 221 were either acquisitions or branches of other previously established businesses.

[11] Sepúlveda et al., *Las empresas transnacionales*; Meyer et al., *La política exterior de México*; Fernando Fajnzylber and Trinidad Martinez Tarragó, "Las empresas transnacionales, expansión a nivel mundial y proyección en la industria Méxicana," cited in Meyer, "The Origins of Mexico's Authoritarian State, Political Control in the Old and New Regimes."

[12] Jorge Navarrete, "Desequilibrio y dependencia," p. 176.

reflecting its recent promotion of export-oriented industrialization. With respect to imports, Mexico acquires more capital goods than all but one Latin American country. It is freeing itself from the necessity of importing manufactured goods consumed domestically, but it is correspondingly increasing its dependence on imported capital goods.

The distribution of the labor force, however, does not reflect the productive significance of the different sectors of the economy. Since World War II employment in the services, the least productive nonagricultural sector, has been growing most rapidly.[13] While Mexican industrialization had a positive effect on employment in manufacturing in the 1950s, since then large modern firms utilizing capital-intensive technologies have been displacing older and smaller firms, to the extent that the overall rate of increase in industrial jobs has declined.[14] Employing approximately one-fifth of the labor force, the increasingly productive industrial sector absorbs only about 5 percent more of the economically active population than it did at the eve of the revolution.[15] This non-labor-absorbing industrialization reflects the government's policy first of "import-substitution" and, more recently, of "export-substitution"-industrialization, policies which encourage the substitution of capital for labor.[16] The capital-intensive tend-

[13] ECLA, *Economic Bulletin for Latin America* 18, pp. 49-51, 89. In socialist Cuba the proportion of the population employed in service activities also has increased, but the proportion employed in commerce has decreased, unlike in the capitalist countries of the continent. Kalman and Frieda Silvert, "Fate, Chance and Faith," p. 5.

[14] Trejo Reyes, p. 63.

[15] According to Cumberland, only in 1960 did the proportion of the labor force employed in industry surpass its 1930 peak. Charles Cumberland, *Mexico*, p. 367. However, the composition of the industrial sector has changed significantly since the revolution: The proportion of artisan activities diminished from 70 percent to 32 percent whereas industrial jobs increased from 30 percent to 68 percent between 1925 and 1970. *Simposio Latinoamericano de industrialización en América Latina* (Santiago, Chile: CEPAL, 1966), p. 13, and José Luis Reyna, "An Empirical Analysis of Political Mobilization," p. 67.

[16] The Law for New and Necessary Industries exempts industries importing capital goods from import taxes, and the overvaluation of the exchange rate implies a subsidy to imports of capital. For a discussion of Mexico's import and export-substitution policies see René Villarreal, "External Disequilibrium, Economic Growth without Development." For a discussion of the latter see also *Policies and Institutions for the Promotion of Exports of Manufactures*.

ency is furthered by national businessmen's bias toward "modern" technology and by direct foreign investments which import mechanized production methods.

While the expansion of industrial and other production, facilitated by such capital-intensive development, has been impressive by international standards, the distribution of the newly generated wealth has not been. According to rough estimates, the poorest 80 percent of the population in Mexico receive only slightly more than 40 percent of the national income,[17] and other Latin American countries have comparable or more egalitarian income distribution structures. The revolution does not seem to have given the Mexican masses a significantly larger share of national income, and available income data suggests that they are not increasing their share of the national income as domestic production expands.[18] Regressive fiscal policies and protection of oligopolistic enterprises, together with government inflationary policies, contribute to the high concentration of income.[19]

Income distribution is particularly inequitable within the commercial sector, dominated economically by large banking and commercial interests but numerically by the rapidly expanding class of shopowners and small merchants,[20] street vendors, and

[17] Irma Adelman and Cynthia Morris, An Anatomy of Patterns of Income Distribution in Developing Nations, Part III. According to ECLA statistics for a select number of Latin American countries, only among the top 20 percent of the population does income distribution compare favorably in Mexico. Economic Survey, p. 65.

[18] According to Navarrete, the poorest 70 percent of Mexican families earned 27.46 percent of the total national wealth in 1963, compared to 31.6 percent in 1950. Ifigenia M. de Navarrete, "La distribución del ingreso en México," p. 37. For somewhat different estimates which also suggest that wage and salary shares of income have fallen since World War II, see Clark Reynolds, The Mexican Economy, p. 84; Roger Hansen, The Politics of Mexican Development, pp. 8, 72, 74; Banco de México, S.A., La distribución del ingreso en México.

[19] For a discussion of the effect the tax structure and government inflationary policy have on income distribution, see Leopoldo Solís, "Mexican Economic Policy in the Post-War Period," pp. 28-46, and the references therein.

[20] Five percent of the commercial industry controls 84 percent of commercial capital. Carlos Fuentes, "The Other Mexico," p. 19. On the distribution of income within the diverse sectors of the economy, see Richard Weiskoff, "Income Distribution and Economic Growth in Puerto Rico, Argentina, and Mexico."

other "penny capitalists,"[21] that is, by self-employed people whose labor generates little income. Such "penny capitalists" are subject to market forces over which they have little control. However, government laxity in taxing them, and regulation of government-controlled consumer markets enables some of them to withstand competition from better capitalized, better organized commercial entrepreneurs. But they do so by exploiting their own labor and, when possible, the labor of others. They work long hours with limited compensation per unit of effort expended. As a result, income is perhaps better distributed than it otherwise would be: the sector can absorb persons unable to find other urban or rural employment, including persons displaced during periods of economic retrenchment and mechanization of agriculture and industry.

Desire for legal title to land was a major factor inspiring Mexican *campesinos* (peasants) to revolt in 1910, especially those associated with the Zapata movement, and the large *latifundia* landholding economy had to be destroyed for the revolution to occur. Therefore, one might expect the distributive impact of the revolution to be more impressive with regard to land than to income. In fact, land was redistributed to *campesinos* in conjunction with the agrarian reform provision of the 1917 Constitution. However, because the reform was only partially implemented, land in present-day Mexico is distributed as inequitably as in many Latin American countries which never experienced a comparable peasant-supported revolution.[22] Instead, the revolution

[21] This term was coined by Sol Tax, in *Penny Capitalism*. Tax implies by the term "capitalist on a microscopic scale . . . no machines, no factories, no co-operatives or corporations. Every man is his own firm and works ruggedly for himself. Money there is, in small denominations." In addition, he notes that there is trade, free entrepreneurs, an impersonal market place and competition, but commerce is without credit and production is without machines (p. ix). Thus, although he argues that "underdeveloped" economies are capitalistic, on the basis of his work on Panajachel, Guatemala, he recognizes that such capitalism differs qualitatively from capitalism in advanced capitalist economies. For Marx, cooperation, that is, the simultaneous employment of a large number of wage-laborers in one and the same process and access to capital to hire wage-laborers and purchase machinery, distinguish capitalist from other modes of production. See Marx, *Capital*, Vol. I.

[22] See Rodolfo Stavenhagen, "Social Aspects of Mexican Agrarian Structure," and Solon Barraclough and Arthur Domike, "Agrarian Structure in Seven Latin American Countries," in Stavenhagen (ed.), *Agrarian Problems and Peasant Movements in Latin America*, pp. 41-96, 225-70. Land-

brought the country "into line" with other countries on the continent, for by the eve of the 1910 revolt the country had come to
have an unusually large proportion of landless peasants. Land
has been redistributed mainly in those sections of the country
where peasants rebelled most strongly.

The main difference between landholding structures in Mexico
and in most other Latin American countries is the form of tenure:
Mexico has a sector of agriculture—the *ejido* sector—which is
legally noncapitalist. It represents an old Indian form of landholding which was reinstituted as a consequence of the civil war.
Land in this sector is collectively owned but generally parcels are
individually operated by *ejido* families. *Ejidal* holders are prohibited from selling, mortgaging, or renting their land to persons
outside the *ejido* village community,[23] although many violate or
circumvent the law without being punished.

While the *ejido* system is precapitalist in inspiration, the Mexican government, through deliberate policies, has increasingly
promoted a highly productive agrarian capitalism, in the sector
of the rural economy *not* covered by the reform.[24] Non-*ejidal* agri-
culturists have more access to private capital, fertile land, and
productive public assistance, including infrastructure, irrigation,
and marketing assistance. Agrarian capitalists are favored over
ejidatarios (recipients of *ejido* land) not because they are inherently more productive. They are more productive in part because
they have more resources, in part because the government makes
more resources available to them. There is some evidence that
production within the *ejido* sector compares favorably with that
in the private sector, when all inputs are taken into account.[25]

---

holdings at times exceed the limit specified in the Constitution, including
the amended Constitution, because the government is lax about enforcing
the law, because members of families at times legally each claim title to
land but operate their land jointly, or because there are no restrictions on
renting land. R. S. Weckstein, "Evaluating Land Reform," p. 399.

[23] If *ejidal* land had been alienable, a repetition of the "land-grab" that
followed the agrarian reform law of 1856 might have occurred, dispossess-
ing a large proportion of the *ejidatarios*. Without the labor-absorbing *ejidal*
sector there might be vast influxes of poor migrants to the urban areas or
increased misery and tension in the countryside. In this respect, the land
reform program serves certain stabilizing political "functions" for the government and those with a vested interest in the status quo.

[24] Reynolds, *Mexican Economy*; Stavenhagen, pp. 249-51.

[25] Marnie Mueller, "Changing Patterns of Agricultural Output and
Productivity," p. 253; Eckstein, *El marco macroeconómico*.

President Echeverría's policy to collectivize *ejidos* seems to reflect the state's basic commitment to capital, not a break with it. Economically, the program is designed to boost recently faltering agricultural production by increasing output both on inefficient individually operated *ejidos* and on private lands threatened by peasant invasions. The program also will augment the economic resources of the state, perhaps increasing its autonomy *vis-à-vis* both peasants and agrarian capitalists.

Not only is wealth—as reflected, conservatively, in income statistics—increasingly inequitably distributed. In addition, the populace has unequal access to the economically rewarding jobs. In industry and agriculture the most lucrative enterprises are owned by a select group. When it changed agrarian property relations the government altered the class structure of agriculture more than the composition of agrarian classes. The contemporary agrarian elite includes families who prior to the revolution were agrarian capitalists and former landed oligarchs. And leading domestic industrialists rarely are of humble socioeconomic origins.[26]

Despite limited access to top entrepreneurial positions, other noncapitalists—especially salaried employees, professionals, and organized workers—enjoy privileges, but less lucrative ones. In comparison to villagers and townsmen, urban residents in general are better off. City dwellers, particularly in Mexico City, enjoy a higher material level of living than people in villages and towns: they have access to more schools, medical facilities, and other social and urban services, more factory and white-collar jobs,[27] and higher income.[28]

The extensive migration to cities in the last three decades suggests that Mexicans realize where opportunities are concen-

[26] Flavia Derossi, *Mexican Entrepreneur.*

[27] On regional inequality, see Paul Lamartine Yates, *El desarrollo regional de México*; Reynolds, *Mexican Economy*; David Barkin (ed.), *Los beneficiarios del desarrollo regional.* The government has encouraged industry to locate in the capital partly by subsidizing the distribution of wheat and corn, low-grade gasoline and diesel fuel, electricity, and natural gas at prices favoring the city. Yates, p. 127, and Laura Randall, "The Process of Economic Development in Mexico from 1940 to 1959." However, the government currently seems to be promoting decentralization by extending tax breaks and eased credit facilities to provincial enterprises.

[28] Over two-thirds of the poorest 20 percent of the Mexican population live in rural areas. ECLA, *Economic Survey,* p. 66.

trated. The proportion of the population living in urban areas (over 25,000 inhabitants) more than doubled since the 1910 revolt, with the largest cities experiencing the largest population increases. Mexico City grew from 721,000 in 1910 to more than 8.5 million in 1970;[29] it grew especially since World War II, when the government slowed down its land redistribution program and shifted its emphasis toward industrialization. Thus, the concentration of social and economic opportunities and, as a consequence, population concentration, reflect the impact of capitalist forces, and government policies promoting such development. Currently the distribution of the Mexican population between rural and urban areas is increasingly resembling that of other semidependent Latin American countries without peasant-fought revolutions and official agrarian reforms.[30]

Although economic conditions generally are better in the cities

[29] Harley Browning, "Urbanization in Mexico"; Jane Cowan Brown, "Patterns of Intra-Urban Settlement in Mexico City," p. 50. However, the proportion of migrants moving to the Federal District has been decreasing since 1950. Centro de Estudios Económicos y Demográficos, *Dinámica de la población de México*, pp. 90-91. Unless otherwise specified in the text, the term "Mexico City" refers to the old municipal district, Mexico City Proper, the Federal District, which includes the surrounding twelve *delegaciones* (territorial administrative units), and the contiguous metropolitan area in the State of Mexico. In 1970 the new organic law for the Federal District divided the old core city into four new delegations. These new delegations and the original twelve now compose a new administrative unit called interchangeably Mexico City and the Federal District.

[30] For comparisons of Mexico's levels and rates of urbanization with those of other Latin American countries, see Gerald Breese, *Urbanization in Newly Developing Countries*, Tables 6 and 7, and John Durand and César Pelaez, "Patterns of Urbanization in Latin America," pp. 166-96, and for a general review of the recent literature on Latin American internal migration see Richard Morse, "Trends and Issues in Latin American Urban Research, 1965-70, Part I," pp. 17-56, and "Recent Research on Latin American Urbanization," pp. 35-74. Nathan Whetten and Robert Burnight, "Internal Migration in Mexico"; Randall, "Labor Migration and Mexican Economic Development"; and Jorge Balán, Harley Browning, and Elizabeth Jelin, *Men in a Developing Society*; and Luis Unikel, "El proceso de urbanización en México," pp. 139-82, focus on internal migration in Mexico. The Mexican and general Latin American patterns of urbanization contrast with that of socialist Cuba. In the latter 1960s Havana grew at a rate two and one-half times below the national growth rate, and the proportion of the population in cities with more than 50,000 tended to remain stable. Jorge Hardoy, "Spatial Structure and Society in Revolutionary Cuba," in Barkin and Nita Manitzas, *Cuba*, pp. 3, 9.

than in the countryside, including the lowest socioeconomic stratum, most city-dwellers remain ill-housed and ill-fed. Moreover, the proportion of low-income families in the cities has increased as peasants have migrated.[31]

The urban poverty partly reflects industry's failure to expand rapidly enough to absorb the growing urban population.[32] While industry generally offers workers more social and economic security than agriculture or small-scale commercial and service ventures,[33] in Mexico City the proportion of the labor force employed in industry has barely increased since World War II, even though per capita industrial production has increased there more than anywhere in the country, except in the north.[34]

Thus, private capitalist forces, both domestic and foreign, along with government policies, have facilitated economic growth since the revolution, but in a way which has generated regional and class inequalities and contradictions. Social and economic benefits within the industrial sector are more equitably distributed than in other sectors of the economy, but the emphasis on capital-intensive industrialization has generated new bases of inequality within the society as a whole, including within the industrial sector. Workers in large enterprises earn higher wages and qualify for more social security benefits than workers in small enterprises, but not necessarily because they are more productive; and the gap in earnings between the two is rising.

THE STATE AND THE POLITY

Political factors have shaped the country's pattern of development

[31] José Iturriaga, *La estructura social y cultural de México*, p. 29; Arturo González Cosío, "Clases y estratos sociales," p. 55.

[32] John Isbister, "Urban Employment and Wages in a Developing Economy," pp. 24-46.

[33] Although income is most equitably distributed within the industrial sector of the economy, labor's share of the national income actually decreased between 1939 and 1958. Not until 1959 did its share surpass what it was in 1939, despite the fact that its contribution to total productivity increased throughout the twenty-year period. As of 1960, labor's share of national income still was only 31.4 percent. Pablo González Casanova, *Democracy in Mexico*, p. 222. His sources of data include Comisión Mixta, *El desarrollo económico de México y su capacidad para absorber capital del exterior* (México, D.F.: 1953) and Nacional Financiera, S.A., Dirección de investigaciones económicas.

[34] Yates, p. 42; Reynolds, p. 174.

somewhat independently of market and production forces. Consequently a complete understanding of postrevolutionary Mexico requires an elucidation of the structure of the polity as well as the economy. To protect primarily the interests of capital and, to a lesser extent, the interests of the salaried "middle class" and organized working class, the Mexican state has had to limit demands by urban and rural poor.[35] Since the 1930s the Mexican government has rather successfully done this by centralizing power and forming a corporately ordered populist party.[36] Although the government actually has encouraged the urban and rural poor and the working-class to organize, it has not concomitantly extended effective and autonomous power to these groups. It at times mobilizes these groups to reinforce its own legitimacy and enhance its ability to bargain with dominant classes;[37] and it encourages members of the organized groups to impose minimal demands on capital and on the government itself.

[35] For an analysis which attributes Mexican political stability to the government's effectiveness in controlling the demands of diverse groups, particularly those of popular groups, see José Luis Reyna, "Control político, estabilidad y desarrollo en México." Earlier commentators on Mexico argued that the regime's stability derived from a political culture emphasizing acquiescence, effective socialization, balanced group interests, cohesion among elites and a sufficiently expansive economy to satisfy the mobility aspirations of mestizos. See Hansen, *Mexican Development*; Robert Scott, *Mexican Government in Transition*; L. Vincent Padgett, *The Mexican Political System*; and Frank Brandenburg, *The Making of Modern Mexico*.

[36] Corporatism—as defined by Schmitter—refers to a social order comprised of organized groups which exchange a legal monopoly on representation and guaranteed access to decision-makers for compliance with certain limitations on behavior. The existence of such semiautonomous but cooperating groups enables the state to play a moderating role. Philippe Schmitter, *Interest Conflict and Political Change in Brazil*, p. 111. While Mexico has successfully institutionalized a modern corporately structured regime, largely in the process of consolidating the revolution, other Latin American societies are corporatist. However, they have less institutionalized modern corporatist political orders. The Mexican case suggests that revolutions may facilitate the establishment of modern polities which incorporate and regulate citizens with use of force. For a discussion of types of Latin American corporatism see Schmitter, "Paths to Political Development in Latin America." For a somewhat different but not contradictory definition of corporatism—based on a categorization of political processes—see Ronald Rogowski and Lois Wasserspring, *Does Political Development Exist? Corporatism in Old and New Societies*.

[37] Tuohy, "Centralism and Political Elite Behavior in Mexico," pp. 265-66.

The administrative bureaucracy is extensive and centralized. Requiring large resources to operate, it depends heavily on revenues generated directly by state enterprises and by taxes imposed on capital. It therefore is closely linked with capitalist interests. Moreover, since appointments and promotions are hierarchically controlled and since high-level functionaries typically are professionals of wealthy social origin,[38] bureaucrats in general are biased toward elites. And since the bureaucracy provides many opportunities for graft, and since officeholders are frequently rotated, it captures over the years the loyalty of a large segment of the population. According to Frank Brandenburg, in every six-year change of presidency there is a turnover of approximately 18,000 elective offices and more than 25,000 appointive posts, about half of which provide good to excellent incomes.[39] He notes that the top administrative posts—which include the executive, heads of government ministries, management of the major state industries, and directorships of the large semiautonomous government agencies, commissions, and banks—furnish the most lucrative opportunities for financial rewards: The average minister or director finishes his term with two or three houses, two or three automobiles, a ranch, and $100,000 in cash; and about twenty-five directors and ministers hold posts from which they can leave office with fifty times that amount in cash.[40]

Not only the bureaucracy but also the PRI operates as a patronage system contributing to the regime's stability and legitimacy, and class biases. Although a postrevolutionary innovation, the PRI identifies itself with, and indeed legitimates itself in terms of, the revolution. It helped consolidate the upheaval, but neither inspired nor directed the rebellion. Initially a loose affili-

[38] Peter Smith, "La movilidad política en el México contemporáneo," pp. 379-413. Although the bureaucratic and entrepreneurial elite both come from well-to-do families and are highly educated by Mexican standards, their backgrounds differ somewhat. Fathers of bureaucrats tend to be professionals, civil servants, politicians, and military careerists, not businessmen as are fathers of contemporary business elites. Partly because of their somewhat contrasting backgrounds but more importantly because of the different positions they hold, their interests at times conflict even though they both are committed to capitalism and capitalist interests. On areas of tensions between economic and political elites, see Derossi, *Mexican Entrepreneur.*

[39] Brandenburg, pp. 157-58.

[40] Ibid., p. 162.

ation of regional and personal parties, ever since its reorganization by Cárdenas in 1938 it has been structured along geographical-occupational sectoral lines. While its sectoral organization, together with its populist ideology, convey the impression that it represents the interests of affiliated groups—mainly *campesinos*, labor, and "middle-class" groups—it in fact is dominated largely by "middle-class" interests, particularly through the Popular sector.[41] The Party is run oligarchically and has a nominating procedure which assures elite control.

The PRI has won all presidential and most other elections since its founding. Yet it is a weak institution. Though formally autonomous, it enjoys no decision-making or budgetary authority.[42] It exercises little power except for putting people into office, and it is ultimately subservient to the executive and the interests the executive favors, for the president appoints and removes the Party head at his own discretion.[43]

At the same time, though, the Party helps channel and limit popular demands, distributes patronage and welfare benefits which increase popular loyalty to the administration, and mobilizes

[41] In 1970 the Popular sector held half of PRI's seats in the Chamber of Deputies (Congress), and the National Executive Committee of PRI has been mainly composed of members of this sector since its creation in 1943. Also, since 1946 about two-thirds of all deputies have held professional titles. A. Delhumeau et al., *México: Realidad política de sus partidos*, p. 80; Scott, *Mexican Government*, pp. 81-83, 193-94; Padgett, p. 125.

[42] According to Linz, one of the main characteristics differentiating "authoritarian" from "communist" and "democratic" regimes is a "dominant" party which is neither powerful nor autonomous. Juan Linz, "An Authoritarian Regime," pp. 297-301.

[43] See Patricia Richmond, "Mexico: A Case Study of One-Party Politics"; Brandenburg, *Modern Mexico*; Padgett, *Mexican Political System*; and Hansen, *Mexican Development*, esp. Chapter 5. In contrast, in *Mexican Government* Scott generally attributes to the PRI decision-making power and balanced representation in policy formulation and outcome (see esp. pp. 29, 32, 108, 145, 146). He, too, though, emphasizes the authoritarian elitist aspects of the political system in his "Mexico: The Established Revolution." The PRI's lack of effective autonomy was demonstrated when President Díaz Ordaz appointed Carlos Madrazo Party head in 1964. Madrazo advocated the following changes which would have established the PRI as an independent party: open party primaries to nominate candidates for municipal elections and the collection of individual financial pledges in order to build the Party's own resources, independent of official subsidies. When he attempted to implement these proposals he was forced to resign, at which point plans to democratize the Party subsided.

public support for the regime. Through the PRI, popular groups automatically are publicly associated with the government in a way which causes them to share responsibility for government policies that they themselves do not make, including policies that discriminate against them. However, the support of these groups is largely based on passive acceptance, not intense commitment.

To influence the executive and gain access to top patronage, groups generally must rely on personal ties with high-ranking functionaries. Pressured to cooperate with the national leadership of the "revolutionary family," the Party serves as a useful mechanism of political control, not interest "articulation" and "aggregation." Because the PRI has no authoritative power, the interests of capitalists have not been undermined despite their exclusion from the Party: their interests are well represented in the informal deliberations central to decision-making. Representatives of business often sit on government boards, consult with political leaders, and have established channels of communication with policy-making officials.[44]

Intra-Party relations are structured in such a way that "popular" forces associated with it are unable to use their formal power to generate and exercise real power. The interests of affiliated sectors are largely kept in check by the way inter- and intrasectoral relations are structured, by market forces, and above all, by government manipulation of power. As a result, even though organized *campesinos* constitute one of the main divisions of the Party they are a disfavored group. They exert limited political influence through the PRI because many leaders of the *campesino* sector, appointed by the national executive committee of the Party, have been nonpeasants; because many of the *campesinos* appointed to top political positions have been co-opted—that is, absorbed into official administrative-political groups to the extent that they advance their own interests more than those of their constituents; because the private landowners, who receive more income-generating benefits from the government than the *campesinos*, are incorporated into the politically more important "middle-class" dominated Popular sector of the Party; and because recipients of patronage congressional and senatorial seats allotted to the *campesino* sector of the PRI do not vote as an

---

[44] Robert Shafer, *Mexican Business Organizations*, esp. Chapter V; Brandenburg, *Modern Mexico*.

interest bloc.[45] Their political ineffectiveness also stems from discriminating administrative actions: functionaries have prevented peasant–working-class alliances, regulated peasant access to agricultural resources, harassed peasants through agrarian bureaucracies, and repressed peasant movements they could not otherwise control.[46]

Similarly, organized labor has not been able to wield effective economic and political influence through its formal affiliation with the Party as a distinct sector. Labor also does not act as an interest bloc in the legislature,[47] and co-optation and imposition of leadership, occasional violent repression, and periodic concessions to workers have served to regulate labor.[48] And labor's as well as peasants' weakness stems not primarily from incorporation into the official Party but from specific discriminating actions by postrevolutionary governments, both prior and subsequent to the founding of the Party.[49] Even though the government encouraged labor's affiliation with the PRI and even though it has, over the years, extended certain benefits to labor—e.g., social security benefits, wage increases, and profit-sharing—it divided the labor movement,[50] thereby limiting and regulating organized workers' political strength. Furthermore, the Constitution ties labor to industry,[51] divides workers socially and economically as a class,

[45] Scott, pp. 65, 69, 163; Bö Anderson and James Cockcroft, "Control and Co-optation in Mexican Politics," pp. 366-89; and Eyler Simpson, *The Ejido.*

[46] Elena Montes de Oca, "State, Agrarian Reform and Peasant Organizations in Mexico."

[47] González Casanova, p. 15.

[48] For an analysis of state control over organized workers, see Aurora Loyo Brambila and Ricardo Pozas Horcasitas, "Notes on the Mechanisms of Control Exercised by the Mexican State."

[49] See Morris Singer, *Growth, Equality and the Mexican Experience,* p. 67; González Casanova, pp. 15, 295; Frank Tannenbaum, *The Struggle for Peace and Bread,* p. 51; Moises Troncoso and Ben Burnett, *The Rise of the Latin American Labor Movement;* Joe Ashby, *Organized Labor and the Mexican Revolution under Lázaro Cárdenas;* and Hansen, pp. 114-15.

[50] Even though Cárdenas originally encouraged the trade union movement he subsequently split the agrarian, civil service, bank employees, teachers, and employees in state-owned industries from the labor central into separate unions. Brandenburg, p. 82.

[51] According to the Constitution, labor is subordinated to capital by the following provisions: strikes are regarded as legal only when they are peaceful and in harmony with the rights of capital; arbitration boards are to be comprised of representatives of labor, industry, and the government;

and restricts the rights of labor.[52] Workers' interests have been linked to managements', even though their interests are not legally considered identical. The Constitution specifies that manual workers are subject to a different pay scale than nonmanual workers and that manual workers may not participate in management. Since the Constitutional provisions, as developed in the Labor Code, are enforced primarily in large industries, workers have the greatest vested economic interests in the status quo in the least competitive sector of the economy.

Nonetheless, not merely rural and urban laborers but also industrial and commercial capitalists are subject to certain government controls and divided as a class.[53] However, the government regulates—or attempts to regulate—capitalists mainly through negotiations, not through co-optation and force, as in the case of "popular" groups. All but the smallest businessmen are required to affiliate with divisions of formally autonomous chambers that deal individually with the state. The government decides which chambers are to be set up, the chamber with which given enterprises should affiliate, and attends the national meetings of the chambers. Because votes in the national assemblies of the chambers are proportional to the amount of dues paid by the affiliates, the richer and larger units dominate the executive positions and largely orient the chambers' policies in their favor.

---

workers are to share in company profits; and management is to provide workers with housing and other social services and community facilities in firms employing more than one or two hundred workers.

[52] The government does not automatically tolerate strikes. The two presidents under whom there were most strikes were Cárdenas and López Mateos (1958-64), even though labor did not experience its greatest setbacks under these presidents. Both periods of major strike activity came after extensive repression of labor. Comparative statistics reveal that although there were twice as many strikes in Mexico in 1939 relative to the total population as there were in the U.S., since then there have been, on the average, more than three times as many strikes in the United States. Similarly, with respect to the ratio of strikers to the total population, the percentage was exactly the same in the two countries in 1939, but since then the proportion of strikers relative to the total population has been, on the average, ten times as great in the United States. For more detailed comparative data see González Casanova, pp. 15, 295.

[53] For a discussion of issues dividing capital, see Hansen, pp. 108-9; Sanford Mosk, *Industrial Revolution in Mexico*; and Marco Antonio Alcázar, *Las agrupaciones patronales en México*.

Although the government partially regulates capital, the two share common interests. The government depends on capital to provide wealth for the political-administrative apparatus and the balance of payments. Moreover, high-ranking functionaries themselves develop a vested interest in capitalist enterprises: Many top-level officials establish their own lucrative businesses through government contracts that they arrange, including ones linked to public sector enterprises. And because upper-level politicians and administrators switch from the public to the private sphere when their political careers terminate, they seek a strong business community as a safeguard.

As in industry and commerce, power within the service sector does not derive from formal PRI membership. Some service groups, such as government employees and teachers, belong to the Popular sector of the PRI. Yet the patronage and favoritism they receive—which includes access to social security benefits—largely stem from their direct negotiations with the government, and from the generally favored status they enjoy within the society as a whole.[54]

Because real power is not vested in the formal political apparatus, the franchise also serves mainly the same limited legitimating function as the PRI.[55] The electoral process serves to incorporate the populace symbolically into the body politic. It does not serve as a channel through which "popular" forces, on the basis of its numerical strength, gain institutionalized access to the government decision-making process and assurance that the government responds to majoritarian interests. For this reason the recent creation of two new parties, the Mexican Workers' Party and the Socialist Workers' Party, in line with the government's proclaimed concern with *apertura democrática* (democratic opening), reflects the further expansion of formal, not real, democracy.

Despite the PRI's close association with the government and the inegalitarian social order, the PRI registers its greatest elec-

[54] Brandenburg, p. 86; Antonio Ugalde, *Power and Conflict in a Mexican Community*, pp. 85-92.

[55] On the PRI's significance as an electoral agent for the government, see Manuel Moreno Sanchez, *La crisis política de México*, pp. 51-63, 136-65. Generally when the PRI registers defeat at the polls, elections either are annulled or elected officials are harassed by higher-level bureaucrats. For example, in the 1960s in Baja California the PAN's electoral victory was annulled, and in Mérida, where the electoral results were validated, the state government assumed control of the city's police force. Hansen, p. 122.

toral support in the states which benefit least under the present government.[56] Urban and rural poor vote overwhelmingly for the PRI partly because the conservative National Action Party (PAN), a party closely aligned with the Church, big business, and the upper and "middle" classes, is the only officially recognized opposition party that runs its own presidential candidate,[57] and partly because the PRI has substantially larger financial and organizational resources than other parties. In addition, rural voting at times is rigged.

The legislature also is subservient to the government and its interests, even though it is formally independent. It appears as if PRI commands legislative power since it holds all senatorial and most congressional seats. But because of its subordination to the executive, the Party in fact wields no autonomous legislative influence. The legislature exercises negligible control over the federal budget,[58] and ratifies almost all laws backed by the executive.[59] Thus, neither the laws passed in the 1960s and early 1970s entitling minority parties to limited numbers of congressional seats nor the PRI's allocation of congressional and senatorial seats to corporate groups provides the beneficiaries with an institutionalized base by which to influence the decision-making process. Instead, both measures cause groups to share responsibility for political decisions which they themselves do not make. The legislature, as a consequence, mainly provides a sanction of legality to presidential actions.

[56] González Casanova, pp. 124-25; Reyna, "Political Mobilization," pp. 7, 121. In part, the PRI fares better in the poorer states because electoral fraud is more possible there.

[57] Not all parties are granted the right to participate in elections. The government has prohibited the Communist Party from running candidates in elections, even though it complies more with official electoral requirements than the Authentic Party of the Mexican Revolution (PARM), which does participate in elections. PARM is a conservative and insignificant party. For an analysis of Mexico's opposition parties see Delhumeau et al., *México*; Luis Medina et al., *La vida política en México, 1970-74*.

[58] James Wilkie, *The Mexican Revolution*, p. 17.

[59] González Casanova, pp. 17-18, 201. The proportion of congressional votes in opposition to projects proposed by the executive branch between 1935 and 1964 was never more than 12 percent. The situation, however, was not always that way. Initially after the revolution the executive used strong repressive measures to assure its political hegemony over Congress: When the opposition permitted in Congress immediately following the enactment of the 1917 Constitution almost overthrew Obregón, the executive repressed and then removed the opposition from Congress. Only in 1940 were "opposition" parties reinstated.

The power of the executive has been further increased by the diminution of regionalism. While the civil war had left the political system fragmented along territorial lines, many state and regional *caciques* and *caudillos* (political bosses) either were co-opted or eliminated. The National Revolutionary Party (PNR), the forerunner of the PRI, restricted the importance of regional politics through its control over patronage and political recruitment and its ability to remove candidates not to its liking. Furthermore, insubordinate state governors have been dismissed or kept in line by threats of dismissal, and governors no longer control the security apparatus they once commanded. Since, in addition, elected officials cannot succeed themselves, the likelihood that *políticos* become subservient to local pressures is kept in check. Also, even though states and municipalities remain formally autonomous, they have come to receive a smaller share of the public treasury, and grown increasingly dependent on the federal government for public works, schools, and other social services.[60]

Because local functionaries—as we shall see in the three areas—owe their positions to, derive much of their support from, and have to be responsive to higher levels of leadership, territorial based politics now is intimately tied and subordinated to national politics: This is particularly true in the capital, since the municipal government is a national ministry. As a consequence, local politics must be understood in the broader national context. The territorial political-administrative apparatus provides opportunities for private gain generally sufficient to make *políticos* loyal to the federal government, even though the stakes here are much less than in the national, ministerial, and semi-public sector bureaucracies.[61]

Military control was a problem closely linked to regionalism. Since the revolution the government has reorganized and reconstituted the military and restricted the military's ability to wield power. The established military, which had been allied with the Old Order, and the various revolutionary armies that developed in the course of the civil war had to be controlled for the new

[60] González Casanova, pp. 24-30, 201. While the average share of the public treasury disbursed to states and municipalities decreased between 1929 and 1962, the average share distributed to the Federal District increased. In general, the wealthiest states receive the largest share of the treasury, although political contacts also are important.

[61] Smith, "La movilidad política."

government to remain intact.[62] There had been major military rebellions in 1923 and 1927 and bloodshed during the 1928-29 succession crisis when dissident generals openly revolted against Calles' imposition of Portes Gil as president. When Cárdenas restructured the Party he made the military one of the four sectors he established, so that they had to compete with members of the other three sectors for political patronage. Cárdenas also controlled the selection of military sector delegates to the Party. Once the military were allowed the right to act corporately only in nominating presidential candidates their political strength was further undermined. Moreover, the military sector subsequently was dropped from the Party altogether and the military bloc in Congress was abolished.

However, as in the case of territorial-based politics, the reduction in military strength—in absolute terms and relative to other groups—stemmed largely from official actions. Generals were eliminated who opposed the government and officers were routinely rotated without their troops to keep them, like regional *políticos*, from building loyal political bases. Cárdenas also undermined the military's monopoly of the instruments of force by arming peasants and workers. The strength of the armed forces was especially curtailed by administration cutbacks both in the number of cabinet posts allotted to military men and in financial support. The proportion of the national budget distributed to the military dropped from 53 percent in 1921 to 1.5 percent in the early 1970s.[63] Its share of the budget has been reduced to the extent that the military now receive a smaller percent of federal allocations in Mexico than in almost any other Latin American country.[64]

Not only has the power of the military been reduced but the military now also recruit from a different stratum of the population and serve different class interests than they did prior to the revolution. Formerly, military officers were primarily of upper-class background and closely aligned with the landed oligarchy. Now men of more humble socioeconomic origin fill the military

[62] For a general description of changes within the Mexican military subsequent to the revolution, see Edwin Lieuwen, *Mexican Militarism*; and Jorge Lozoya, *El ejército Mexicano (1911-1965)*.

[63] Wilkie, pp. 102-3; *New York Times*, February 5, 1974, p. 4.

[64] José Nun, *Latin America: The Hegemonic Crisis and the Military Coup*, p. 11.

ranks. One of the three main divisions of the military, the division of rural defense, is comprised almost exclusively of *campesinos*. While the government initially encouraged this division to help wrest power from the landed oligarchs and the Church, the government currently utilizes it to help maintain internal social and political order. The division provides the government with information concerning subversive activities, although the regular line army is responsible for crushing local insurrections. Since the division of rural defense is not a paid force, the actual federal budget allocated to the military does not accurately reflect the significance the military currently assumes.

Despite such changes, the military remain a privileged group, even if less privileged than before the revolution. The prerogatives they enjoy—which include access to political posts, such social benefits as pensions, life insurance, credit facilities, hospitalization, training in civilian professions, housing, discount shops, and schools for their children—stem from government favoritism secured through direct dealings with the president, not from their direct contribution to the capital accumulation process or to their affiliation with the PRI. The benefits they enjoy suggest that their informal influence is far greater than their formal power.

Whether Mexico's civil-military balance will continue intact remains to be seen. Despite a small military budget, the armed forces have lately assumed important internal political functions, although perhaps less than in other Latin American countries. They were used in 1968 to crush a strong antigovernment student movement preceding the Olympics, and, since then, to quell other student demonstrations. They also have been used to track down rural guerrilla groups, fight urban terrorism, clamp down on *campesino* land seizures, officiate elections, forestall the collapse of local governments, and dislodge labor protestors.[65] Since the military in the early 1970s received a pay raise, an improved pension program, access to new middle-level government jobs, and control of the lucrative customs posts along the United States border, they seem to be gaining benefits at the same time that their informal political importance, as an instrument of repression, seems to be expanding. Their stake in the civilian regime

[65] David Ronfeldt, *The Mexican Army and Political Order Since 1940*; *New York Times*, February 5, 1974, p. 4; Cockcroft, "Coercion and Ideology in Mexican Politics," pp. 253-54.

is therefore increasing. To the extent that they are resuming pre-eminence, though, they represent somewhat different interests than they did prior to the revolution.

The formal power of the Church, like that of the military, has been restricted since the revolution. According to the Constitution, the Church may not own property or comment on political issues. Religious orders are illegal and by law all cemeteries are secular. While these prohibitions already were included in the 1857 Reform Constitution, the current Constitution further limits the potential influence of the Church politically and spiritually: now clergy may not vote, hold office, comment on politics, or criticize civil law; states have the right to limit the number of priests within their territorial domain; the Church may not sponsor elementary and secondary schools; and no new churches may be constructed without federal government authorization.

Although the Church initially refused to accept the restrictions imposed on it and although it aligned with counterrevolutionary forces in the 1920s, since the Cárdenas era overt Church-State conflict has subsided. Ostensibly the two institutions at that time reached a *modus vivendi*: each granted the other autonomy within its own institutional sphere.[66]

As a result, once again the Church, and Catholic culture, enjoy national preeminence. The country is dominated by a Catholic ethos[67] and, according to the Census, almost all Mexicans continue to consider themselves Catholic. In comparison with other Latin American countries, available data suggest that the Mexican Church recruits more clergy and participants in such lay groups as the Christian Family Movement; offers more Church-sponsored hospitals than all but Brazil, and more charitable institutions than all but Brazil, Colombia, and Argentina; and enrolls more school-aged children in Church-affiliated schools than all but Brazil and Colombia.[68] Politically, the Church hierarchy par-

[66] For a historical account of the Church's relations to the polity since Independence see J. Lloyd Mecham, *Church and State in Latin America*; Robert Quirk, *The Mexican Revolution and the Catholic Church, 1910-1929*; Ralph Beals, Jr., "Bureaucracy and Change in the Mexican Catholic Church, 1926-50"; and Frederick Turner, "The Compatibility of Church and State in Mexico."

[67] Octavio Paz, *The Labyrinth of Solitude*; and Samuel Ramos, *Profile of Man and Culture in Mexico*.

[68] Luigi Einaudi et al., *Latin American Institutional Development*, pp. 20, 26.

takes in national moral and civic activities,[69] and socially it supplements the government's public education system even though Church-sponsored schools are illegal. Economically, however, Church influence *has* been curtailed. Once a large property owner, as a corporate entity the Church now is propertyless. Consequently, while the Church formerly impeded the free mobility of land as a factor of production, it no longer represents a force antithetical to capitalist expansion.

Nonetheless, the shift in the government's de facto stance toward the Church parallels structural, ideological, and personnel changes within the Church itself. Since the 1930s the national hierarchy has been staffed mainly by Mexicans rather than foreigners.[70] Also, it now is stronger and functionally more independent of the international Church,[71] and more closely identified with the government and its publicly expressed concerns: both the Church and State address themselves to problems of development and order.[72]

The reemergence of the Church as a major pillar of the social order does not stem from affiliation with the PRI, just as the power wielded by capitalists and salaried "middle-class" groups, including the military, does not. In fact, the Church, government, and the PRI to date maintain an uneasy alliance, since the only sizable officially recognized political opposition to the government, the National Action Party, is closely associated with the

[69] For example, when Cárdenas expropriated oil companies the Archbishop of Mexico exhorted the people to support the government, and in 1951 the Church took an active part in a national moralizing campaign by encouraging Catholic organizations to participate. In addition, important public works projects at times are inaugurated by clergy as well as by high government officials. González Casanova, p. 39.

[70] See Beals, pp. 61-62.

[71] Ibid., p. 76.

[72] The public identification of the Church with the regime is expressed, for example, in a pastoral letter issued in 1968 by the Bishop of Mexico. "Carta pastoral del episcopado Mexicano sobre el desarrollo e integración del país." In this letter (esp. pp. 24, 25, 49, and 50) the Bishop condemned the pervasive inequality of present-day Mexico. The solution he offered stressed "integral development" and "harmony," and the organization of society along organic and functional rather than class lines. In an episcopal letter the Church also has endorsed the government's new anti-papal birth control program.

Church through lay Catholics.[73] Accordingly, the Church indirectly represents and strengthens conservative capitalist interests.

Even though the state facilitates capitalist expansion and maintains political order with the support of most groups, the political economy contains internal tensions and contradictions which may eventually threaten its legitimacy. The disjunction between the government's populist ideology and its inegalitarian policies and between the real and the formal power structure are sources of potential overt conflict. Groups with symbolic power may come to demand effective power. Conversely, groups with effective but merely "behind the scenes" power may come to want and demand formal power, in order to deny those with formal power access to the graft and patronage that they now enjoy.[74] In addition, foreign economic interests conflict with the national ideology the government propagates and with the interests of competitive domestic capitalists. Above all, since the government attempts to satisfy all groups, should some of them come to believe that they warrant more government favoritism than they presently receive or that they have more to gain by withdrawing their support from the status quo, the government would be unable to maintain order, except by much more widespread use of force than it now employs.

Until recently the government resolved conflicts by allocating resources to co-opt, repress, or distribute benefits to dissident sectors. Yet recent urban and rural guerrilla activities, peasant land invasions, labor strikes, local electoral victories for the PAN, and student-led protests—especially those in 1968 and 1971— suggest that the government's legitimacy is becoming precarious once again, despite continued official presidential and gubernatorial electoral landslides. The state has responded to the recent crises, heightened by inflation and a declining economy, by revitalizing its ties with the popular sectors and by expanding formal democracy in conjunction with its proclaimed *apertura democrática* goal. Its ability to regulate opposition, though, may well deteriorate if economic conditions worsen or capital resists the costs of the concessions made to popular groups.

[73] The PAN espouses a more Christian ideology and draws more of its leadership from lay Catholic groups (e.g., Catholic Action) than does the PRI. On the PAN's Catholic orientation, see Donald Mabry, *Mexico's Acción Nacional.*

[74] The concern with "administrative reform" reflects this tension.

CONCLUSIONS AND IMPLICATIONS

Hierarchically structured corporate groups form the basis of the social, economic, and political order. The groups include some which assumed national preeminence during the course of the revolution, some which have been fostered by deliberate post-revolutionary government policies, and some antedating the upheaval. However, the old groups incorporated into the new political-administrative apparatus have been partially restructured and realigned with new interests.

The state now exercises considerable direction over the economy and polity, particularly over the "popular" groups which are most closely identified with it publicly. The mass-based party is subordinated to the central government so that the socially and economically deprived cannot use their numerical strength to elect into office politicians who regularly exercise official power in their interests. The formal exclusion of capitalists from the PRI enables the government to sustain its avowed commitment to "popular" sectors and the populist goals of the revolution while simultaneously favoring capitalists over other groups. The government does not thereby open for question the revolutionary bases on which it legitimates itself.

The centralization of power and manipulation of power in favor of capital reflect deliberate government policies serving to resolve the economic exigencies of a capitalist state. Consequently, even though the government and the PRI legitimate themselves in the name of a revolution, Mexico has been developing along similar lines as other Latin American governments dominated by capitalist interests. In fact, as conditions in the three areas reveal, political institutions identified with the revolution have enabled the Mexican government to do less for the lower socioeconomic stratum (except through its limited *ejido* program) and more for industrial and commercial agricultural elites than any other major Latin American country.[75]

[75] Hansen, p. 87.

CHAPTER TWO

The Rise and Demise of Autonomous Communities

An inner city, a self-made, and a planned low income urban set-tlement.[1] They look different and seem to have contrasting effects on inhabitants. Yet the impact of the dwelling environs over the years has proved to be limited, for social and economic condi-tions within the areas have been shaped by contemporary and historical economic and political forces linked to the country's capitalist development: No architectural planning has been effec-tive in countering the impact of these societal influences. Even initial political differences between the areas owing to their dif-ferent origins have diminished, as the communities have become more integrated into urban and national structures and as rela-tions within the communities have been routinized.[2]

Nevertheless, because the areas were formed under diverse circumstances, during contrasting periods of the nation's history, the areas differ somewhat. The center city area, notorious for its crime, deteriorated low-rise tenant-occupied tenements, and un-sanitary living conditions, was already settled prior to the Span-ish Conquest. The now legalized squatter settlement is of much more recent origin. It was first inhabited in the mid-1950s by a

[1] Throughout the study the terms "community," "neighborhood," "settle-ment," and "area" are used interchangeably. Unless otherwise specified, they refer to administratively delineated units. The extent to which these units form socially meaningful entities is discussed below.

[2] Until the 1950s and 1960s studies ignored communities *within* cities. The social and economic background of inhabitants of diverse types of set-tlements and early organizational life differ among areas, depending on how and when the areas initially were settled, and especially on land-tenure conditions. Although differences attributable to the histories of the areas have not entirely disappeared, I found that economic conditions and political life within the areas increasingly have been shaped by national class and political forces. Thus, I would predict that such larger forces increasingly will shape opportunities and organizational life in the more recently formed low-income areas on the periphery of Mexico City, including those studied by Cornelius (*Politics and the Migrant Poor in Mexico City*).

group of persons who illegally staked out claims to the land. Compared to the center city area it appears tranquil and rural now. It is comprised mainly of small self-constructed houses. The government-financed housing development is even newer. It opened in 1964. Spacious and carefully planned, it contains low-cost, solidly built "middle-class" style homes. Because of different origins the areas initially attracted somewhat different types of residents and exposed residents to different types of experiences.

However, despite these differences, the three areas currently are integrated into the national society through many of the same institutional linkages, and through ties the residents individually have both within the areas and outside of them. Through such linkages the national pattern of stratification has been reinforced locally, to the extent that class standing more than community of residence now shapes inhabitants' lives.

Even though residents remain near the bottom of the urban socioeconomic hierarchy, for most of them—particularly in the two newer areas—their economic situation has improved over the years. Most migrants feel that they are better off in the capital than they were in the provinces, and migrants and nonmigrants alike almost uniformly agree that their economic situation has improved since living in Mexico City. Some of them even are property-owners for the first time in their lives. Such improvements are not surprising, in view of Mexico's economic growth and pattern of urbanization in the postwar period. We must remember, though, that the improvements these individuals have had the good fortune to experience do not necessarily represent changes in their relative economic standing: wealthier socioeconomic groups, as we saw in the previous chapter, have been even more fortunate.

SUBORDINATE INTEGRATION INTO MUNICIPAL AND NATIONAL INSTITUTIONS

El Centro: The Center City Area

The center city area, a notorious inner-city slum (*tugurio*), covers about sixty small city blocks.[3] Housing approximately 100,000 people, it is one of the most densely populated areas of

[3] The urban poor families depicted in Oscar Lewis' *Five Families* all lived in this center city area. Armando Ramírez Rodríguez's novel *Chin-Chin, El Teporocho* portrays this area as well.

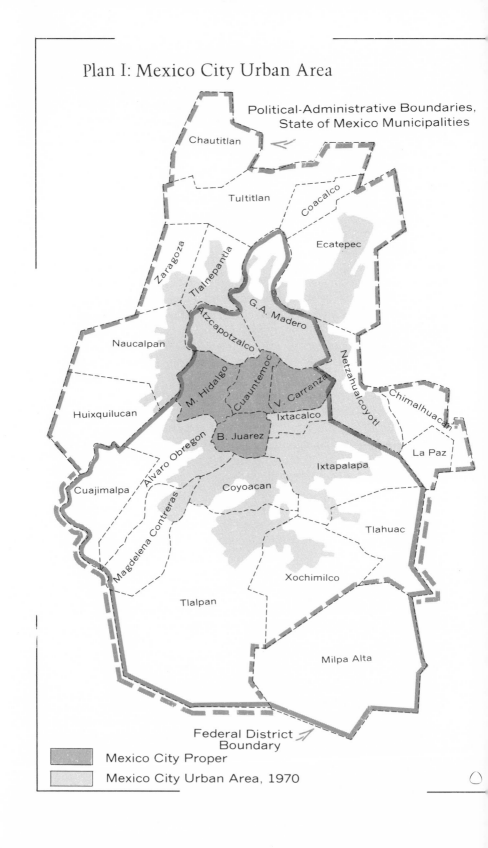

Plan I: Mexico City Urban Area

Political-Administrative Boundaries,
State of Mexico Municipalities

Chautitlan

Tultitlan

Coacalco

Ecatepec

Zaragoza

Tlalnepantla

G.A. Madero

Naucalpan

Atzcapotzalco

Netzahualcoyotl

Chimalhuacan

Huixquilucan

M. Hidalgo

Cuauntemoc

V. Carranza

Ixtacalco

B. Juarez

La Paz

Cuajimalpa

Alvaro Obregon

Coyoacan

Ixtapalapa

Magdelena Contreras

Tlahuac

Xochimilco

Tlalpan

Milpa Alta

Federal District
Boundary

Mexico City Proper

Mexico City Urban Area, 1970

the city. Along with other contiguous areas, it forms a horseshoe of housing around El Zócalo, the hub of Mexico City under colonial rule. These *tugurios* form part of the inner core of the city, known until recently as Mexico City Proper (Plan I). Until World War II they housed most low-income families in the city, including most migrants from the provinces, and approximately one-third of the city's total population.[4]

Referred to as a *"zona típica,"* the part of the center city area closest to El Zócalo has a long history. The oldest standing church in the area serves as a contemporary symbol of the area's heritage. Built under the Spaniards in a colonial style with Indian labor, the church rests on the site of a former Indian temple and bears both a Spanish and an Indian name.[5] The area initially had been inhabited by Aztecs, but after the Conquest it became a center of colonial life. Under Spanish rule the Indians had their own political organization, but one which was subordinate to Spanish political authority. And although the community established by the Spaniards resembled the indigenous *capulli,* the colonizers imposed their own social and economic institutions on the native population. Thus, present-day street names in the area —for example, the Streets of the Bakers, Cobblers, Barbers, and Tinsmiths—reflect trades in which Franciscan missionaries trained local Indians.

Over the centuries the area has continued to be a vital economic center, although local economic activities have changed, as socioeconomic conditions in the society at large have changed. In the late nineteenth century, after the abolishment of regional tariffs, the creation of political stability, and the introduction of a railroad system which linked the city and the hinterland, the area became an increasingly important commercial center. Today the buildings, streets, small shops, and local markets are filled

---

[4] Studies of low-cost housing up to and including 1953 in Mexico City are reviewed in Banco Nacional Hipotecario Urbano y de Obras Públicas, *Estudios, No. 6: El problema de la habitación en la Ciudad de México,* pp. 3-12. Studies of more recent housing include Instituto Nacional de la Vivienda, *Colonias proletarias* and *Herradura de Tugurios;* Instituto Mexicano de Seguro Social, *Investigación de vivienda en 11 ciudades del país;* Jane Brown, "Intra-Urban Settlement"; Jorge Alberto Harth Deneke, "The Colonias Proletarias of Mexico City."

[5] The Spaniards, in their effort to win converts, typically destroyed Indian temples, constructed Catholic churches in their place, and attached Indian as well as Spanish names to the churches.

with people selling a wide array of goods to customers from diverse parts of the city. In the afternoon the streets are crowded with men returning from elegant sections of the capital wheeling pushcarts full of secondhand clothing and other used items to be sold at the large local markets. In addition, since the turn of the century, the area has been a major center of shoecraft production, early industries,[6] and craftwork—such as automobile repair work—linked to the nation's mechanization and "modernization." Women sit at the entryway of their living quarters selling *tacos, tortillas, frijoles, enchiladas,* and other flavorful Mexican favorites to the multitude of men who work in the area.

The residential composition and physical appearance of the area also has changed dramatically over the years. Once intraurban transportation and communication improved, wealthy inhabitants moved to more luxurious quarters farther from the city center. While now deteriorated, surviving nineteenth century Porfirian "modernist" architecture is living testimony to the elegance which pervaded the locale in the nineteenth century, when well-to-do persons lived there. The transformations have been so great that the area now resembles what E. Burgess called an "area of blight."[7] The area remains largely residential;[8] increasingly *comerciantes* ("petty" merchants), artisans, factory workers, and lower "middle-class" salaried and clerical workers have replaced their wealthier predecessors.

As the area became more commercial, a huge *tianguis* (an In-

[6] The factories within El Centro date from the early twentieth century and are either small or medium in size. The large factories are mostly on the periphery of the Federal District, in the north. Similarly, in England historically major industrial cities arose in places where there previously had been no settlement at all or only small villages or hamlets—in places with no long urban tradition of guilds, market privileges, and other vested interests. The new cities grew faster and ultimately became larger than the older, preindustrial cities. Bert Hoselitz, "The City, the Factory and Economic Growth," pp. 74-75.

[7] Ernest Burgess, "The Growth of the City," in his *The City.*

[8] Under Porfirio Diaz the "center" of the city shifted westward from El Zócalo to the area around the avenues named Reforma and Bucareli. Enrique Valencia, *La Merced.* Consequently, the area under study never was transformed entirely into a business district, as probably otherwise would have occurred with the expansion of the city economy. Initially, under the urban "grid-pattern" introduced by the Spanish colonizers the rich lived in the center city. For a discussion of the conditions under which the Burgess model applies to Latin American cities, see Leo Schnore, "On the Spatial Structure of Cities in the Two Americas," pp. 347-98, and the references therein.

dian word for an outdoor market) market came to clutter the streets and patios of the houses. Many *comerciantes* began to live in the newly constructed but rat-infested wooden market stalls as well as in the large old houses which were subdivided into small apartments. In addition, new, less elegant buildings were constructed, particularly in the section farthest from El Zócalo. These one-room, one- and two-story tenements, known as *vecindades*, are built inward from the street around courtyards.[9] They now constitute the most typical dwelling unit in the area, housing approximately three-fourths of the residents. The largest ones contain about 1,000 people, but generally the *vecindades* house one-fifth as many people. Absentee-owned, some by proprietors of Spanish descent, the *vecindades* are densely populated, unsanitary, and poorly ventilated. Plumbing facilities frequently do not function properly, and buildings at times are so run down that sections occasionally collapse, leaving survivors injured and homeless.

Conditions in many old buildings, particularly those which are rent-controlled,[10] have deteriorated over the years, except when tenants invested their own time and money to improve the edifices. Some tenants, for example, pooled *centavos* and labor to paint the facades of their *vecindades* in bright colors, in conjunction with a government beautification program publicly associated with the Olympics.[11] Families also invest in their own

[9] *Vecindades* are known as *callejones* in Lima, *conventillos* in Chile and *avenidas* or *vilas* in Rio de Janeiro. See R. W. Patch, "Life in a Callejón"; L. Salmen, "The *Casas de Cômodos* of Rio de Janeiro."

[10] According to rent control legislation enacted in 1948, which in modified form remains in effect, rents cannot be increased in those dwelling units still occupied by the families which inhabited them when the law was established. The section of Mexico City with *tugurios* includes the highest proportion of rent-controlled units. Harth Deneke, "*Colonias proletarias.*" Housing falls under the rent-control law as long as the original tenant, or members of his permanent family who resided with him in 1948, remain in the dwelling. The rights to rent control do not terminate with the death of the original occupant: unless previously agreed upon with the landlord, occupancy may be inherited. Brown, p. 84.

[11] At the same time that Mexican sponsorship of the Olympics in 1968 provoked a serious student-led challenge to the government's legitimacy, here as well as in the other two areas the government publicized the occasion, in the months preceding the sports events, in a way which generated national pride, unity, and sacrifice for the nation: Tenants and shop-owners were encouraged to paint their buildings to give "foreigners a good impression of Mexico."

1.

2.

3.

4.

5.

7.

9.

EL CENTRO

1. The old barrio church
2. Athletic field at the government-run sports and social center
3. A nineteenth century building
4. Busy commercial street
5. *Ambulantes,* ambulant "penny capitalists"
6-8. Scenes from *vecindades*
9. A new prefabricated government-administered market
10. Local police

individual quarters: for example, when they build a mezzanine floor, fix a broken door, or make other alterations, they either pay for a portion or all the materials and generally for all the labor. In the process the tenants increase the value of the property which the proprietors can absorb when there is a changeover of occupants.

Because of low returns to investments, the slum landlords increasingly are abandoning or selling their buildings. And because the value of the land is high the new owners replace the old constructions with modern apartment buildings, which they rent at prices the former tenants cannot afford. Accordingly, the socioeconomic level of the community has risen.

While not evident from the street, social and economic life within *vecindades* varies markedly. On the one hand, there are large *vecindades*, such as the one known as the Casa Grande in Oscar Lewis' *Five Families*.[12] Spread out over an entire square block, this *vecindad* almost forms a world of its own. Together with the neighborhood market and nearby public bath it supplies most of the daily "needs" of tenants. It is enclosed by high cement walls and rows of shops. People enter and leave through two gateways which are open during the day but locked at night. Within the *vecindad* are several cement patios, filled with children. The patios are surrounded by unventilated one-room apartments which generally house individual families. Many of the inhabitants have washtubs, toilets, modern furniture and appliances, radios, television sets, phonographs, beds, and tables. Some of them even have refrigerators, and washing and sewing machines. Their quarters at times are carefully decorated with linoleum flooring, fresh paint, picture calendars, plastic ornaments, porcelain trinkets, and religious objects. Overcrowded in their cramped quarters but sufficiently well-off financially, many have constructed mezzanines which hold an additional bed or two besides those for which there is space on the ground floor. They also use the exterior of their quarters as an extension of their home. They dry laundry, raise chickens, and grow flowers and medicinal herbs on the roofs.

Socioreligious customs and activities bind *vecindad* residents together. The *vecindad* is protected by patron saints at the entryways. Surrounding the images of the saints are offerings of flow-

[12] Lewis, *Five Families*. Part of the Sanchez family, one of the families discussed in *Five Families* and the subject of the entire book, *The Children of Sanchez*, lived in the Casa Grande.

ers and candles, and small medals which are testimonials of the miracles saints performed for residents. The socioreligious life of the *vecindad* also includes collectively celebrated pilgrimages and festivities, particularly on the annual Commemoration of the Feast Day of the Virgin of Guadalupe and during the Christmas *posadas*, but also, for example, on the *barrio* Saint's Day and on the day of the annual pilgrimage market vendors organize to the Basilica of Guadalupe. The latter event first was introduced in 1931. Thus, not all of the seemingly traditional socioreligious activities in which such *vecindad* residents participate are surviving Indian and Colonial customs.

On the other hand, there are smaller and poorer *vecindades* which are neither as self-contained nor as well-furnished as the Casa Grande. Built of adobe brick, they are physically more deteriorated and they tend to have only communal toilet and washing facilities. They also tend not to be integrated through collectively celebrated socioreligious festivities, largely because the inhabitants are too poor to afford such luxuries. These *vecindades* have no gates and no patron saints, and the *viviendas* (individual living units) are filled with few of the manufactured goods which clutter the larger, more opulent *vecindades*.

The variation in cost of rented quarters in the area depends not so much on the quality of housing as on whether or not *viviendas* are rent-controlled.[13] Only the units with regulated rents, which represent an indirect income subsidy, are inexpensive. Of the tenants interviewed, about 40 percent reported paying less than $11.00 a month rent, 20 percent reported paying between $11.00 and $16.99, and the remainder reported paying $17.00 or more. The actual cost of housing, however, tends to run higher. To circumvent the law and capitalize on the great demand for quarters in the area, *vecindad* owners generally insist that tenants pay "under the table" to get housing. Moreover, as previously noted, whenever tenants fix inoperative facilities and upgrade their living quarters they must invest their own money.

The most far-reaching change in the area since World War II, however, has not been the housing alterations but rather the re-

[13] While free market rents increased five times between 1942 and 1963, rents in rent-controlled properties remained much more stable. Oliver Oldman et al., *Financing Urban Development in Mexico City*, p. 139. The rent control law, initiated during World War II when domestic industrialization was expanding, facilitated rural to urban migration since it kept the cost of urban living down. In effect, the law helped provide urban-based businesses with a large supply of labor, which they could hire at low wages.

placement of the sprawling *tianguis* market with several closed, prefabricated government-administered modern markets. The government now controls—as it does in all the markets it administers—the size of stalls and working hours, thereby limiting the profits vendors are likely to earn, but preventing a small number of merchants from monopolizing local market opportunities. Thus, vendors benefit from indirect government protection without which their businesses could not readily remain solvent.

The introduction of covered markets had important social and political implications. Most of the *comerciantes* who had booths in the *tianguis* market were allotted stalls in the new markets, but those who formerly slept in their stalls were left homeless. Their flight to outlying areas of the city—some, with government permission, to the then recently settled but still illegal squatter settlement I studied—depopulated the area. Yet the community as a whole benefited from the new markets, mainly because of the resultant improvement in local sanitary and safety conditions. Now rats much less frequently scurry through the streets, traffic moves more freely, and Mexicans feel more secure when entering the crime-ridden area than they did before.

The municipal government took advantage of the occasion to introduce new political-administrative controls locally. However, even though most of the local markets in 1968 were administered by retired policemen and even though policemen patrolled the markets and adjacent streets, the area continues to be a thriving hub of underworld and other illegal activities. Local vendors still peddle goods illegally in the streets, maintain ties with the "international mafia," and participate in well-organized crime networks. Because of the illicit way much of the merchandise is obtained, the secondhand markets are known as the "Thieves' Market." In addition, near the markets are large, illegal houses of prostitution and stores selling alcohol after legal hours, guarded by policemen. The government functionaries and policemen, while commissioned by Federal District agencies to maintain "law and order" locally, protect such illicit activities because they in return receive graft. In this way national political and economic forces are subordinated to local interests, but residents must pay for the laxity in law enforcement.[14]

[14] Reflecting the close ties policemen have with the community, people living and working in the area know locally stationed Secret Police to the extent that they hide stolen merchandise when they see the Police approach-

The area is exposed to national influences not only through the market administration and the police but also through other institutions. There now are several new government schools, along with old run-down ones functioning since the Porfiriato (the reign of Porfirio Díaz, preceding the revolution), and a few private primary and commercial schools. In addition, there is a newly renovated government-run sports center, National "Popular" Subsistence Corporation (CONASUPO) shops where residents line up at 5:00 a.m. in order to get milk at one-third the commercial price,[15] and medical clinics for government employees and organized workers.[16] Religious institutions include two Catholic churches besides the colonial *barrio* church, a Church-affiliated charity hospital and primary school, and several Protestant churches—including Pentecostal, the Salvation Army, and Methodist[17]—serving small sect-like congregations. One Catholic parish was run by U.S. and French priests, and two of the Protestant

---

ing them. When goods were stolen from my car I had the opportunity to observe relations between the Secret Police and local market vendors. I reported the theft to the market administrator, a retired policeman. Since I was an American and a personal acquaintance of his he assigned the Secret Police to my case, even though the merchandise was not valuable or easily identifiable. While waiting for the Police, I saw a large crowd suddenly gather around two men. I subsequently realized that *comerciantes* had gathered around the "Secret" Police to find out what case they were beginning to investigate. Once the Police learned what had been stolen from me they visited certain *vecindades* near the market where they knew thieves generally stored such goods before selling them in the secondhand market.

[15] Goods in CONASUPO shops, which include mobile trailer units, sell at lower prices than goods in private stores.

[16] There are no public ˙clinics within the area for artisans, *comerciantes*, and others not covered by medical insurance through work, although such clinics exist in the vicinity.

[17] A group which split from the Salvation Army started a Methodist congregation. The first Protestant sect in the area was established in the early 1900s. According to Willems, Protestantism in Latin America has made its greatest inroads in cities undergoing urbanization and industrialization, owing to a concomitant weakening of traditional controls and migrants' marginal status within the cities. Emileo Willems, "Culture Change and the Rise of Protestantism in Brazil and Chile," pp. 187-93. Since foreign missionaries introduced Protestantism within the *tugurio*, urbanization and industrialization do not explain the *emergence* of Protestantism locally. However, it is plausible that the ability of the missionaries to win converts is linked to the loose social controls which prevailed in the area as the local population expanded and the local economy underwent change.

churches were founded or financially supported by American missionaries. Although the ministers were Mexican, they were partly trained by Americans. They also received spiritual guidance from U.S. missionaries.

These various social and religious services and facilities all were administered locally by nonresidents who had been temporarily assigned to the area by higher-ranking personnel in the respective institutional hierarchies. Local residents, despite their deep roots in the community, rarely have been able to influence the appointments, much less determine the facilities locally available.

In contrast to most low-income sections of Mexico City, residents here tend to be long-term urban dwellers who have lived almost exclusively in this one urban neighborhood. Most of the migrants have lived in the capital at least fifteen years: they are mainly from shoemaking communities in Guanajuato and Jalisco, although there are migrants from all states living in the area. While residents generally have always lived in this section of Mexico City, they often resided in one or two other domiciles, having moved either when they married or when they were able to find improved living quarters.

Among the core of residents who were born and raised locally is a group known as *el núcleo* (the nucleus). They identify strongly with and take great pride in the area, the community's bad reputation and physically deteriorated state notwithstanding. They even have their own subculture which partly contrasts with the culture of other poor, as well as with the culture of other socioeconomic classes. Their subculture includes *modismos* (slang) referring to local economic activities, and distinct norms and values. The "nucleus" have their own criteria for evaluating people. They praise, above all, individual prowess. Thus, the most outstanding local figures in their minds are not local industrialists, politicians, and government functionaries whose importance derives from national political and economic power, but old, established store owners, certain *comerciantes*, and some owners of *vecindades*. They also have their own local heroes, such as the nationally renowned boxers, Raúl "Ratón" Macias and José "Huitlacoche" Medel. These heroes, particularly the athletes, never entirely leave the area, even when, with newly acquired wealth, they move to more socially and economically respectable neighborhoods. For example, one of the nation's outstanding boxers, who earned his fame when growing up in the area, comes back daily to visit his mother, family, and friends, and regularly frequents the newly renovated sports center to help train a new generation of boxers. Moreover, the nucleus assigns limited importance to conspicuous consumption. As a consequence, their wealth is not evident from the way they live.

Although some of the young generation of this nucleus have moved away because they wanted and could afford their own home, many of them have stayed in the area by choice. They find people on the city's periphery too "provincial" and not as virtuous and "dignified" as local residents.

Those who are most anxious to move and dissociate themselves from *barrio* life are the petty bourgeoisie—small shopowners, low-level bureaucrats and clerical workers—or persons actively seeking "middle-class" status. However, most residents do not wish to leave the area. They appreciate the area's central location and the friendliness of local people. What they dislike are the alcoholics who roam the streets,[18] the homeless men who sleep in the streets, particularly near the old church plaza, and the low "culture" of some residents. Those who want to move generally are interested in acquiring their own home. The congested, deteriorated state of most local buildings is not of particular concern to residents.

In sum, as the society at large has changed so too has the *tugurio*. Residents, though weak in shaping national political, economic, and social policies, have been able to adapt some of those policies to their own needs and wants. This is particularly true of the nucleus of old-time residents. They remain somewhat apart both from other residents and from persons in the society around them.

La Colonia: The Legalized Squatter Settlement

Situated on the northeast periphery of the Federal District, the legalized squatter settlement, which in Mexico is called a *colonia proletaria*,[19] is much less densely populated than the inner-city

[18] There are more bars in this district than in any other district in the city. Valencia, p. 38.

[19] The term *colonia proletaria* refers to low-value land on the outskirts of Mexican cities which generally houses low-income families. Although this term generally is used in reference to several different types of low-income neighborhoods, the name *"La Colonia"* is used euphemistically

area. Whereas the population of *tugurios* has remained stable in recent decades as the city has grown in size, to the extent that *tugurios* currently house only about 6 percent of the urban population, outlying *colonias proletarias* have steadily increased in number and have come to house an increasing proportion of the city's population.[20] *Colonias proletarias* now represent the most typical pattern of low-income urban housing settlement in Mexico, as in other Latin American countries (Plan II). They are a response to the regional imbalances generated by capitalist development, imbalances which attract the populace to the centers of industrial production, commerce, and services.

This particular *colonia proletaria*—called euphemistically *La Colonia*—is approximately 1½ kilometers long and 1 kilometer wide, and presently houses an estimated 60,000 families. Until 1952 the area belonged to an *ejido*.[21] In that year the Department of Hydraulics expropriated the land to better control the water of the lake which underlies and surrounds the city of Mexico.

One night in October 1954, several hundred families occupied

---

here specifically in reference to the legalized squatter settlement. Similarly, the term *colonos*, residents of *colonias proletarias*, here refers specifically to residents of *La Colonia*. *Colonias* are known by other names in other Latin American countries, for example as *callampas* in Chile, *villas miserias* in Argentina, *barriadas* in Peru, and *ranchos* in Venezuela.

[20] The population of the Federal District residing in *colonias proletarias* increased from approximately 14 percent in 1952 to an estimated 50 percent in 1970. *Colonias proletarias* covered 21 percent of the city's surface area in 1940, and an estimated 40 percent in 1970. Brown, p. 72. This proliferation of lower class settlements on the city periphery goes contrary to the Burgess model which states that the wealthy, not the poor, live on the periphery. While there are a few sections on the outskirts of the city, particularly in the southeast, which are inhabited by wealthy Mexicans, most peripheral settlements in Mexico, as in other major contemporary Latin American cities, house people of low socioeconomic status. Latin American cities do not conform to the Burgess model (of limited applicability to most U.S. cities as well) largely because, in comparison with the U.S., Latin American cities have been growing more rapidly and not expanding their low-cost inner-city housing supply sufficiently to house the urban poor.

[21] In the Federal District, between 1950 and 1960 alone, the number of *ejidos* declined by 80 percent. Oldman et al., *Financing Urban Development in Mexico City*. To the extent that such *ejido* land is being used to house the expanding low-income population of the city, the cost is being borne by the *campesinos*, not by well-to-do.

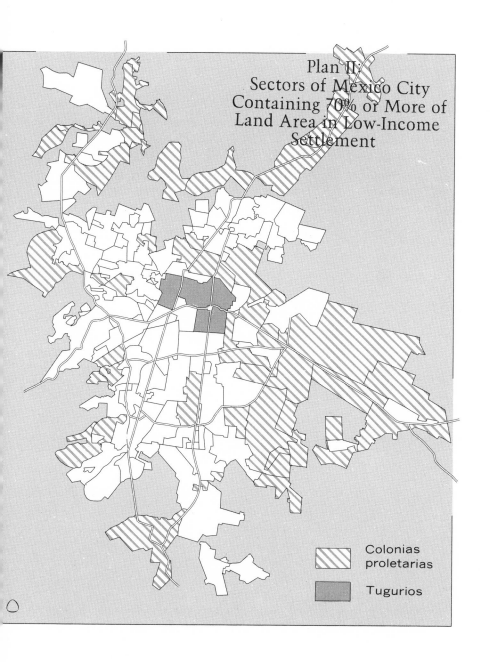

Plan II.
Sectors of México City
Containing 70% or More of
Land Area in Low-Income
Settlement

Colonias
proletarias

Tugurios

—or, as Mexicans say, "parachuted" onto—the land.[22] The invasion was organized by *coyotes* (illicit brokers) who organized the movement in several sections of the city, under the banner of a group affiliated with the Popular Sector of the Party.[23] Some of them assumed colorful pseudonyms such as Piedad Hueso (Mercy Bone) and Samuel El Grande (The Great). These *coyotes* sold so-called *credenciales* (credential cards) to interested persons prior to the invasion for $6.00, although some squatters report that they were charged three times as much. The *coyotes* claimed that those who purchased the cards were entitled to a plot of land. Not specifying in advance where the land would be, the *coyotes* periodically called meetings. At the rallies they informed credential holders and potential customers of their latest plans. While many with *credenciales* realized that they were acquiring title to land which did not belong to the *coyotes*, they wanted property of their own and felt that if they invaded *en masse*, with the protection of the organizers and the Party, they might not be evicted.

At the time of the invasion the area was uninhabitable. It was muddy and partially covered with water. The government initially tried to force the *paracaidistas* (the parachuters) to leave, both by inundating the land with water from the canals and by calling in police. However, it abandoned its effort after meeting persistent resistance from the squatters.[24]

[22] Land invaders in Mexico are called *paracaidistas* (parachuters). Other countries have different words for such squatters: for example, Brazilians call them *favelados*, and Venezuelans call them *rancheros* and *conqueros*. In recent years organized squatter invasions in Mexico have decreased in importance, while land speculators dealing in "subdivisions" have come to play an increasingly important role in the land market. Brown, p. 20. Thus, *La Colonia* represents the initial post-World War II type of self-constructed housing.

[23] In other countries as well squatter settlements, from their very inception, have been plugged into national political or administrative structures. See Talton Ray, *The Politics of the Barrios of Venezuela*. At times governments actually encourage the formation of squatter settlements. See David Collier, *Squatters and Oligarchs*, p. 57, and Henry Dietz, "Urban Squatter Settlements in Peru," pp. 353-70.

[24] Typically, police reaction is milder when invasions are on public land than when they are on private land. Collier (p. 47) reports the same to be true in Lima. In Mexico, government policy toward squatting in the capital has shifted since 1966 from hostility and confrontation to acquiescence and at times assistance in the improvement of illegally formed settlements. See Harold Jackson, "Intra-Urban Migration of Mexico City's Poor," p. 27.

But squatters' problems did not end then. Property allocations became a source of corruption and manipulation. The *coyotes* and their resident collaborators, as well as district *políticos* and local "natural leaders" who acquired posts in the PRI and government-linked groups, illegally sold property which they did not own at increasingly higher prices after the invasion, and regularly charged squatters fees ostensibly to arrange for legalization of land claims. Some squatters were robbed, and removed by force. Others had parts of their rudimentary houses confiscated. Most of them were helpless, fearing that they would be ousted if they failed to acquiesce. Squatters even fought among themselves over claims to land, sometimes because the *coyotes* and *políticos* had knowingly sold "landrights" to more than one party. *Políticos* also increasingly fought among themselves, accusing one another of illegally forming groups, and of illegally using the groups for their personal aggrandizement both by selling "rights" to property they did not own and by collecting money without authorization for civic events and the community's anniversary celebration. In the course of the feuding, local leaders who never successfully secured or maintained the support of higher-ranking functionaries experienced unfortunate consequences: One small-scale entrepreneur in charge of a local PRI and government-affiliated group was threatened with a pistol by a collaborator of his arch-enemy and was subsequently imprisoned for fraud; one unlicensed lawyer was informed by the police that he would be arrested if he continued mobilizing residents; and one low-level local government functionary was assassinated.

Material conditions also remained bad for several years. The unpaved streets were muddy during the rainy season and dusty during the dry season. Squatters initially had no running water, no *molina* (mill) where they could buy *tortillas*, no officially recognized public school for their children, and no public transportation connecting the area to sections of the city where they worked. They had to go to neighboring *colonias* to get prepared *tortillas*, and they had to wade through the canal and walk about twenty minutes to the closest bus stop. After the construction of a bridge over the canal, buses and itinerant water dispensary trucks entered the area. Squatters then had to line up early in the morning to get small, limited quantities of water.

Gradually, after the area was officially recognized as a *colonia proletaria* in 1958, *colonos* (residents of *colonias proletarias*) ob-

11.

12.

13.

14.

15.

16.

17.

18.

19.

LA COLONIA

11-13. Housing, reflecting the area's socioeconomic diversity

14. Advertisements: multinationals, gifts for Mother's Day, public toilet facilities

15. Itinerant water distributor

16. Store selling *tortillas*

17. An ambulant unofficial market

18. The official prefabricated market

19. Local residents

20. A garbage heap

20.

tained legal access to electricity; running water, first in public taps, then on the individual plots of land they claimed for themselves; public primary schools and a kindergarten; paved streets; additional public transportation; police protection; a social center; and a medical clinic. Several religious institutions also were established: a Catholic church and a chapel; a parochial school; Jehovah's Witness and spiritualist centers, and Evangelical, Methodist, and Pentecostal "temples."

As the locally available facilities have improved, so too has the quality of the housing. Once squatters accumulated money and became confident that they would not be evicted, they began to replace the cloth-covered posts which they initially used to stake claims to the land with scraps of tin sheets and wooden boards, and, increasingly, adobe bricks and cement. They constructed their homes with little if any help from professional architects and engineers, and minimal help from paid construction workers. Their homes now typically are one story high, and contain one or two rooms. The exteriors, frequently painted colorful pinks, greens, and blues, are adorned occasionally with "branches," or with other objects, to protect residents from "evil spirits."

Many *colonos* raise a few pigs or chickens to help minimize the cost of city living, and have dogs, which though costly to feed, help protect them from thieves. A few of them even have cows and mules.

Home improvements especially stepped up once the government legally recognized the area in 1958, in accordance with the Law of the *Colonias Proletarias*. Technically this law protects the interests of urban poor as land covered by it is sold for a nominal fee, may not be absentee-owned, must be inhabited by lower- and working-class persons, and is inalienable (*patrimonio familiar*). Were the law strictly enforced it would create a class of small-propertied urban poor, just as the government's *ejido* program has created in principle a small-propertied peasant class in rural areas: The law prohibits land speculation and land-grabbing by well-to-do persons who can afford housing on the non-subsidized market. Although *colonos* had to finance their own housing, the government sold the property to them for the nominal fee of eighty cents a square meter, payable in monthly installments over a ten-year period.

The government, however, has been lax in enforcing the Law of *Colonias Proletarias*, to the disadvantage of resident poor. In

1968 residents still had not received the official scriptures authorizing their legal property rights. In violation of the law, one-third of the residents by the late 1960s were tenants, and most of the largest *vecindades* were illegally owned by persons who never lived in the area.[25] While these *vecindades* contrast markedly in size with those in *El Centro*, rents compare favorably even with rent controlled center city quarters.[26]

Also in violation of the law, professionals and other "middle class" people are increasingly buying land locally.[27] Many squatters left when the government began to charge for sidewalks, street pavement, and drainage facilities as well as for land. However, since then the value of the property has increased, to the extent that only the "middle class" can afford to purchase local housing: local residents claim that an average-sized house currently sells for approximately $3,000, and the largest homes for $8,000-$16,000. Expensive as the land has become, it remains cheaper than the cost of comparable property in legally-formed areas in the city limits. Thus, the area increasingly is becoming a subsidized housing for the "middle class." Economically more secure than the original *colonos*, the new residents have enlarged, partially reconstructed, and redecorated their homes. Their two- and three-story tiled homes contrast markedly with the makeshift quarters of the first *paracaidistas*.

Because of the increasing number of tenants and the change-over of proprietorship, the composition of the area has shifted since 1954. As housing density has increased, the original squatters have come to comprise an ever-smaller percentage of the total population. Only about 15 percent of the present-day residents lived in the area since the first years after the invasion. Furthermore, according to early leaders of local squatter organizations, at most 25-50 percent of the original squatters still live in the area.

[25] By the early 1960s renters constituted almost 50 percent of the general *colonia proletaria* population. Brown, p. 101.

[26] Rents on the whole are lower in *colonias proletarias* than in *tugurios*. Instituto Nacional de la Vivienda, *Colonias proletarias*, unnumbered chart, "Rentas de casa," and Instituto Nacional de la Vivienda, *Herradura de Tugurios*, unnumbered chart, "Rentas de casa."

[27] Cornelius (*Politics and the Migrant Poor*, p. 51) reports a similar transference of property to more affluent newcomers in return for cash payments when the government began to collect money from squatters for land and improvements.

Consequently, as in *El Centro* the government, legally and officially, protects urban poor, but it does not prevent class forces
from asserting themselves locally, to the increasing advantage of
the "middle class."[28] The socioeconomic level of *La Colonia* has
been upgraded over the years, but largely because of an influx
of petty bourgeoisie.

Despite the imposition of such class forces, the area remains
somewhat distinct from other types of low-income dwelling
areas. In comparison to the *tugurio*, the legalized squatter settlement continues to look more rural, partly because its population
is more rural. According to interviews with residents, about
twice as many *colonos* as center city dwellers are migrants, although only about 6 percent of the *colonos* moved to the area
directly from the provinces.[29] Furthermore, the migrants in *La
Colonia* tend to come from smaller towns and to have lived fewer
years in Mexico City than the migrants in *El Centro*. The contrasting backgrounds of residents reflect the fact that the two
areas were settled during different time periods: *La Colonia*
houses a later generation of migrants.

Nonetheless, despite the provincial appearance of the area and
the rural origin of most *colonos*, the area lacks both the rich network of informally organized activities so frequently attributed
to village life, and a local subculture comparable to that found
among the old-time residents of the center city area. No set of
customs and beliefs unite all or part of the community, differentiating it socially and culturally from other sections of the city.
Not even the original settlers maintain close contact any more.
Precisely because the *colonos* are not united by sustained com-

[28] Not merely the government but private economic institutions discriminate against urban poor. Mortgage, savings, and loan banks rarely
finance site improvements for low-cost settlements, and only a few banks
accept unimproved land as collateral for loans for the purpose of urbanizing
such settlements. Moreover, banks generally only make money available
for city residents earning more than $60.00 a month, which only approxi-
mately one-third of the *colonia proletaria* population earn. The 1962 credit
reforms did not ameliorate credit opportunities for urban poor. See Oldman
et al., *Financing Urban Development*; Raúl Cacho, "La Vivenda," p. 45.

[29] According to Turner, the more industrialized and urbanized a country
is, the less likely are migrants to settle first in the center city area, and the
more likely are they to move directly to *colonias proletarias*. John Turner,
pp. 354-63. For additional evidence on the Mexican pattern, see Brown,
Chapter Five.

munal activities and a long tradition, they are subject to the class biases operating in the society at large.

Few residents partake in community-sponsored religious pilgrimages. In contrast to center city area residents, groups of *colonos*, even when they come from the same provincial community, rarely celebrate together the day of the patron saint of their town of origin. Moreover, the emergent *vecindades* in *La Colonia* are not protected by saints, and inhabitants rarely collectively celebrate socioreligious festivities. However, it is their poverty rather than their social and cultural background which impedes such organized activities, just as finances constrain poor residents in the center city area: When *vecindad* people in the legalized squatter settlement were asked why they did not partake in more community activities, their most frequent answer was that they could not afford to do so.

While there is less informal sociopolitical and religious organization in *La Colonia* than in *El Centro*, so too is there less "disorganization" and organized illicit activity. *Colonos* complain of robberies and assaults, but trade in drugs, theft, and prostitution is not nearly as extensive and organized in *La Colonia* as in the center city area. Rates of homicide also appear to be lower in *La Colonia*: local leaders estimate that there is less than one killing per month in the area, whereas leaders in the center city area estimate that a killing occurs there on the average of once a week. For such reasons *colonos* feel that their settlement is a safer place to live and to raise children than the inner city, even though there are only two policemen permanently stationed in *La Colonia*, compared to approximately six dozen in the center city area.

Not only informal but also formal organized activities fail to bind *colonos* together. There are less and less community-wide sociopolitical activities, and attendance at the remaining few has declined over the years. The insecurity and excitement which initially brought *colonos* together has subsided and residents have been exposed to general political constraints to the extent that the area now is little more than an aggregate of families each interested, as they themselves acknowledge, primarily in themselves.

The prospect of home ownership above all attracted people to the area. However, over the years residents have also come to like the urban services which the area now offers. Their main complaints about *La Colonia* are the dust that continues to whirl through the streets during the dry season and the smelly garbage-cluttered canal which borders on the area; however, few residents currently organize collectively to pressure the government to remedy their grievances, as they did initially.

La Unidad: The Housing Development

Southeastward from *La Colonia*, on the eastern periphery of the Federal District, is the housing development. Also on a former *ejido*,[30] the area, covering over 1,000 hectares, had the uniformity of a Levittown when it first opened. Larger than any other housing project built by the government of the Federal District,[31] and much less characteristic of low-income housing than *La Colonia*, it served as a showpiece project for the outgoing president in 1964, López Mateos.[32] According to the original plan, the government intended to build 18,000 single-occupancy homes to house 59,526 persons. By 1968 approximately 10,000 units had been built, but they housed approximately 80,000 people.[33] Initially the different sections included a combination of

[30] Initially the *ejidatarios* received no compensation for their land, although two years after the development opened and several years after the *ejidatarios* lost their land, some of the families received retribution in the form of partial credit toward a house in the development. However, those *ejidatarios* who were *campesinos* were provided with no alternative means of employment in the city, although they were given the option to acquire agricultural land in the provinces.

[31] The Department of the Federal District (the DDF) is the principal organ of local government for Mexico City, excluding the contiguous urbanized sections in the State of Mexico. The head of the DDF, a presidential appointee, is a member of the president's cabinet.

[32] Between 1925 and 1960 the government of the Federal District constructed only 2.6 percent of all the housing sponsored by the public sector, or 1,800 homes. Over half of the housing in the public sector was sponsored by groups such as El Instituto de Seguridad y Servicios Sociales de los Trabajadores al Servicio del Estado (ISSSTE). El Banco Nacional Hipotecario Urbano de Obras Públicas (BNHUOPSA) built 18 percent and the Instituto Mexicano de Seguro Social (IMSS) built 12 percent. Therefore, access to most housing sponsored by the public sector during the thirty-five-year period depended on membership in corporate occupational groups associated with the two social security institutions. Sociedad de Arquitectos Mexicanos y del Colegio Nacional de Arquitectos de México, *La vivienda popular en México*, page unnumbered.

[33] This study focuses on the sections of the development completed by 1968. However, between 1968 and 1971 several thousand additional houses were built: some were prefabricated, others were constructed by individual families with no-interest government loans.

one- and two-story houses, except one section which contained only the least expensive, small single-story homes.

Despite the inaccurate population estimation, the development is less densely populated than either of the other areas. Also, the quality of the housing for the most part is better. Although residents complain that their houses are poorly ventilated, that the walls leak during the rainy season, and that they have drainage problems and occasionally no running water, the house frames tend to be sturdier and the interiors more spacious and better equipped with electricity and plumbing than housing in *El Centro* and *La Colonia.*

According to the statutes, recipients of houses are to buy the property from the government in monthly installments ranging between $9.60 and $28.00, over a fifteen-year period. The price varies according to the size of the house and its location. Most residents interviewed paid between $11.00 and $17.00. This amount is higher than that generally paid by tenants in *La Colonia* and those center city tenants who live in rent controlled quarters. It approximates the amount paid by other center city area tenants, but the dwelling units in the development are larger and better constructed. Moreover, recipients of homes here become property-owners after fifteen years.

Novel to Mexicans, the design of the area draws on U.S. city planning concepts. However, it never produced the intended effect: Like the Clarence Perry plan, the development is designed to promote privacy, neighborliness, and community-wide solidarity.[34] Thus, homes include separate rooms for sleeping, cooking, and everyday living. The area is divided into several distinct neighborhoods, each of which is separated by major through streets and minimally contains a primary school, market, central plaza, and, generally, a church (see Plan III). Each neighborhood also includes open space, pedestrian paths, and small streets designed to foster friendliness among neighbors. In line with the Perry plan, there also are community-wide facilities to tie the entire community together. There is a park with a zoo and lake, sports centers, a children's hospital, and technical and academic secondary schools. There also is a government social center with a pool and other athletic facilities, a movie house, a post office, and a funeral parlor. Until this social center opened in

---

[34] Clarence Perry, "The Neighborhood Unit," pp. 22-140. Use of U.S. planning concepts may stem from the fact that the chief architect of the program studied in the United States.

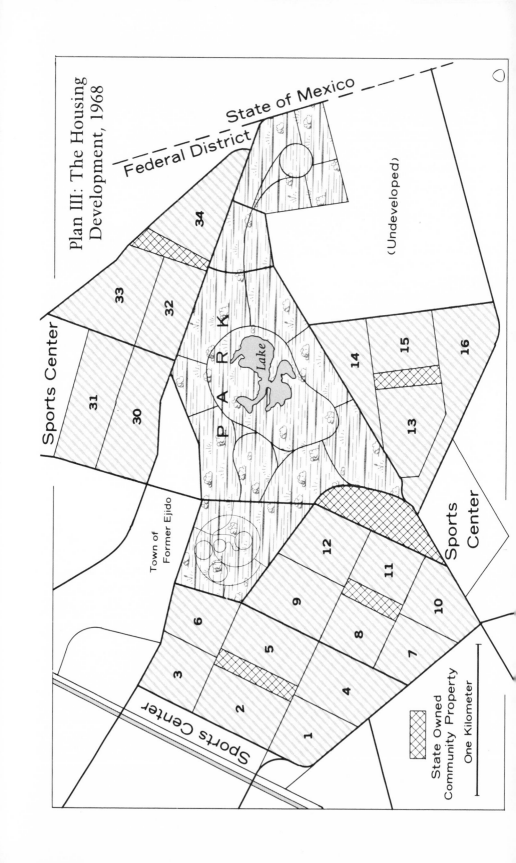

Plan III: The Housing
Development, 1968

State of Mexico

Federal District

Sports Center

Sports Center

34

33

32

31

30

P A R K

Lake

Town of
Former Ejido

(Undeveloped)

14

15

16

13

Sports
Center

12

11

9

10

8

7

6

5

3

2

4

1

State Owned
Community Property

One Kilometer

1968 there was a small one operating in the poorest section of the development, but there never have been indoor places where residents could informally intermingle. *Pulquerias* (places selling *pulque*, an inexpensive alcoholic beverage) and *cantinas* (bars) are outlawed. A *preparatoria*, the three-year school preceding the university, and a large commercial center with a movie house, bank, and supermarket, included in the original plan, had not been built by 1971.

To what extent the area was supposed to be specifically for urban poor is unclear, even though officials claimed that the houses were mainly for families displaced by public works projects and for families living in unsanitary squatter settlements and slums. Public proclamations, administration policies, and statements by officials and planners suggest that the government never intended that the housing be mainly for the socially and economically underprivileged. Some of them all along doubted whether displaced squatters and slum-dwellers could afford living in the area. Moreover, according to an official statute, the area was to house workers earning the legal minimum wage, significantly more than what most of the city's poor earn. The government's intent is even more suspect since it allocated a large number of houses to various working- and "middle-class" groups —to units of the police force, industrial unions, journalists, municipal government functionaries, the army, "opposition" parties and the PRI—to distribute, in turn, to select members of their respective groups.[35]

In addition, housing qualifications and the manner in which homes were allocated to squatters and slum dwellers reflect the government's "middle-class" biases and its insensitivity to the concerns of urban poor. Abandoned women in the areas destined for demolition could not qualify for homes in the development unless they lied about their marital status, and displaced persons of ill-repute were not given homes. Those who were eligible claim that they were carted in trucks, with only those belongings that they could readily transport. Materials which they had in-

[35] An even larger proportion of the houses constructed since 1968 have been allocated to occupational groups—primarily to the unions of taxi drivers and electricians, and to the Mexican Federation of Laborers (the CTM), but also to municipal government employees, airline and transport workers, and professionals (especially doctors). Thus, these houses from the onset were not allocated to poor people. Moreover, the housing—ranging from approximately $12,000 to $16,000—was costly for urban poor.

21.

22.

23.

24.

25.

26.

27.

28.

LA UNIDAD

21. Typical housing, large and small
22. Expansion and modification of housing
23. Housefront converted into store
24. Landscaping, border of sub-community
25. A government social center
26. A playing field
27. A prefabricated public elementary school
28. A local prefabricated government-run market
29. A prefabricated Catholic church building

29.

vested in their former quarters had to be left behind. Moreover, they were neither shown the development beforehand nor given a clear idea of the place to which they were being moved. Assigned to houses on numbered streets which to them all looked more or less alike, they recall incidences of spending endless, fearful hours at first, searching for their homes when returning from work and shopping.

Although, as in *La Colonia*, the property here is technically inalienable (*patrimonio familiar*), over half of the homes in the poorest section and about one-third of the homes in the other sections had by 1971 changed hands illegally. Mainly the poorest families left. Current residents and the housing administrator claim that poor families moved largely because (1) they never entirely adjusted to the new environment, (2) they preferred living closer to where they worked, (3) they could not afford the monthly payments,[36] and (4) they were tempted by the money others were willing to pay them to relinquish their property.

While most families who left did so "voluntarily," the government forced some to move who ostensibly were guilty of crimes. According to one of the local priests, the government, pressured by "middle-class" residents of the development, evicted one hundred pickpockets it had transplanted from an inner-city area. In so doing, government functionaries used the pretext of eminent domain to remove avowed criminals from the city center and then denied the displaced persons the right to live in another section of the city.

The original inhabitants are increasingly replaced by working- and particularly by "middle-class" families. The new residents consider the housing both inexpensive and highly desirable, even though they generally pay up to twice as much as the original price set by the government. In addition to paying the monthly installments in the name of the initial housing recipients, they pay the original to-be owner an amount approximately equal to the total cost of the home to forego the property. Since only "middle-class" persons can afford such cash outlays, the development more than either of the other areas is proving to be a "middle-class" subsidy, and the government is not preventing this trend.

[36] The government reserves the right to evict residents if they fail to meet three consecutive monthly installments.

In general, the values and priorities as well as the budgets of these "middle-class" persons differ from those of their predecessors. Many of them have built additional rooms and elaborately decorated and painted the facades of their dwellings. They are more preoccupied with respectability, housing quality, conspicuous display of wealth, and safety for their children.[37] According to original recipients of homes who have not moved, those who left, in contrast, were more concerned with securing inexpensive shelter.

In addition to homes being occupied increasingly by people for whom they were not intended, the homes are not being used according to design: While buildings are supposed to be for single-family occupancy and while residents are not to take in tenants, raise animals on their premises, or use their homes for commercial purposes, many residents do not comply with these stipulations. They cannot afford to do so. To cover the high monthly "rent," they tend to take in boarders. As many as twenty people sleep in some homes: the living room becomes used as a bedroom, and children and adults share rooms, even though the houses were designed to assure privacy for adults. In addition, some families raise a few chickens or pigs, or operate small shops in their homes.

The "middle-" and, to a lesser extent, working-class occupants are financially better able to use the house in the manner intended.[38] However, they too at times violate the regulations by adding stories to their homes.

Although about 40 percent of the residents of the development are migrants—compared to 30 percent of the center city dwellers and two-thirds of the *colonos*—most of them already lived in the capital by the time they were fifteen. As in *La Colonia*, the majority both of migrant and nonmigrant residents previously lived in other sections of Mexico City. And like *colonos*, residents of the development consider the urban services and the opportunity to own a home the most attractive aspects of the area. What they dislike about the community depends mainly on their socioeconomic status. The lower-status residents are discontent with the

[37] On the relationship between economic status and housing priorities see John Turner, "Housing Priorities."

[38] Epstein argues, on the basis of his study of Brasilia, that because planners themselves are elites, they tend to see the city as an elite process and design housing accordingly. David Epstein, *Brasilia, Plan and Reality.*

area's location: They would prefer living closer to the city center or their place of work. Those who formerly lived and worked far from the development now must commute several hours a day by public transportation to get to their job. Above all, women raising families frequently had to quit their previous jobs, being unable to spend up to four hours daily in transit. In addition, poor residents are unhappy with the high cost of local living.[39] Except for goods under government price control, food costs tend to be high here, particularly in comparison with prices in the center city. Moreover, many former squatters and slum-dwellers previously paid little or no rent, and no electricity or water bills.

In contrast, the more affluent residents are displeased with the "culture" of their poor neighbors. Because they moved to the area to live a "middle-class" life-style which they could not otherwise afford, they are particularly anxious to differentiate themselves from their poorer neighbors.[40] As a result, interclass relations here are highly formalized. Dress, skin color, house size, house decor, and, on occasion, automobiles, serve as visible cues to the degree of intimacy lower, working, and "middle" class neighbors can expect from each other. Interclass tensions are such that more employed artisans and unskilled laborers in the development feel socially and economically inferior than people similarly employed in the other two areas, and more salaried white-collar workers in the development feel socially and economically superior than people similarly employed in the other two areas. In addition, the desire of salaried "middle-class" residents of the development to affirm their social status inclines them to accumulate more possessions than their economic counterparts in the other areas, even though they have to go more into debt as a consequence. The strains produced by this situation are exemplified by a shoe artisan, a former squatter whom the government forced to move to the housing development. He noted that the area imposed new social, economic, and psychological

[39] According to a small consumer price census I conducted of goods merchandized in markets and shops in the three areas, the cost of living is highest in *La Unidad* and lowest in *El Centro*. Of the three areas, only *El Centro* has a local second-hand "market economy."

[40] Similarly, Wagley notes that normally latent racism in Brazil becomes manifest when socioeconomic classes feel threatened and when interclass contact is most intimate. Charles Wagley, "From Caste to Class in Northern Brazil," pp. 55, 57.

strains on him: "I feel intimidated by my new neighbors. They see that I am of lower status, because they see I am poorly dressed." Similarly, a family who moved from the poorest section of the development to one of the better sections in order to obtain a larger house, complained that their new "middle-class" neighbors snubbed them, while their former neighbors never did. They felt so uncomfortable that they continued to go to church in their former neighborhood. Thus, the disdain of resident "middle class" for their poor neighbors suggests that social and economic heterogeneity may generate tensions and resentments, rather than tolerance and class homogenization.

Yet despite such class tensions and complaints, the development tends to be viewed as a success. At least those persons who have remained in the development view their residency more positively than *colonos* and center city dwellers view theirs.

However, measured against the original plan, the area in many respects is a failure. Houses are not used as specified in the original design, and paradoxically, there is much less sense of community here than there presently is among the center city area "nucleus" and formerly was among the squatters, despite the architectural efforts to create a viable community.

Residents, unlike *el núcleo* in *El Centro*, do not share a common socioeconomic background routinely reinforced through local work, and they, unlike squatters, were not initially drawn together by a common crisis. For these reasons they do not have a distinct subculture or extensive and intensive community ties which significantly shape their outlook and involvements independently of forces operating in the society at large.

COMMUNITY-BASED PARTICIPATION

Participation in community-based activities also varies among the three areas. While almost one-fourth of the center city area residents interviewed worked in their home or neighborhood, only 1 percent of the *colonos* and 5 percent of the residents in the housing development worked in their respective areas. The business opportunities situated in the center city area reflect specific historical artisan, industrial, and commercial economic developments and government policies. Since those economic conditions no longer exist and since zoning laws now limit the range of businesses locating in residential sections, *La Colonia* and the development are unlikely ever to provide a great variety of economic opportunities for their residents.

Local church participation also varies in each area. While over 90 percent of all residents interviewed considered themselves Catholic, 73 percent of the center city dwellers compared to 64 percent of the *colonos* and 54 percent of the residents of the development said they attended their local church when they went to religious services. However, since church involvement is highly individualistic,[41] and since no more than 10 percent of the Catholics in the three areas go weekly to church services, and no more than a few hundred in each parish jointly participate in church-sponsored groups,[42] the Church hardly serves as an institution integrating the communities. Nonetheless, it is the only formal institution which regularly brings a substantial number of neighbors in each area together.

In addition to the formally sponsored church activities, residents independently organize socioreligious activities, at times despite the priests' disapproval. They organize fiestas and pilgrimages in conjunction with important saints' days. Yet once again this is most true of center city dwellers: According to estimates by local priests and participants, approximately 3,000 center city dwellers compared to 400 *colonos* and only 50 development-residents participate in locally organized pilgrimages. Similarly, the festivities in honor of the patron saint of local parishes are best attended in the center city area. Such community festivities are nearly nonexistent in *La Unidad* because the parishes there are controlled by American priests who are determined to destroy the saints' cults which "distract from true Catholicism." Although several of the center city area pilgrimages have been initiated only in recent decades, comparable community-organized socioreligious activities are unlikely to become equally popular over the years in the two newer areas: They tend to attract residents with a modicum of financial security who both live and work in the same area, particularly those who originate

[41] The individualistic nature of their Catholicism is not a specifically urban phenomenon. On the individualistic nature of Catholicism in rural Mexico, see George Foster, "The Dyadic Contract," pp. 225-30.

[42] While estimates by priests reveal that no more than 10 percent of the parishioners attend church weekly, approximately four times as many of the persons interviewed claimed they frequented church weekly. Residents reported the behavior prescribed of them as Catholics, not their actual behavior.

from the same provincial communities. Thus it is primarily the local *comerciantes* and shoe artisans who are active in community-wide socioreligious festivities in the inner-city area.

INFORMAL INTERACTION

Despite little community involvement, particularly in the housing development and *La Colonia*, residents of the areas are not anomic, lonely, and isolated. They engage in highly personalized social networks which crosscut community lines, networks which vary more according to inhabitants' socioeconomic status than to their place of residence.

Among residents interviewed, those who were most successful economically generally had the largest and highest-status network of kin and nonkin with whom they were friendly. The economically least successful had few ties with nonkin, largely because they felt they could thereby "avoid problems." Those nonkin with whom residents of low socioeconomic standing cultivated friendships often were asked to become *compadres* (fictive kin).

Although residents tended not to see their *compadres* frequently, they considered the relationships important: through *compadrazgo* ties residents institutionalized feelings of trust and respect.[43] As the prefix "co" implies, the sponsor-parent relationship was more important than the sponsor-child godparent bond for which the relationship was nominally intended.[44] Yet these *compadrazgo* ties generally were neither an alternative to other types of personal relationships nor a means by which many resi-

[43] For example, one of the men in Lewis' *Five Families* bought a television, partly under the supposition that by charging neighbors who come to watch programs he could get a return on his investment (p. 192). However, his wife would not allow him to take advantage of their neighbors, since many of them were her *comadres* (the fictive kinship relationship among women). In contrast, the case studies are replete with examples of theft, exploitation, and dishonesty among urban poor who are not restrained by *compadrazgo* ties.

[44] On the other hand, in southern Europe the sponsor-child relationship is more important. Sidney Mintz and Eric Wolf, "An Analysis of Ritual Co-parenthood (*Compadrazgo*)," pp. 174-99. On the secular functions of *compadres* in Mexico, see Douglas Butterworth, "A Study of the Urbanization Process Among Mixtec Migrants from Tilaltongo in Mexico City," pp. 257-74; Robert Redfield and Alfonso Villa Rojas, *Chan Kom*, pp. 98-100; Lewis, *Life in a Mexican Village*, p. 351; Andrew Whiteford, *Two Cities in Latin America*, p. 100.

dents could formalize links with wealthy persons. The persons interviewed with the most extensive networks of intimate relations were also the most apt to have *compadres*, and more salaried white-collar workers than residents otherwise employed in *La Colonia* and *La Unidad* had at least one salaried white-collar *compadre*. However, in *El Centro*, where class barriers were least clear-cut, *compadrazgo* ties varied less by socioeconomic class.

Since the *compadre* relationship implies reciprocity, it serves to inhibit the poor from exploiting one another. Informal interviews with residents suggest that the more equal the status of the parent and sponsor, the more equal the exchange relationship. When the two parties were of roughly equal socioeconomic standing they generally felt that they could count on one another for personal support and small loans. The more unequal the status of the parent and sponsor, the more different the favors generally exchanged. For example, residents who had employers as *compadres* felt compelled to work hard and be dependable, in exchange for occasional financial assistance.

Social ties were stronger among center city dwellers than among residents of the other two areas, particularly among those employed as artisans, *comerciantes*, and factory workers: They tended to have more frequent contact with their network of friends, *compadres*, and relatives, and they were a bit more inclined to be friendly with their neighbors. Patterns of sociability have been alleged to be a function of provincial upbringing, residential stability, and density.[45] But since most *El Centro* residents were either urban-born or urban-raised, since residents living equally long in the three areas were not equally involved in extensive and intensive network ties, and since not all center city area residents were equally involved in friendship networks, other forces must shape patterns of sociability in the three areas. The contrasting community patterns in part reflect an element of choice: The economically least successful persons, when interviewed, often expressed a preference for the social isolation which *La Unidad* and *La Colonia* offered, so as to avoid inter-

---

[45] Sylvia Fleis Fava, "Contrasts in Neighboring," pp. 122-131; Herbert Gans, *People and Plans*, pp. 12-24. Sociability within rural communities may be less than heretofore assumed, as is suggested in the works of Maccoby and Nash. See Michael Maccoby, "Love and Authority," pp. 336-345, and Manning Nash, *Machine Age Maya*, pp. 72-76.

family problems. Poor and working-class residents in the outlying areas in fact found the privacy and tranquillity which their homes provided one of the most attractive aspects of their new residency. They felt that they thereby avoided problems, quarrels, and gossip.

There are differences in patterns of neighboring not only between the three areas but within each area. The differences tend to follow socioeconomic lines, particularly in the housing development. There, the class tensions which are so characteristic of the area were reflected in a limited amount of intimate cross-class ties between the salaried "middle-class" residents and their lower-status neighbors. Thus, residents' informal interpersonal ties are shaped by a combination of territorial and class forces.

CONCLUSIONS AND IMPLICATIONS

While one community was officially planned, another illegally and surreptitiously formed, and the third prerevolutionary in origin, all three have been permeated by the same class and administrative forces that dominate in the society at large. The state has made education and medical and sports facilities available locally, regulated dwelling costs and opportunities for home ownership, and influenced local economic possibilities. Class forces, in turn, have shaped the formation of the areas, local economic conditions, the composition of the areas, and patterns of socializing, at times in opposition to official policies, laws, and plans.

Thus, conditions in the three areas must be viewed within the context of the national political economy. Societal forces have had a more pervasive impact than urban design on patterns of formal and informal community life, but they have assumed somewhat different meanings in the different community contexts owing to the contrasting historical origins of the areas.

As the following chapter shows, such general social forces have increasingly affected not only informal social life but also formal organizational life locally: Initial territorial-based differences, owing to the different origins of the communities and distinct community problems, have diminished.

CHAPTER THREE

The Irony of Organization

The state appears to be responsive to and protective of the interests of resident poor. Residents have access to legitimate political and government organizations which espouse populist goals, but the groups provide them with no assurance that the government will act in their interests. They do acquire certain goods and services through the groups; but these benefits tend to reinforce the established urban stratification, since more privileged classes receive more substantial benefits. Above all, the extension of government benefits serves to subject residents to social and political controls, and expand the regime's support base, regardless of the residents' intention when establishing political ties and pressing for benefits. As a result, state involvement in the local communities has facilitated the extension of social forces dominating in the society at large, even though the grass-roots organizations convey the impression, as they do nationally, that the politically hegemonic forces operate in opposition to the dominant capitalist economic forces. This process works both through formal groups, and through informal social pressures rooted in the national class and power structure.

FORMAL GROUPS

In addition to political and administrative groups, there are social and economic associations in the three areas. Altogether, there are approximately three dozen locally operating, formally recognized, groups or divisions of groups: these include territorial units of the municipal government and the PRI electoral apparatus; union locals (and factions within the locals) of market vendors, school teachers, and a few center city factories; lay groups associated with parish churches; independent, government, and PRI-linked social groups, including community associations and athletic groups; and groups formed to promote government social-athletic centers. Through divisions of the electoral organ of the PRI and the municipal administrative apparatus residents enjoy formal power; through economic associations they ostensibly "articulate" and "aggregate" their class interests; through social groups they nominally satisfy their nonpolitical, noneconomic interests. However, most of the groups are formally affiliated with national PRI or government-linked organizations,[1] and even the nominally independent ones are subject to PRI and government influence because the leaders overtly or covertly associate with PRI or government groups, or persons associated with such groups. The former set of groups provide residents with no institutionalized authoritative power or budgetary discretion; the latter set do have authoritative power, but they are constrained by their limited financial resources.

The groups officially include an executive board. The geographically organized groups, in addition, have a hierarchy of officers, extending to the block level. The groups, however, do not function according to their "organizational chart": they are dominated by the top-ranking officer, and most low-level officers do not regularly attend group meetings. Members actively participate more out of loyalty to the leader and anticipation of ensuing benefits than out of commitment to the group per se. Thus, if the leader, in their estimation, proves ineffective they generally cease to attend group meetings and to partake in civic and political activities requested by him or her; and if the group leader leaves his or her formal post members still may collaborate with him or her if they see a reason to do so. The importance of groups rests more in their informal network of communication and control than in their formal structure and official objectives.

Active group participation varied in the three areas and, within each area, over the years. We saw in Chapter One that regional politics since the revolution has diminished in importance,

---

[1] Except for certain organized workers affiliated with the Party's Labor sector, local PRI-affiliated groups are incorporated into the Popular sector, the CNOP. This multistatus "middle-class" dominated sector is increasingly absorbing the expanding urban population, particularly through the territorial based Federation of Proletarian Neighborhoods (FCP) and, to a lesser extent, through economic associations of small-scale *comerciantes*. The growth of the CNOP reflects an adaptation to historically rooted structures and processes. The corporate-occupational, mass-based party which was formed to help consolidate the revolution under Cárdenas, was organized prior to the country's mass rural-urban migration. Now that the urban lower stratum is expanding numerically, the state attempts to formally incorporate them into the established politico-administrative structure.

being superseded by occupation-based politics: the local areas reflect these trends. Residents were least active in groups organized along geographical lines in the center city area, where group life was most routinized. There, adults are most active in occupation-based groups. In the two newer areas rank-and-file participation in community groups has declined since the areas first were settled, except around specific issues such as legalization of illegal property transferences (in the housing development). However, participation in the planned community never was as extensive as in the squatter settlement, largely because initial settlers there never were faced with the same pressing problems: unlike *colonos* they had legal property rights and basic urban services when they moved to the area.[2] Participation initially depends on prevailing local conditions, not formal organizational affiliations.

Whatever specific concerns initially led to the formation of groups, most groups now claim a general concern about the welfare of members. For example, the first groups in *La Colonia* began as loosely structured "followings" around particular leaders who attended to the problems of securing legal title to residents' illegally held land and basic social and urban services. Now, though, the leaders of these groups proclaim a general commitment to the moral, social, and economic defense of residents, and they claim to head associations with complex hierarchical structures.

Local groups which formally affiliate with national organizations do so in one of two ways. Either residents more or less spontaneously join together and subsequently, through dealings made by the group leaders, associate with supra-local groups as branch affiliations. Alternatively, local groups begin at the initia-

[2] When areas are formed by gradual attrition community-based groups apparently are less likely to emerge. See Larissa Lomnitz, "The Social and Economic Organization of a Mexican Shantytown," pp. 135-55. Goldrich also argues on the basis of his comparative analysis of urban poor in Lima and Santiago, Chile, that the initial experience residents of urban communities have with authorities shapes subsequent political patterns. If residents immediately face limited government opposition, they are most likely to establish groups and initiate demands for community improvements. Daniel Goldrich, "Toward the Comparative Study of Politicization in Latin America," pp. 361-78. My findings support his conclusions, except that differences between the areas I studied tended to subside as relations within local groups became formalized.

tive of higher-level hierarchical divisions, in which case nonlocal authorities assign, or agree to allow, someone to establish a local division.[3] The former method occurred especially after the land invasion, when the squatters, in self-defense, organized so as to deal more effectively with the government. In either case, though, local groups initially address themselves to local problems. Since the problems of residents of each area differ somewhat, not all divisions of the same parent organization at first concern themselves with the same sets of problems. In this respect the organizations are adaptive to the interests of their members.

When informally organized and first affiliating with national PRI and government groups residents successfully petitioned government offices for a variety of benefits they coveted, including health clinics, social centers, water and drainage, electricity, schools, roads, pavement, markets, and public transportation. *Colonos* also finally secured property rights, thus ending abuse by *coyotes* and *políticos.* Yet, over the years, residents found it increasingly difficult to secure goods and services, and not because these were no longer needed. Above all, school and medical facilities remain inadequate, as do individual incomes. Residents never collectively insisted on redistributive benefits which would have directly reduced income inequality.[4]

Occasionally, directly or through intermediaries, including through the press, local divisions of national organizations manage to convince the government to respond to their complaints about hierarchically appointed leaders, in addition to their complaints about inadequate facilities.[5] For example, they sometimes

[3] Schmitter calls these two processes of group formation "natural" and "artificial" corporatism, respectively. Schmitter, *Interest Conflict.*

[4] Legalization of squatter land claims and access to homes in *La Unidad* transformed previous tenants and squatters into proprietors. While property ownership improved such persons' standing relative to nonpropertied poor, wealthier segments of the society were not compelled to rescind any of the privileges they enjoy in the process. As previously noted, these property owners benefited at the expense of the *ejidatarios* who formerly had legal rights to the land.

[5] Similarly, Cornelius found that residents in the low-income areas he studied did not influence government policy formation, although they did effectively informally demand benefits from the government. Since the demand-making he describes is not a formally prescribed mode of political participation outlined in the statutes of political and administrative groups, it corroborates the point made here that the formal political apparatus pro-

successfully pressure higher-ranking functionaries to remove corrupt local leaders. However, they have no way of preventing subsequent appointees from being equally abusive. Thus, during both of my visits, four years apart, I found center city market vendors complaining about corrupt market administrators.

Even congressmen, the only locally elected *políticos* with institutionalized power, do not exercise their Constitutional authority on behalf of residents. They do not view their main task as one of representing their constituents' interests in the legislature. They spend little time in the local districts. At most they visit local district party offices every week or two. One congressman rarely had been to his district. They explained to me that they rarely go to their districts because they consider their main function to be legislative, and because they identify mainly with their occupational group.[6] As one member put it: "Congressmen have two representations—the group with which they are affiliated and the citizens of the district who elect them to office. In session, though, we vote more in the name of our group." Nonetheless, as one legislator correctly noted: "The executive sends us the laws, even though, according to the Constitution, Congress is supposed to determine the laws." Congressmen, as noted in Chapter One,

---

vides resident poor with no guaranteed, institutionalized means by which to influence decision-making. Cornelius, "Urbanization and Political Demand-Making," or *Politics and the Migrant Poor*, Chapter Seven.

[6] While the regional office of the PRI ran some local PRI district offices, others were run by such "corporate-functional" groups as the union of Social Security workers, the Revolutionary Confederation of Workers and Peasants (CROC), and the Mexican Workers' Confederation (CTM). These groups paid for the maintenance of the district quarters and the salaries of group members who worked in the districts for the Party. They also provided some patronage to local residents and gave financial support to the Party. Interestingly, the congressman in the district controlled by CROC gave fabric away during the campaign which he obtained from the industries employing members of his union. This case illustrates a way in which industry is indirectly linked to the PRI through district-level politics, but through the coordination of national political offices. Industry thereby helps support the Party even though it enjoys no formal power within the Party. These political districts are more integrated into a national "machine" than were districts in city "machines" in the U.S., probably because that segment of the economy which subsidizes the Mexican political apparatus today is more concentrated and national in scale than was the corresponding economic sector in the U.S. which historically supported urban "machines."

give near-unanimous support to all legislation. Thus, institutionalized power, as well as organizations with no local formal authority leave residents with no reliable protection of their interests.

But while the legislators' role is largely symbolic, they do not entirely ignore their electoral constituents: They act extra-officially as influential solicitors (*gestores*) to government agencies at the request of district residents. For example, on behalf of local leaders they ask for schools, markets, and urban services.

Nonetheless, through congressmen as well as through formally and informally organized local groups incorporated into national organizations, demands and constraints are placed on residents, to the extent that rank-and-file group participation changes. Upon affiliation with national groups, associations which once had large and highly active memberships became largely inactive,[7] and members increasingly came to deal with their group leaders on an individual basis about individual problems. Most group activities in which members now collectively participate center around civic and political rallies, not as formerly around local concerns. Those who continue to partake in group-sponsored activities generally do so in return for or in anticipation of favors from the group leaders. Participation has become ritualized; no longer is it an effective form of collective power from below.[8]

[7] Cornelius (*Politics and the Migrant Poor*, Chapter Five) also argues that participation depends on community conditions, and not merely on individual attributes or social status. In contrast, the literature on social "mobilization," "political participation," and "marginality-integration" assumes that participation is an ever-increasing phenomenon. See, for example, Karl Deutsch, "Social Mobilization and Political Development," and Daniel Lerner, *The Passing of Traditional Society*.

[8] On ritualistic, system-supportive participation in the Mexican political system, see Richard Fagen and William Tuohy, *Politics and Privilege in a Mexican City*, pp. 38-39. In contrast, Almond and Verba assume in their five-nation study, which includes Mexico, that involvement in local politics reflects civic responsibility and competence. Gabriel Almond and Sidney Verba, *The Civic Culture*, esp. pp. 117-207. Even *if* this were true in "Western democracies," people in other sociopolitical contexts may engage in identical political behavior for different reasons and their behavior may precipitate different consequences. In terms of the U.S., Verba subsequently has distinguished between "instrumental" and "ceremonial" or "support" participation. See Verba and Norman Nie, *Participation in America*, p. 2.

Yet the decline and change in rank-and-file participation has occurred not merely because of affiliation with national political and government groups. Members also lost interest in the groups after they either secured the benefits which initially induced them to join,[9] or became completely disillusioned with the leaders.

Groups which do not formally affiliate with national institutions also subject members to political-administrative constraints. Although these groups, unlike the PRI and government-affiliated groups, technically have authoritative power, they have few resources with which to satisfy members' concerns because of the poverty of their constituents. Therefore, they too turn to *políticos* for help. Leaders of these groups, either because they formally affiliate with PRI and government-linked organizations as individuals or because they anticipate political patronage, operate their groups almost as if they were PRI or administratively linked affiliations. Thus, the head of a Church-initiated social group which was deliberately established as an apolitical group, privately affiliated with the PRI-linked Federation of Proletarian Neighborhoods (FCP). Afterwards, political and civic matters assumed high priority in his own association. Although he maintained that his affiliation with the PRI-linked group was purely as a private citizen, and not as a representative of his group, he subsequently reported regularly on the activities of the PRI group, and allowed the leader of the PRI group to monopolize a number of rallies held by the social group. The head of the PRI-affiliated group used the opportunity largely to talk about his own group, his own leadership credentials, and the various

[9] Paradoxically, once organizations succeed in securing their objectives they may end in failure, for the very conditions which called them into being no longer exist. Organizations may survive under such circumstances if they become concerned with new goals, as Sills discusses in his study of the March of Dimes (David Sills, *The Volunteers*). In the *colonia* we have a case of an informal organization which emerged for specific ends—namely, to secure legalization of illegal claims by *colonos* to land, and social and urban services—subsequently affiliating with a formal organization with more broadly defined social objectives. The interest of *colonos* in the local group waned *in part* because their initial reasons for informally organizing had been satisfied, even though the objectives of the group with which they formally affiliated had not been fulfilled. This situation suggests that both individual and group properties must be taken into account to fully understand organizational behavior.

benefits residents of the housing development enjoy thanks to his efforts. He actually claimed credit for the same improvements that the head of the social group previously said were his doing. Above all, in the process this group was diverted from its original goals which were social and economic.

Another case involves the head of an independent soccer league, the largest in *El Centro* and one of the largest in the entire city. He allows the PRI to offer social services at the group's headquarters, requires members to partake in civic celebrations, and organizes his group by blocks, as the PRI does, so that, as he phrased it, he would be ready if the Party should call on him.

Hence, formal incorporation of established groups into national organizations and overt and covert co-optation of leadership both have similar effects on group members. They serve as mechanisms of social and political control. In the process residents are "demobilized" and made to reduce their demands on the government. Moreover, the groups which formally are incorporated into the national political-administrative apparatus by definition contribute to the government's legitimation.

Residents' difficulties in securing benefits from the government stem not from any "organizational incapacity" or "political incompetence," as some Mexican commentators claim.[10] On their own, residents have organized into groups to deal with the mu-

---

[10] See Susan Purcell and John Purcell, "Community Power and Benefits from the Nation"; Almond and Verba, *The Civic Culture*. The Purcells argue that the ability of Mexican communities to secure benefits from the national government depends on the existence of groups with "organizational capability" which "cooperate on local projects." They therefore imply that the unequal distribution of benefits in Mexico is largely due to the inability of communities to organize. Yet they note cases of "closed corporate communities" with *cooperative and cohesive* political structures which receive *few* public benefits. The government obviously does not reward organization per se: it rewards different groups in different ways. The Purcells also fail to highlight the way in which communities, and groups within communities, are subject to pressures limiting their ability to organize or remain *effectively* organized. In view of the multitude of organizations which have operated in the three areas I studied, it is striking how few benefits residents have secured from the government. Furthermore, were the Purcells' thesis correct one would expect that once groups developed organizational capabilities they would maintain them and thereby continue to secure public benefits. However, the experience, particularly of *colonos*, demonstrates that this is not necessarily the case.

nicipal government. They also have joined established national groups which deal with municipal authorities, including some which publicly profess a concern with their social welfare and have grass-roots organizations. Their organized efforts have met with limited success because most of these groups have no institutionalized access to power and because affiliation with PRI and government-linked groups has undermined their organizational effectiveness. Covert as well as overt co-optation have left local groups without effective power, as has anticipated co-optation, and co-optation and incorporation have served regulatory and legitimizing functions. Even groups with formal power subordinate local to nonlocal interests. The constraints on the residents' organizational effectiveness stem mainly from the impact of informal, institutionalized processes rooted in the national class and power structure. They shape residents' actions and attitudes to the extent that residents now manifest some of the characteristics of the so-called culture of poverty.[11] In particular, most of them have become politically apathetic.[12] This change came about when local groups, or their leaders, established extralocal ties, and when relations within the groups, in turn, were routinized.[13]

[11] Lewis initially developed the concept in conjunction with his work on Mexican urban poor, although his best delineation of it appears in *La Vida*, Introduction. While he argues there that apathy and other characteristics of the "culture of poverty" are particularly characteristic of early stages of capitalism, we see here that political quiescence stems from political as well as economic forces. For critiques of the "culture of poverty" thesis, see Charles Valentine, *Culture of Poverty*, and Eleanor Leacock (ed.), *Culture and Poverty*, and the references therein.

[12] Hansen (p. 207) argues that distrust, hostility, and consequential political apathy are so pervasive in Mexico that cohesive groups rarely form and impose demands on the regime. Our evidence suggests that the limited effectiveness of local groups is largely a structural, not sociopsychological problem, for residents do mobilize for collective concerns under certain social circumstances. Hansen tends to attribute only secondary importance to structural factors. Nonetheless, I agree with Hansen that limited pressure has been put on the regime to redistribute resources, and disagree with Vernon who argues that the government has become immobile because of the broad range of demands imposed by diverse groups. Vernon, *Mexico's Development*, esp. pp. 14-15.

[13] Butterworth's analysis of the Committees for the Defense of the Revolution in Cuba suggests that hierarchically organized grass-roots organizations may become ineffective in socialist as well as capitalist societies, due to increased rank-and-file apathy or withdrawal of higher-ranking leader-

INFORMAL CONSTRAINTS

The informal processes that inhibit the political effectiveness of organized residents are rooted in various national institutional arrangements: mainly in the hierarchical nature of national inter- and intragroup relations, the class structure, the personalistic style of Mexican politics, the multiplicity of groups operating nationally along with the containment of overt elite competition, and the government's threat to apply force. They reflect social structural forces closely associated with the state, but not necessarily deliberate efforts of functionaries to regulate local poor. For these reasons political stability can be maintained with little cost, and the state can nationally advance the interests of capital without using brute repression against a major base of political support.

Local leaders are constrained to conform with national political "rules of the game." Otherwise they can neither personally advance in politics nor secure benefits for their constituents. The prospects of removal from office also compel local subordinates to conform with the expectations (or their perception of the expectations) of higher-ranking functionaries. Thereby, "appropriate" local concerns are delimited and heads of local groups are encouraged to be subservient, although they are not necessarily accordingly rewarded. Thus, a politically ambitious head of a local division of a government agency complained, "If you do more than your boss you're in real trouble," and leaders in general spoke to me about their concern with "controlling" the communities. At their meetings leaders made frequent reference to the "authorities" whose requests "all citizens had the obligation to obey."

Even leaders who establish new groups are subject to such constraints since they command few material resources of their own. For example, the head of the formally independent United Front for the Defense of Proletarian Residents (FUPC), a group formed to assure that the government sell land inexpensively to squatters, to secure urban services, and to help residents get access to additional land elsewhere in the city, publicly claimed

---

ship support. However, in comparison to Mexico, in Cuba urban poor participate more actively in neighborhood groups. Butterworth, "Grass-Roots Political Organization in Cuba," pp. 183-203.

that his association intended to collaborate with "the authorities" and the governing institutions. Accordingly, he even solicited membership in the Popular Sector of the PRI.

Higher-ranking national functionaries also prevent the consolidation of power within local branch organizations by appointing and removing local functionaries at their own discretion. Periodic reassignments keep local officeholders from identifying with local interests. Thus, one market administrator explained to me that the head of the Division of Markets regularly reassigns administrators to different markets so that "no administrator gets entrenched in local 'politics' to the extent that he becomes subservient to local interests and fails to fulfill his obligations."

In addition, the hierarchical promotion system drains local divisions of their best leaders. When the most charismatic leader in *La Colonia*—of a spontaneously formed grouping—was promoted to nonlocal political and administrative posts, outside the area, he was succeeded by someone who was less popular and effective in defending local interests. Even when functionaries remain at their local posts the hierarchical system weakens their groups' political effectiveness because ambitious local leaders recognize that their prospects of political advancement are enhanced if they collaborate with higher-ranking functionaries outside their area. Thus, during the last two national campaigns leading local *políticos*, particularly in the housing development, engaged almost exclusively in political activities in other electoral districts. One of them even worked outside Mexico City.

The hierarchical system also limits the ability of local groups to collectively organize, both within the areas and the city at large. At times, individual divisions are isolated from, and in competition with, other divisions of their same parent organization for favors from higher-ranking functionaries. For example, such local PRI-affiliated social groups as the FCP had to compete with other divisions for favors from municipal offices. Not even all local divisions of unions were incorporated into the same sector of the PRI. Since benefits are allocated separately and unequally to sectors, and to groups within each sector, the unionized workers do not all share a common fate and common sense of loyalty, even when they are affiliated with the same party.

The hierarchical structure of groups also divides workers' loyalty *within* occupational groups, and often makes workers subservient to union leaders' interests. This is best illustrated by the largest locally operating economic grouping involving local residents—the association of local market vendors. Almost all markets have one or more "union" leader. Yet the only contact "union" heads in each market have with one another is through the regional offices of the union. There is no horizontal communication or collaboration. Even within any one market the loyalty of the small-scale tradesmen is divided when there is more than one local leader, as in the lucrative center city markets.[14] Moreover, because the "union" leaders serve as intermediaries linking the government and the PRI with the "petty" merchants, they tend to encourage vendors to be acquiescent, in response to orders from above. As one administrator proudly noted: "*Comerciantes* have become more docile and responsive since I've been working here. If I ask them to do something, they do it. Now they want and accept us as representatives of the 'authorities.'" The leaders do not organize protests to pressure the government for better working conditions, fringe benefits, or social and political justice.

Because of hierarchical constraints the various local functionaries also feel pressured to give residents the impression that higher officials are concerned with local problems and to convince residents that they should obey orders from "authorities." When the "authorities" in 1967-68 were not responsive to local requests several heads repeated to their subordinates what higher-ranking functionaries had told them: that they must wait and make sacrifices, as the Olympics cost the government a lot. And when government functionaries raided homes in the poorest section of the housing development to confiscate animals which inhabitants illegally raised to supplement their income, the local head of the PRI-affiliated FCP made no attempt to retrieve the animals. He expressed outrage over the incident at one of his weekly meetings, but he simultaneously led residents to believe that the intruders were thieves so as to avert resentment of the government. Similarly, the housing administrator who ordered

---

[14] Effective collective organization among market vendors is further inhibited by the competitive nature of their commerce. As one "union" leader in the center city area commented to me: "The *comerciantes* feel that they are in competition with one another. They are jealous. They all want to be the only one selling the goods they merchandise. They talk but really they don't like each other." Similarly, a leader of another group of market vendors noted that "the *comerciantes* don't trust anybody but themselves."

the men to raid the homes confided to me that he intentionally publicly disassociated himself from the men "for fear of making local enemies." The same leader of the FCP publicly condemned lawyers and engineers associated with the PRI-affiliated United Tenants' Front for illegally selling land *credenciales*, but he never insisted that police prevent the illicit activity.

Aside from the hierarchical structure of political and administrative groups, class biases at work in the society at large permeate relations within the three areas, constricting the political effectiveness of local groups. Access to local leadership posts, opportunities for political advancement, and the ability of local groups to secure benefits for members—particularly once relations within the groups are routinized—depend more on the socioeconomic status of group members and leaders than on the grass-roots structure and formal objectives of the national groups.

While local functionaries are not the local economic elite, they tend to be among the economically most successful. In 1968 the top functionaries in *La Colonia* were a market vendor, a shop owner, and a factory worker, and in the other two areas they were almost without exception white collar employees. The highest-ranking local government functionaries in *La Unidad* included a policeman and a union officer in the wealthiest sections, and a factory worker in the poorest section.

Moreover, leadership in the areas has become increasingly "middle class" over the years, as the socioeconomic composition of the areas has improved. Thus, whereas the first government functionaries in the squatter settlement were poorly educated persons holding low prestige jobs, in 1971 the highest-ranking local officer was a secondary school (military school) educated bureaucrat. As the 1971 incumbent noted to me: "Now we need people who are more skilled than we did before. My predecessor didn't have enough technical skills. He did things in his own way —not the way he was asked."

Furthermore, local leaders' prospects of political mobility have come to depend increasingly on their class standing and contacts outside the local areas. Leaders of humble class origin stood the greatest chance of promotion through local groups when their constituents were highly mobilized, a rare situation once relations within the areas were routinized. The most successful *político* these areas produced was the charismatic leader of the squatters (*supra* p. 88), following the land invasion. He subsequently secured several higher-level political and administrative posts, some of which have given him access to so many payoffs that he now is reputedly a "millionaire" and a recipient of a house in the housing development. His advancement has largely been at the expense of urban poor whom he exploited through illicit land transactions.

Economic groups provide greater opportunities for advancement than territorial groups. The head of the FCP in the housing development exemplifies the opportunities unions hold for faithful workers. Originally a railroad worker in the northern state of Sinaloa, he rose to several posts in the local and national division of the union of railroad workers, now holds a salaried white-collar job in a government office, and entertains the idea of becoming a congressman. His social, economic, political, and even geographical mobility derived from his initial union affiliation. Similarly, the congressman in the section of the development controlled by the Revolutionary Confederation of Workers and Peasants (CROC), began his career as a rank-and-file factory hand. He subsequently became a textile engineer and active member of a textile union. After successive union posts he finally obtained the highest position in CROC and, thereby, one of the highest political posts in the country, although one that rarely promises further political advancement. These men both gained political status on the basis of their work status.

Functionaries might serve the interests of local poor, even without being themselves of low socioeconomic status. But because they are primarily interested in their own advancement they tend to be hierarchically rather than community-oriented. Rarely do local leaders collaborate to promote programs for the benefit of local residents. They have much more contact with persons of higher rank in their own organizations, outside the local communities, than with one another.

Class constraints also limit the ability of most local *políticos* to provide guidance and useful political contacts. As a leader of a local group in the housing development explained to me: "We go to the PRI office to try to establish friendships with persons who can help orient us, and to find out what the PRI can do for us. We also can learn from them, because we lack friends who can help us resolve our problems quickly. We suffer because we personally aren't known in the high levels of the government."[15]

The government in general has rewarded residents inversely to their economic "need" ever since organizational life in the areas has been routinized. As a result, residents of the most "middle class" of the three areas, the housing development, receive the most social services, even though they have had better facilities from the start. Moreover, within the development the sections with the largest numbers of "middle-class" residents and "middle-class" leaders receive the largest share of government assistance. Their effectiveness derives not from special formal group affiliations, but from higher-ranking nonlocal functionaries generally favoring their "middle-class" subordinate staff and the "middle-class" interests they represent, and from local "middle-class" functionaries generally having better contacts with regional or national personnel who can help them.

The personal manner in which *políticos* are appointed and removed from office, goods and services distributed, and local demands and conflicts articulated and resolved further limit residents' ability to use local groups to serve their own ends. The groups operate in a highly personalized manner because the structure of power induces politicians to adapt personalistic strategies. Thus, the head of the local branch of a PRI-affiliated group in the housing development, a salaried bureaucrat, regularly reassured followers that he served their interests before the authorities. At a meeting he announced: "We are like your family, in permanent struggle. Our duty is to see that you have few problems, to personally take your problems to the Treasury and other government dependencies. We are at your orders. We do not feel distant or indifferent. We realize that there is misery in many places, but we hope that this will change. That's our preoccupation." Similarly, a former government functionary in the squatter settlement, a *comerciante*, worked hard to become a "broker" between local residents and higher authorities. He explained to me that "I help *colonos*. If they can't afford fines or taxes I connect them with people who can help them for little

[15] Johnson argues that on the national level particular *camarilla* or political clique memberships are generally of greater political consequence than formal political or administrative career patterns. Kenneth Johnson, *Mexican Democracy*, esp. pp. 59-84. The limited access residents have to such cliques informally limits their political power.

money. I am lucky. Whenever I used to go to government offices I spoke with people there. I asked them their occupation. If I thought they could help people here in the *colonia* I became friendly with them. I told them that I'm from here and that I have 'x' number of people behind me. Out of friendship they charged *colonos* less than their usual fee. *Colonos* who know that I have such contacts come to me."

The structurally induced personalistic style of Mexican politics makes residents—particularly in the two newer areas—feel dependent on and indebted to the government for material benefits they receive, including the land and pavement for which they actually pay. These "gifts" are officially "given" to them at public rallies which often are attended by such high-ranking dignitaries as the president of the country and the mayor of the city.[16] Local leaders also periodically distribute material benefits which they acquire through contacts, to entice residents to attend their meetings. The head of the FCP in *La Unidad*, for example, distributed dinner plates and second-hand clothing at gatherings I attended in 1967-68.

Anticipation of rewards also induces residents to collaborate with individual functionaries. Attendants at the above-mentioned FCP group meetings had come because the local leader gave them the impression that he might get them houses in the section of the development under construction. Even a nonresident regularly attended the meetings because the head of the organization led him to believe that he would get a house if he used his connections at the phone company (where he worked) to get

---

[16] Even renovations of such public facilities as the sports center in *El Centro* are causes for public celebrations. Although no comparable study to this one has been made of "middle-" or upper-class neighborhoods, I am under the impression that more benefits are provided unceremoniously to the rich than are provided ceremoniously here to the poor. The rich seem to receive urban services without public fanfare because both they and the government assume that the rich automatically are entitled to the benefits. The government's preoccupation with "giving" and "regiving" benefits is reminiscent of the task Bonaparte took on. According to Marx: "Bonaparte would like to appear as the patriarchical benefactor of all classes. But he cannot give to one class without taking from another. . . . Bonaparte would fain be the most *obligeant* man in France and turn all the property, all the labour of France into a personal obligation to himself. He would like to steal the whole of France in order to be able to make a present of her to France. . . . Marx, "The Eighteenth Brumaire of Louis Bonaparte," p. 347.

telephones installed in the area. But by 1971, when the rank-and-file realized that the *político* would not secure houses for them, they ceased to attend meetings.

Moreover, in the very process of securing personal "favors" from the government the collective effectiveness of residents, paradoxically, was indirectly undermined.[17] Particularly when legalizing illegal land claims local functionaries collaborated with higher functionaries to establish social order and routinize local organizational life in a section of the city where community relations initially had not been institutionalized. In general, group members are instructed by higher-ranking functionaries to personally request, not demand, goods and services, and to petition for benefits either individually or in small groups, not *en masse*, as the squatters initially did. As a local *político* mentioned to me, "If we make demands, the authorities don't listen to us." Local *políticos* conform because they believe that the government otherwise may not be responsive to their concerns. In the process, though, group participation declines and the government is less pressured to provide residents with goods and services.[18]

Because politics is personalized, conflict is also, When residents' expectations are not fulfilled they blame individuals. Above all, competition for political and economic spoils pits local leaders against one another. The petty jealousies weaken the potential collective strength of local inhabitants because divisions are thereby created among different local leaders and their "followers." Thus, while local leaders give lip service to the official concern with unity and order, they accuse each other of being self-serving, corrupt, and having a divisive effect on the community.

---

[17] Cornelius also discusses the impact of government performance in low-income areas in Mexico City, although he focuses more on its impact on the attitudes of urban poor than on its organizational consequences. See his "Impact of Governmental Performance on Political Attitudes and Behavior," pp. 213-51, and *Politics and the Migrant Poor in Mexico.*

[18] Cornelius (*Politics and the Migrant Poor*, p. 80) also notes that the urban poor are limited in the benefits they can extract from the government: "Approaching public officials to seek help in satisfying particularistic personal or local needs is both permitted and encouraged; but demanding major changes in public policy or government priorities is viewed as threatening and illegitimate activity." He adds that "a fairly optimistic view of the community's development prospects . . . may be a necessary precondition for involvement in this (community related) kind of political activity" (p. 99).

Even when local leaders work for their constituents they are criticized by competing *políticos*. For example, heads of several local PRI and government-affiliated groups in *La Unidad* resented a local female government functionary because she devoted more time to local political-administrative matters than they did. Since she received financial support from her husband she did not have to work for a livelihood, as they did. They accused her of creating "disunity," and embarrassed and ridiculed her at their group meetings. The head of the promotion committee for the new social center read aloud at one of his meetings a letter from her requesting assistance in a campaign to clean the plazas. He snidely added that he saw no reason why he himself "should have to go around with a broom." Jealous of her, the head of a local division of a PRI-linked group did not invite her to a dinner he organized which the President of Mexico attended. She, however, managed to get in. In recalling the incident, she snickered and told me: "I went to greet the President outside the center. He saw me there and said we should talk inside. He did not know that I had not been invited."

Such divisions direct residents' energies toward local personalities, rather than toward those national institutions which, on the one hand, generate the conditions giving rise to local conflicts and, on the other hand, have the resources to help improve the level of local well-being. Furthermore, by personalizing conflict residents never criticize political and administrative institutions in ways which might undermine the legitimacy of the institutions which, in effect, subordinate their interests to those of other classes.

Any political power that residents might enjoy through collective organization is further weakened by the sheer number of groups operating locally. This multiplicity is a by-product of the numerous vertically structured groups operating nationally in affiliation with the PRI and the government, and of functionaries tacitly encouraging such an array of organizations by periodically distributing gifts to them,[19] by attending their meetings, and by seeking their support in civic events.

[19] In conjunction with an antipollution program the government planted trees throughout the city. Although the program never accomplished its nominal purpose, since factories and automobiles continued to pollute the air, it served definite political functions. It gave local politicians the opportunity to petition higher-level functionaries for a community benefit

The hierarchical system of appointments induces the various leaders to compete for local support and influence, even when the groups they head are ultimately affiliated with the same parent institution and when the groups concern themselves with the same sets of issues.[20] In the process residents obtain some personal benefits but their potential collective strength is undermined. In recalling the situation in *La Colonia* following the invasion the man who eventually became the leading local government functionary commented to me: "There were always many groups, including some headed by women. The groups were formed in response to the discontent of the people and their desire to obtain municipal benefits. They were formed so that the *paracaidistas* could present their problems to the PRI and the government. There was a lot of competition between the groups because each leader wanted to control *La Colonia* and have the most collaborators." Similarly, when "middle-class" residents of the housing development wished private telephones they did not collectively pressure the phone company. Though ostensibly a nonpolitical demand, it became a political issue. As a leader of a local group noted to me: "There were three groups which collected petitions for phones. The heads of the groups competed to get the most signatures. One of them even lied about the cost

---

and claim credit for obtaining trees, even though the forestation program was city-wide in scope. Because local leaders wanted to impress residents with their political effectiveness and because nonlocal leaders wanted to gain, maintain, or expand chains of indebtedness and probable future support locally, the nonlocal leaders led local leaders to believe that they were instrumental in securing the benefits. Interestingly, pollution became a public issue in Mexico shortly after it did in the U.S., even though Mexico City had polluted air long before.

[20] Similarly, Peruvian urban poor are able to take advantage of ambiguities in jurisdiction among different authorities and dependencies of the state, despite the apparently monolithic military government. Bryan Roberts, "The Interrelationships of City and Provinces in Peru and Guatemala," p. 230. In countries where two or more parties effectively compete for poor people's support, parties, not groups affiliated with a single party or direct appendages of the government bureaucracy, may create division among urban poor. On the divisive effect of political parties among urban poor in other Latin American countries, see Ray, pp. 98-127; and Raymond Pratt, "Parties, Neighborhood Associations, and the Politicization of the Urban Poor in Latin America," pp. 509-10; Roberts, *Organizing Strangers*, Chapter Five; Powell, "Political Participation in the Barriadas"; Rogler, "Slum Neighborhoods in Latin America."

of phones so that people would sign his petition." After collecting signatures the leaders individually spoke to people they knew at the phone company. One leader promised to help persons in the phone company get houses in the area in return for their assistance. Yet, as he admitted privately to me, "It really would have been better if we had formed one big group, because we would have been a much larger force."

Nonetheless, competition among leaders of the diverse groups in itself does not account for the limited political effectiveness of the groups. When members are highly mobilized and nonlocal functionaries want to capture local support, residents, though divided, succeed in securing benefits from the government. The squatters' initial success in acquiring public facilities and private property, even when they were not all united behind a single leader, is a case in point.

At the same time that the government encourages groups it in fact regulates and restricts them. The government requires all groups to be officially registered and the law of "social dissolution" gives it the right to intervene in local associations.[21] The very existence of these laws, and the government's monopoly of the legitimate use of force, inhibit residents both from forming groups and from engaging in activities which challenge the government's authority. Rarely did the government forcefully repress local groups, although some residents of *La Colonia* did have difficulty organizing during the first years the area was inhabited. The law of "social dissolution" served as a useful device by which the government compelled a controversial local leader to dissolve his group, the FUPC, even though he espoused the same objectives and concerns as leaders of officially recognized groups.

The leader was accused of attaining popular support by illicit means, at the expense of *colonos*, by selling *credenciales* for land he did not own. Since the *coyotes* who organized the inva-

[21] The government applies the crime of "social dissolution" against persons who avowedly diffuse ideas or programs of foreign governments which disturb public order or affect Mexico's sovereignty and, more generally, against persons like Demetrio Vallejo and Valentin Campa, who led the 1958 railway workers' strike, and the Communist muralist Alfaro Siqueiros. One of the six demands made by student protestors in 1968 was the repeal of this law, but all crimes covered by the law now are covered in an amended Penal Code. Evelyn Stevens, *Protest and Response in Mexico*, p. 254.

sion of the squatter settlement and the politically most successful *colono* engaged in land fraud, and since persons currently are publicly promoting illegal property transactions in the two newer settlements, it is doubtful that the police threatened to arrest him merely for such activities. Most likely his unlawful activity served as a pretext for repressing his movement, particularly since he was asked not only to stop selling *credenciales* but also to dissolve his group entirely. It seems as if the other local leader, with higher-level contacts, requested the police and government authorities to intervene so that he could—in his words—"control the people better." Since the head of the FUPC held positions in the PRI, he was not reprimanded for supporting an opposition party.

The way the FUPC leader was removed from office typifies the way the government handles nonconformity. Like the woman functionary in *La Unidad*, he was never attacked frontally and the group's dogma was never questioned. Condemnation centered around his personal integrity. Since dissolving his group, he has not held another political position. Because functionaries at the bottom of the social, economic, and political hierarchy have few political prospects outside the confines of their immediate neighborhood, upon being removed from office they commit political suicide. In this manner potential opposition is already curtailed on the local level, since it reminds residents that they may expect a similar fate should they too try to organize in opposition to established functionaries. Anticipation of such consequences probably further reduces the government's need to apply force to maintain order.

Official sanction, however, does not depend on morality or legality. Although the leader of the FUPC was castigated for illegal land transactions and although there was a quick turnover of housing administrators in the development's first four years, ostensibly for accepting large bribes from people illegally trying to get housing there, the underworld and many other illicit activities thrive under the umbrella of the Party, particularly in *El Centro*. For instance, a large well-known house of prostitution in the *tugurio* operates under police protection, supposedly because the owners are high-ranking PRI-officials: at night when the streets of the area generally are quiet and deserted, the only busy street, lined with parked cars and policemen, is the one with the whorehouse. Similarly, many of the *comerciantes* belonging to the PRI-affiliated unions in *El Centro* get their merchandise illegally, with the knowledge of the government and the police. Thus neither the Party nor the government are consistent in their condemnation of illicit activities.

STRUCTURAL BASES OF CO-OPTATION AND INCORPORATION

My personal discussions with local leaders and my observations of local activities suggest that certain groups existed because they satisfied local concerns and interests of leadership. Nonlocal functionaries' involvement in local affairs generally began when ambitious local leaders sought clientage relationships with them.

Leadership co-optation and group incorporation, in turn, took place largely for opportunistic reasons.[22] Leaders were guided above all by a desire for political and economic spoils. The prevailing social order encouraged them to act accordingly, by rewarding them materially and symbolically. They were not primarily prompted by shared ideological commitments, or organizational needs. Viewed from the local level, co-optation and incorporation did *not* necessarily occur, as Philip Selznick contends (see Chapter Three, Appendix), because organizations were threatened.[23]

The varied ways in which leaders were co-opted reflect adaptations to the general class and power structure, in line with their position within that structure. Local leaders generally were encouraged to establish overt institutional ties with national political-administrative groups because they felt that their own prospects of political and economic mobility would thereby be enhanced, and that they thereby would be most apt to secure social and urban services for members. However, they did not by

[22] Perlman also notes that the local leadership in the areas of Rio she studied were readily accessible to control and manipulation from above as they opportunistically sought benefits from the regime. As a result, the leaders supported populist, labor, and military elites under different historical conditions. Janice Perlman, "The Fate of Migrants in Rio's Favelas," pp. 445-47.

[23] Selznick developed his analysis of co-optation on the basis of a study of a co-opting group. I am here viewing the problem from the point of view of co-opted groups. We thus approach the problem from the perspective of groups differently situated in the social structure. Philip Selznick, *TVA and the Grass Roots*, p. 221.

choice establish ties which left them without budgetary resources and decision-making authority.

On occasion, however, local leaders deliberately established covert rather than overt ties with nonlocal functionaries when they felt constituents or potential constituents were antagonistic to the idea of being openly associated with the government or the PRI. For example, the politically ambitious head of the soccer league in *El Centro* never formally affiliated his league with a government or PRI organization because his membership felt that they thus would be compromised. Yet, because of his own political ambitions, he collaborated with political and government functionaries, and ran his group the way he felt pleased those functionaries. Aware that prior leaders of the league and prominent local athletes in the past had been awarded posts in PRI and the government, he hoped to secure political patronage on the basis of his organization. Similarly, the head of the lay church social group in the development never allowed his group to be formally associated with a PRI or government-affiliated group because he thought that he would be forced to resign if he did. Nonetheless, he deliberately affiliated with the FCP individually to secure material assistance for his constituents without which his following would atrophy.

Such opportunism also induced leaders to collaborate with political and administrative authorities even when they personally were dissatisfied with the government. As one of the students arrested in the large 1968 protest, who in 1971 headed the government sports center in *El Centro*, confided in me: "The government is not very effective, but I must conform with it and accept orders from my boss. If I were to do what I would like I would be dropped immediately."

Thus, the situation within the three areas suggests the following hypothesis: that leaders are prompted to establish ties with national political and administrative groups, even when they do not, in the process, gain institutionalized access to power, if they feel such ties enhance their own personal interest. The situation within the areas also suggests that the same selfish concerns of the leaders largely determine whether the ties established are overt or covert, individual or collective. However, while leaders act in accordance with their own interests, their involvements are constrained by formal and informal pressures operating within their groups and the society at large.

Such structurally shaped concerns of leaders help explain why societal resources remain inequitably distributed even when poor people are organized into legitimate political-administrative groups publicly committed to protecting their interests. Organizations do not necessarily serve as instruments of political power if their members gain no institutionalized access to authorities, if the groups lack economic resources of their own, and if informal processes inhibit members from using the groups to serve their collective interests. At the same time organizations of the poor help legitimate the regime, extend the government's realm of administration, and reinforce existing social and economic inequities through overt and covert collective incorporation and through overt and covert individual co-optation of leaders into the official power structure. Of course, members are not necessarily aware of such effects and do not necessarily organize with such effects in mind.

CONCLUSIONS AND IMPLICATIONS

Residents receive limited individual and community benefits not because of a lack of will or ability to organize. To a certain extent organization even contributes to their low material level. Because of collective efforts and persevering leaders, residents secured certain improvements and—in La Unidad and La Colonia—property rights which they otherwise might not have attained. But formal organization per se has proved of limited help. Squatters, in particular, were most effective in securing benefits from the government in the early years following the invasion, when they were least acquiescent (but not antagonistic toward the government) and when their organization was still largely informal and their participation extensive.

Co-optation of leaders and incorporation of local groups has served to establish and reinforce the status quo.[24] Residents have been co-opted into organizations which reinforce and extend the legitimacy of the regime, provide little institutionalized access to power, and subordinate their interests to those of other classes despite the groups' declared objectives. Above all, informal constraints, rooted in the general political economy, inhibit residents

[24] In areas of Mexico, such as Chihuahua, Villa Hermosa, and Durango, where local leaders have resisted being co-opted, there is more opposition to the government.

from using the groups in ways which might significantly alter their position in the urban social and economic hierarchy. Control of the one channel for institutionalized access to official decision-making, Congress, is monopolized by nonlocal residents primarily concerned with their own personal careers and the corporate groups with which they are associated. The effectiveness of this channel of influence is further circumscribed by the fact that Congress actually does not act independently of the Executive.

In addition, local organizations contribute to the formal democratization of the society, for through them the people of the areas are transformed from an "unreliable" citizenry into an "accessible" public. Yet the local groups which legitimate themselves in the name of the revolution are democratic more in theory than in practice. They give residents access to the public symbols of power but only limited, informal, and indirect access to government resources and decision-making.

Viewed from the local level, co-optation and incorporation arise primarily because the "opportunity structure" encourages local leaders to affiliate with PRI and government groups, either individually or together with other group members. The populist doctrine and grass-roots organization facilitate acceptance of the government and enable the government to stand as the champion of local residents, while the co-optative processes contribute to the stability of the capitalist order and the interests of capital which the government above all protects.

It should not be forgotten, though, that co-optation *has*, on occasion, resulted in a commitment of resources to local residents by the government. The co-opting and the co-opted groups, and leaders affiliated with each, generally all benefit from co-optation, even though unequally. The difference in the living standards between local residents and those who co-opt them suggests that local poor benefit least.

APPENDIX TO CHAPTER THREE:
A NOTE ON CO-OPTATION

While co-optative processes help account for the fact that residents have not significantly improved their social and economic lot once relations within the areas have been routinized, the processes operating in the three areas suggest that Selznick's conception of co-optation, the best statement on the subject, should be respecified. The reconceptualization improves the analytic utility of the concept, and facilitates our understanding of why groups with grass-roots structures and populist ideologies do not above all serve the interests of their constituents.

Selznick distinguishes two types of co-optation, formal and informal, and argues that each arises under different conditions, as adaptive responses to different organizational exigencies. To briefly recapitulate his thesis, formal co-optation entails shared public responsibility for authoritative decisions but no actual influence in decision-making, whereas informal co-optation entails the converse, sharing in decision-making but not public responsibility for the decisions.[25] The former type occurs when there is a "need" to establish the legitimacy of authority or the administrative accessibility of the relevant public. It tends to fulfill both the political function of defending legitimacy and the administrative function of establishing reliable channels for communication and direction. In contrast, informal co-optation occurs when there is a "need" to adjust to pressure from specific centers of power within the community. It occurs when persons or groups either are brought into the leadership or policy-determining structure or are conceded resources which they can independently command after previously being deprived of them.

Selznick's two defining characteristics of co-optation, public responsibility and actual influence in the decision-making process, imply four, not two types of co-optation.

1. *Overt (formal) non-power-wielding co-optation*, when public responsibility is shared but actual power is not;

2. *Overt power-wielding co-optation*, when public responsibility and actual power are shared;

3. *Covert power-wielding co-optation*, when public responsibility is not shared but actual power is; and

4. *Covert non-power wielding co-optation*, when neither public responsibility nor actual power is shared but co-opted groups are influenced by other groups.

There is no resaon to assume that accountability for and involvement in decision-making are mutually exclusive, even though Selznick notes that access to power occurs only when co-optation is covert.

[25] Selznick, *Grass Roots*, pp. 13-16, 259-61.

Selznick's distinction between formal and informal co-optation also implies that co-optation transpires because groups have conflicting interests and because power is unequally distributed in the society. Should co-opted groups not get institutionalized access to power but be publicly identified with co-opting groups that wield power, they are likely to share responsibility for policies which do not above all serve their own immediate interests. Alternatively, if groups in the process of co-optation gain institutionalized access to power, the likelihood that co-opting groups act in their own self-interests is diminished. Overtly co-opted groups by definition are associated with the policies of the co-opting group, whereas covertly co-opted groups are not. If the policies are publicly regarded as unpopular, or if they do not operate in the interests of co-opted groups, it is disadvantageous for the co-opted groups to be held accountable for the policies since they cannot under such circumstances criticize the policies.

Yet, in this context Selznick's distinction between formal and informal co-optation is itself misleading. In reference to co-optation Selznick seems both to confuse public accountability for decision-making with institutionalized access to decision-making, and to view real power as necessarily informal. The term "informal" in organizational analyses generally refers to nonsanctioned, nonprescribed relations which are unintended by those responsible for the organization, relations which arise despite or because of the formal organizational structure. However, since the exercising of power may be anticipated and indeed encouraged but deliberately concealed in order to avert the repercussions which public recognition might generate, it is more useful to distinguish between institutionalized and noninstitutionalized access to power than between formal and informal power. Individuals or groups which lack institutionalized access to power may, on occasion, exercise power. They may also articulate their interests and periodically influence decision-makers, but their ability to do so is not guaranteed. Conversely, individuals or groups with institutionalized access to power on occasion may not exercise power. Yet their abstention, especially if it is deliberate, in itself reflects a form of power, as they can, if they choose, employ the power.

Selznick's distinction between formal and informal co-optation is confusing also because it suggests that formal and informal processes associated with co-optation are mutually exclusive. But Selznick himself notes that they are not. He rightly points out a fundamental contradiction inherent in formal co-optation: lest groups with public access to power take advantage of their position to encroach upon the actual arena of decision-making, informal controls must operate.[26] Whether overt co-optation becomes more than symbolic depends not on the stated objectives of groups or on the group's formal organizational command structure but on the actual structure of inter- and intra-group relations. Since Selznick's conception of formal co-optation, by definition, involves informal processes, his hypothesis, that "co-optation which results in an actual sharing of power will tend to operate informally" is non-testable.[27]

The distinction between institutionalized and noninstitutionalized power avoids confusing so-called informal co-optation with informal processes operating among formally or overtly co-opted groups. His hypothesis can now be restated: co-optation which involves an actual institutionalized sharing of power will tend to operate covertly. The respecification of co-optation, however, suggests several alternative outcomes, which if not equally plausible empirically, are each equally plausible logically: overt co-optation and an actual institutionalized sharing of power; covert co-optation and no institutionalized sharing of power; and overt co-optation and no institutionalized sharing of power.

Finally, while Selznick refers to "incorporation" and "corporation" in his discussion of co-optation,[28] incorporation is best kept analytically distinct, with co-optation referring to individual and incorporation to group processes. Co-optation and incorporation need not occur coterminously, and, if they do occur simultaneously, they may each take different forms: one may be covert, the other overt. For example, individuals may be co-opted while groups are not, and individuals may be overtly co-opted while groups are covertly incorporated. However, incorporation does imply co-optation of affiliated individual members.

Selznick's failure to distinguish between the individual and group processes reflects the systemic bias of his conceptualization. He views organizational behavior in terms of organizational responses to organizational "needs"[29] and implies that leaders put their group interests over their individual interests. Yet because

[26] Ibid., pp. 232, 251, 261.
[27] Ibid., p. 260.
[28] Ibid., pp. 220, 260.
[29] Ibid., p. 259.

leaders assume posts as organization heads with their own sets
of interests, as Selznick himself recognizes,[30] and because they
are subject to multiple influences through other present and previous affiliations of theirs, they may, if they can, use the posts to
serve their own interests. The distinction between the individual
and group processes provides a theoretical basis for understanding these potentially conflicting tendencies, including the conditions which give rise to them and the effects they have. One
would expect that the less leaders are accountable to rank-and-
file members because of membership apathy and leadership involvement in covert extraorganizational relations, the more they
are likely to use the groups for their own interests even if against
the best interests of rank-and-file members.

Because of his systemic bias, Selznick also attributes co-optation, even by definition, to be associated with organizational
weakness—a "survival" mechanism whereby an organization
comes to terms with forces in its institutional environment. He
fails to recognize that co-optation and incorporation may serve
other organizational ends, or individual ends quite independently of organizational ones. Why might not leaders co-opt individuals or incorporate groups because they view it as a means by
which to extend their personal range of influence and control?
Power may become a goal in itself, and aspiring leaders may use
co-optive or incorporative tactics to achieve it. Furthermore, co-
optation may have a legitimating impact even though it is instituted to serve the opportunistic concerns of group leaders. The
distinction between co-optation and incorporation provides a
basis for differentiating between individual intentions and organizational consequences.

It is by distinguishing between overt and covert co-optation,
institutionalized and noninstitutionalized access to decision-making through co-optation, and between individual co-optation and
group incorporation, that this concept gains analytic cogency.
Applied to conditions prevailing in *El Centro, La Colonia,* and
La Unidad, the reformulation helps one to understand why societal resources can remain inequitably distributed even when poor
people are organized into legitimate groups publicly committed
to protecting their interests. Organizations may not serve as instruments of political power even if they have "popular" objec-

[30] Ibid., p. 256.

tives and grass-roots structures if they lack institutionalized access to authoritative power and independent economic resources, or if informal social forces inhibit members from using the groups to serve their own interests. Moreover, the reconceptualization helps us understand that if members are overtly or covertly collectively incorporated or if group leaders are overtly or covertly individually co-opted into institutions affiliated with official power structures organizations of the poor will help legitimate a regime, extend a government's realm of administration, and reinforce existing social and economic inequities.

CHAPTER FOUR

Políticos and Priests: Oligarchy and Interorganizational Relations

Not only groups and institutions legitimated in terms of the revolution but also organizations formally restricted since the upheaval serve to subordinate the interests of local poor to those of capitalists and other privileged groups. The Church, and individuals and groups affiliated with it, violate the Constitution in ways which extend the political reach of the state apparatus. Conditions within the three areas studied suggest that the disappearance of overt Church-state conflict in the course of this century stems *not*, as is commonly believed, from each institution respecting the independence of the other. Rather, it derives, at least in part, from groups affiliated with each institution being directly and indirectly interlinked and thereby mutually restrained. These linkages are not mere "survivals" from Mexico's prerevolutionary past, for many have been recently established. They reflect the failure of the two institutional hierarchies to control their affiliated units,[1] in compliance with the Constitution and their own formal command structures.

Interviews with local leaders reveal that the same structurally induced forces which induce secular leaders to retain and expand their power, wealth, and prestige account for Church-state ties. Leaders of Church- and state-affiliated groups seem to engage in extraorganizational relations in addition to or in lieu of internal manipulation of their own groups for several reasons: because their positions give them access to little if any formal

[1] Ivan Vallier, in his analysis of the Catholic Church in Latin America (*Catholicism, Social Control and Modernization*), also argues that the Mexican Church is institutionally weak, even though it appears not to be. According to him, its weakness stems, in part, from its religious hegemony. Vallier adds that the Church's religious hegemony precipitates other consequences as well. For example, he attributes the unprogressive orientation of the Mexican Church partly to the absence of religious competition. The Church's inability to own property and therefore acquire sizable financial resources undoubtedly also contributes to its institutional weakness.

economic and political power, because rank-and-file members are apathetic, and because the organizations with which they are affiliated enjoy a hegemony of influence within their respective institutional domains. Thus, co-optation and incorporation do not merely undermine the organizational effectiveness of residents. They also give rise to extralegal relations and interorganizational oligarchy, through which government influence extends into nominally autonomous realms.

STRUCTURES AND PROCESSES LINKING
CHURCH AND STATE

Both local Catholic groups, and groups affiliated with the PRI and the government, are incorporated into national institutions which are hierarchically structured but not well-integrated and monolithic. Parishes, like local divisions affiliated with the PRI and the government, do not all function identically. In both cases differences between local units are partly attributable to the contrasting social and economic concerns of local residents and partly to the extraorganizational ties which the leaders of the local units established prior and subsequent to the time they assumed their present posts.

The differences reflect the fact that local units actually operate with a modicum of autonomy despite formally imposed hierarchical constraints. Leaders tend to use the groups as bases for expanding their range of contacts and generating new sources of influence, wealth, and prestige. To do so they at times establish ties with other divisions affiliated with the same parent organization as, for example, when parish priests get together. Less frequently they meet with heads of other organizations within their institutional domain: for example, some priests and ministers occasionally communicate. However, even when intrainstitutional ties are formally encouraged,[2] heads of local Church- and government-affiliated groups instead tend to seek links with leaders of groups in the other institutional realm. The ties between priests and heads of government groups are in contravention of rules of

[2] Since the Second Vatican Council (1962-65) the parishes have been organized into *decanatos* and groups of *decanatos* into *gerencias*, each meeting several times a year, as part of the Church's effort to improve both horizontal and vertical integration within the institution.

the respective national institutional hierarchies.[3] They tend to be direct and indirect, formal and informal, legal and illegal.

Direct ties are largely illegal or in violation of the spirit of the Constitution, as exemplified by government subsidization of Church and Church-sponsored activities and involvement of priests and government functionaries in matters which by law fall within the other's domain. The government in effect gives land to the Church since it does not require Catholics to buy the property on which they construct places of worship, and government agencies provide material assistance to Church-sponsored social programs. The public school administration, for example, supplies books and part of the salaries paid to teachers in local parochial schools, even though such schools are outlawed.[4] It also supplies books for literacy programs sponsored by lay groups lacking legal recognition.

Priests and *políticos* at times collaborate in other ways as well. They periodically make announcements for each other, jointly promote and conduct collective matrimonial services for local residents living in free union, and together participate in official celebrations as they occasionally do nationally. In one case, priests actually collaborated with the Secret Police to crush a youth group allegedly infiltrated by Communists. The collaboration included deliberately organizing a church dance the same place and evening that the group scheduled a talk featuring a speaker who the police claimed was a Communist, subsequently refusing to allow the 100-member group to meet in the church social room, the only large indoor meeting place at the time in the area, and actively promoting a competing youth organization.

However, such Church-state collaboration is limited mainly (though not exclusively) to local priests, leaders of formally autonomous groups, and heads of geographically based government

[3] Viewed from a "higher" level of analysis—taking the Party, government, and Church as national organizations (or the Church as an international organization)—the relations depicted here are "intraorganizational." If such an approach were taken, the leaders discussed here would constitute low-level functionaries, and their "extraorganizational" ties, in defiance of hierarchically imposed orders, would reflect the disjunction between informal and formal *intra*organizational relations.

[4] Mexico and Cuba are the only Latin American countries which legally prohibit the Church from establishing educational institutions. Vallier, pp. 36-37.

and Party-linked groups. All priests have ties of some sort to the
state, directly or indirectly. But heads of locally operating social
and economic agencies rarely have contact with local leaders
within their own institutional realm, much less outside it. Consequently, unless otherwise indicated, the analysis below focuses
on relations among the area-based local groups affiliated with the
Church, the Party, and the government, and formally independent area-based groups.

Probably because direct Church-state collaboration is illegal,
linkages between the two institutions mainly are indirect. The indirect ties are a by-product both of formal and informal structural forces. They derive in part from the same persons occupying leadership posts in groups affiliated with both institutions.
Such linkages come about because both institutions generally
seek leaders with similar skills—persons who are responsible, cooperative, known, liked, respected, and effective—but not spe-
cially trained (except for parish priests).[5] Since few residents
combine all these attributes, the same leaders sometimes are independently recruited for both a Church- and a government-affiliated organization.

On other occasions leaders were deliberately recruited into
groups affiliated with one of the institutions on the basis of their
ties with groups in the other institutional realm, although individuals never automatically assumed membership in government-linked groups on the basis of their religious affiliation. Such
intentional "overlapping leadership" occurred in part because
leaders attempted to extend their sphere of influence through as
many existing groups as possible. For this reason several functionaries incorporated leaders of Church-affiliated groups into
their formal political and administrative apparatus.[6]

In one section of La Unidad the Church trained men in leadership skills through Cursillo and Vanguardia programs. After

[5] Bendix argues that bureaucratic autonomy depends on the degree to
which functionaries have a monopoly of particular skills. He qualified
Weber's thesis that bureaucratic autonomy varies according to the degree
to which officials possess indispensable skills. Reinhard Bendix, "Bureaucracy and the Problem of Power," pp. 114-34.

[6] Similarly, in Peru a government-sponsored "grass-roots" organization
co-opted the leadership and adopted much of the organizational structure
of the Pueblos Jóvenes del Perú (PUJOP) and, in the process, emasculated
the Church-linked organization. See Sara Michl, "Urban Squatter Organization as a National Government Tool," p. 170.

briefly leading a lay group, these men secured posts in the PRI and government-affiliated groups. The Church in these instances unintentionally trained leaders for the PRI and the government. Since the co-opted persons technically joined the political and administrative groups as individuals, and not as formal representatives of the Church group, the Church did not as a consequence formally become involved in politics and government, in violation of the Constitution.

In part, however, common recruitment occurred through consultation between leaders of both institutions. For example, when a functionary of a city-wide government agency formed a local group in one of the areas to promote interest in a newly renovated social center, he asked the local priest for names of capable and dependable residents, and the priest recommended persons active in lay groups.

Moreover, the Church and state are intermeshed through complementary activities sponsored by divisions of the two institutions. Under the auspices of ostensibly lay *patronatos*[7] several parishes offered medical services, including one hospital and a few clinics, and such educational facilities as literacy classes, courses in sewing and cooking, and elementary schools, where the government provided insufficient facilities or none at all. Thus, the Church provides services to the government at the same time that it extends its own sphere of influence. However, this influence remains within parameters set by the state, for Church-sponsored schools and hospitals are regularly inspected by government agents and forced to conform with government standards.

In addition, Church and state indirectly collaborate through inaction. Functionaries, for example, not only permit, assist, and regulate Church-affiliated schools and hospitals, but even allow local priests to hold religious services outside Church edifices in violation of the Constitution, when such services promote public morality and "law and order." For example, an American priest in the housing development held open-air mass in the section inhabited by pickpockets, and another American priest held house mass in one of the oldest, most dilapidated, crime-ridden apart-

---

[7] To circumvent the Constitutional restriction prohibiting the Church from directly engaging in nonreligious matters priests organize civic groups with lay boards of officers (*patronatos*).

ment buildings in the center city area. Both priests hoped thereby to reform the criminals.

Just as government functionaries are tolerant of the Church, so too are priests tolerant of the government. Church-affiliated leaders do not pressure the government in the local allocation of resources. The local priest in the squatter settlement never asked either for legalization of the squatters' land claims or for needed social and urban services.

Church, PRI, and government institutions also are linked through the religious, political, and civic activities of their members. Members of many work associations participate in civic and political manifestations, and in religious activities. They collectively partake in pilgrimages, activities associated with the patron saint of their work places, and at times, sponsor special church services. While the civic, political, and religious activities are distinct, they all reinforce a sense of docility and commitment to the status quo through their emphasis on hierarchy.

In contrast, the various small Protestant and other sectarian groups are not nearly as closely linked with the Party and the government as is the Catholic Church. Compared to priests, ministers have few contacts with *políticos*, and their congregations are not subsidized by the government. There are no "temples" on public land. All the denominations bought their property before turning it over to the state. Moreover, ministers are more reluctant than priests to hold outdoor services or otherwise evade the Constitution. The ministers fear that the government might use such occasions as a basis for denying them the religious freedom they now enjoy. Since most state officials are Catholic, ministers feel that the functionaries favor the expansion of Catholicism, at the expense of Protestantism.

Not only is the Catholic Church more closely intertwined with the state than the Protestant sects but also its ties to the government are closer than to Protestant groups. Only one minister and one priest reported having contact with one another, and that consisted merely of a conversation. Thus, ties among groups in different functional spheres in this instance are greater than among groups in the same functional sphere. Such common interests as religion and antipathy to government restrictions on religious activities are not sufficient bases for establishing intra-institutional ties. Ministers and priests consider themselves in competition for religious domination within their areas; thus they rarely communicate or collaborate. As long as Protestantism remains a minority and sect-like religion and priests tolerate the PRI's political hegemony, government functionaries probably will continue to give the Catholic Church preferential treatment over Protestant groups.[8]

EFFECTS OF CHURCH-STATE LINKAGES

The linkages between groups affiliated with the Church and state affect leaders and rank-and-file members of the respective groups, the structure and functioning of the groups, and, as a consequence, the institutions with which the groups are affiliated —indirectly if not directly. The full impact of the ties, however, is not obvious to leaders, much less to rank-and-file members, and the effects frequently are quite different from the reasons which induced the leaders to initiate them. To rank-and-file members the implications are even less apparent because frequently the groups remain nominally intact while leaders alter the purposes of the groups.

Leaders and rank and file of interlinked groups are both affected, but in different ways. Leaders tend to receive symbolic rewards associated with overt co-optation, such as access to political and civic posts having no decision-making power. They also acquire access to new channels of influence and control, and new prospects for attaining higher-ranking positions by acquiring new dependable collaborators. Occasionally, leaders who used the groups almost exclusively to advance their own interests were forced to resign, because of members' resentment. But because the conditions which accounted for the political manipulation remained, namely the state's near-monopoly both of the resources available for lower-class communities and of channels for

[8] This finding corroborates conclusions of studies of church-sect relations which posit that church or ecclesiastic groups are more involved than sect-like groups in the "establishment." See, for example, N. R. Niebuhr, *Social Sources of Denominationalism*; Bryan Wilson, "An Analysis of Sect Development," pp. 3-15; J. Milton Yinger, *Religion in the Struggle for Power*. Since church-sect theory includes little analysis of processes through which religious-secular involvements occur and the "churchly" mode of religion gets absorbed in the society (and vice versa) this chapter has implications for sociology of religion theory, as well as for organizational theory.

individual political advancement, their successors also tended toward similar abuses.

The interinstitutional ties do not work entirely to the detriment of rank-and-file members. They gain limited material benefits, especially when their groups are publicly incorporated into others that provide no institutionalized access to power. Thus, a Church youth group acquired athletic uniforms, and a social group which worked closely with one of the parish priests received a movie projector in exchange for their affiliation with the PRI.

While the official goals of the groups tend to remain intact, the actual concerns of the groups subsequently change, particularly when leaders of lay groups are co-opted formally into PRI and government-affiliated groups. Lay leaders and incorporated groups were constrained to collaborate with those who co-opted them, to the extent that lay leaders who previously had been critical of the government and the PRI and suspicious of the motives of *políticos*, came to involve their followers in civic manifestations and political rallies and to report regularly on political and civic matters at their group meetings. After the leader of the lay group in *La Unidad* joined the PRI-affiliated FCP his group actually ceased to meet. But had the leader not affiliated with the PRI, he and the remaining active members would not have become subject to its political influence.

The ties between Church and state-linked groups also affect the institutions with which they are affiliated. Because of such linkages the Party and government secure support from skilled and enterprising people, and extend their sphere of influence and control. While the leaders, as a consequence, may be torn by "cross-pressures," the favors exchanged induce them to be passively if not actively predisposed toward the institutions with which they affiliate.

Inaction on the part of these lay groups also serves to strengthen the Church, the Party, and the government. Government laxity in enforcement of the law enabled the Church to extend its secular and religious influence, in that Catholic schools were allowed to supplement official textbooks with books more in line with the Church's point of view, start school days with prayers, offer classes in ethics and morals, invite priests periodically to lecture, and encourage students to go to church. Similarly, religious activities held outside church buildings and foreign priests who supplemented the shortage of Mexican priests, in violation

of the Constitution, helped reinforce and extend Church influence. In turn, priests who made announcements for PRI-affiliated
groups (but not for Socialist and Communist parties) limited the
likelihood that groups challenging the regime's legitimacy would
gain force, and priests who participated in official ceremonies
helped legitimate the regime and the inegalitarian social order.
Since PRI functionaries frequently also attended the same ceremonies, priests in the process indirectly lent support to the PRI,
even if unwittingly. Furthermore, the very extension of Church
activities contributes to the expansion of the government bureaucracy, and reinforcement of the status quo, for the government
regulates and monitors the Church.

BASES OF CHURCH-STATE LEADERSHIP LINKAGES

The conditions inducing leaders of Church- and state-affiliated
groups to involve themselves in proscribed Church-state relations
and to adopt permissive postures toward each other's activities
were mainly structural in origin. The leaders were prompted by
group exigencies, situational constraints, and, above all, by the
same societal forces which induced group leaders to co-opt and
be co-opted. Local leaders who felt that they could not maintain
or significantly enhance their power, wealth, and prestige merely
by concerning themselves with intragroup matters overstepped
their organizational boundaries when opportunities arose and
appeared propitious. However, because rank-and-file members
occasionally were able to pressure higher-ranking functionaries
to replace exploiting local leaders, there were limits to the degree
to which ambitious leaders could manipulate their groups.

   Extraorganizational ties also were established to gain access
to resources otherwise difficult to obtain, so that interests of residents could be satisfied and groups would not atrophy. Here the
interests of ambitious leaders coincided with those of members.
Groups comprised of members of low socioeconomic status were
unable to generate sizable economic resources internally, and the
institutions with which they were affiliated did not regularly provide them with compensatory resources. To gain access to goods
and services for constituents and to enhance their personal standing local leaders accordingly sought extraorganizational contacts.
For example, priests and lay leaders were able to raise few funds
within their parishes to finance benefits for residents because

most parishioners were poor, and heads of PRI- and government-linked groups informed me that they wanted the support of Catholic lay groups in order to enlarge the size of their following and thereby their prospects for political advancement.

Local leaders generally seemed to feel that they maintained more autonomy when they collaborated with leaders in other institutional spheres than when they collaborated with leaders in their own sphere.[9] Local government functionaries, competing for favors from their hierarchical superiors, were reluctant to collaborate with each other. In contrast, leaders of groups affiliated with the different institutions at times viewed their interests as complementary rather than antagonistic, especially when they shared common institutional memberships. The collaboration which ensued did not, however, stem merely from overlapping memberships, as overlapping intrainstitutional affiliations—e.g., among PRI-affiliated groups—rarely led to comparable cooperation.

The local leaders were not driven by any ideological commitment to rectify Church-state ties. Quite the contrary. Priests typically viewed the National Action Party as more pro-Catholic than the "official" Party, reflecting the Catholic orientation of the former on the national level. Even in the one instance in which ideology appeared to have precipitated collaboration—a shared hatred of Communism—at least one of the parties involved saw its own immediate interest at stake: the priest in the housing development colluded with the Secret Police to dissipate the reputedly infiltrated Catholic youth group, partly because he felt his authority being challenged since the group did not want to be subordinate to him.

Structurally induced opportunism contributed to interorganizational and, in the process, interinstitutional alliances, as the following cases make clear. One case, previously discussed, involves the leader of the PRI-affiliated FCP in *La Unidad* who formally co-opted the head of a Catholic lay group in order to enlarge his constituency and thereby his chances of political advancement. Until then the head of the PRI-linked group had had little influence in the section of the development where the lay

[9] William Reid, "Interagency Coordination in Delinquency Prevention and Control," pp. 418-28, and Harold Guetzkow, "Relations among Organizations," also report that interorganizational ties had a similar effect in the respective organizations which they studied.

group operated. Another case involves some *políticos* who asked an American parish priest to oversee a rigged local election to give it an air of legitimacy, and the priest accepted the invitation because he felt he would then be identified as an important community leader. Still another case involves a female government functionary, a nonpracticing Catholic, who sought the collaboration of a Church youth group because she felt the group could assist her in civic tasks which would impress higher-ranking functionaries and increase her chances of political promotion. And in one other case a government functionary offered a priest authority to close down an illegally operating bar, even though law enforcement is the responsibility of the government, because the functionary did not want to incur public disfavor by closing it himself.

In turn, the heads of groups least anxious to extend their sphere of influence and control had fewest interinstitutional bonds. One American priest in the center city area, who had studied at Louvain where he had become influenced by the Christian Workers Movement, was critical of the established Church and the government. He was not well integrated into either institutional hierarchy. He permitted few religious rituals in his parish, and published a local newspaper in which he publicly criticized local *políticos*. He had contact only with functionaries concerning official business.

Occasionally collaboration occurred even though leaders felt competitive toward each other. Several priests, for example, cooperated with government functionaries because they recognized that they needed government support, but privately viewed themselves as competitors for domination over the local communities. The American priest who had officiated the rigged local election in *La Unidad* told me that he was in a race with the government, the PRI, and the Communists for control of the area, that he did not want the literacy class he sponsored to be officially recognized by the government because then the government would subsequently "take it over," and that he symbolically wanted to assert the superiority of the Church by building a tower taller than the edifice of the adjacent government social center. Another American priest in the area noted that he had his church built during Holy Week when the government was on vacation so ". . . that way the government had no choice. It had to allow the church on the plaza because by the time the functionaries re-.

turned to work the building was already up." Still another American priest told me that he was striving hard to finish his census before the local leader of the PRI-affiliated FCP and the head of the Promotion Committee of the new social center finished theirs. Similarly, structural pressures induced a Protestant *político* in one of the areas to have more contact with the local priest than with local ministers: he considered seeking the priest's support politically more expedient.

OLIGARCHY AND INTERORGANIZATIONAL TIES

The conditions which here have induced leaders to overstep their organizational and institutional boundaries are an extension of those which Robert Michels argued induce leaders to manipulate intraorganizational relations.[10] Michels held that both democratic-egalitarian and conservative-inegalitarian organizations tended to become oligarchic, because of the desire of leaders to maintain their positions of influence, the inability of the masses to participate in the decision-making process, and the tendency of large-scale organizations to give officers a near-monopoly of power. How does this analysis apply to the case under study? Conditions within the three areas suggest that organizational hegemony combined with organizational weakness, and membership passivity, contribute to the extraorganizational ties which leaders establish.

Hegemony of organizations within their institutional domain, even if the organizations include multiple affiliated units, affects group leaders, rank-and-file members, and the groups themselves. The organizational near-monopoly of the Church and the PRI within their respective spheres seems to induce leaders of affiliated groups to seek new spheres of influence, in the other institutional domain. When each organization is hegemonic within its institutional sphere leaders are subject to few pressures inhibiting them from overstepping organizational and institutional boundaries. Under such conditions the leaders can quite freely use their positions to further their own ends. Such hegemony, however, does not necessarily imply organizational strength or power, or forceful intrainstitutional oligarchy, for many local leaders established the interinstitutional ties in *defiance* of hierarchical orders.

[10] Michels, *Political Parties.*

Lack of formally prescribed financial and decision-making power as well as institutional hegemony seem to contribute to interorganization oligarchy, as heads of powerless groups have restricted means—though more than rank and file—by which to increase their personal wealth, power, and prestige and satisfy their constituents. Their superior knowledge and control over communications both within their organizations and between their own and other organizations, however, are assets they can use to establish extraorganizational relations to enhance their personal and possibly also their constituents' interests.

Finally, membership apathy seems to have contributed to interorganizational oligarchy. Since local leaders believe that they must have a large following in order to advance politically, and since leaders of lower-status groups must deliver material benefits to maintain and enlarge their following, local leaders sought extraorganizational ties to expand their sphere of local influence. Yet when members are apathetic leaders need not be regularly accountable: Under such circumstances the extraorganizational relations in which leaders engage may go unnoticed or unchallenged by rank-and-file members. The leaders therefore are subject to somewhat conflicting constraints.

Mass apathy frequently develops where group membership is automatic and requires no strong commitment;[11] where co-optation into national political and administrative organizations has discouraged active participation; where intrainstitutional competition is limited because of the near-hegemony organizations enjoy within their institutional realm; and where groups fail to achieve their stated purpose. However, such apathy does not stem from the "incompetence of the masses," as Michels argues,[12] for rank and file, as we know, were not always inactive.

[11] In general, even though Mexican poor are religious people, they adhere to a fusion of Catholicism with "folk" beliefs which does not generate great interest in parish churches. Since many of them have small wall "altars" where they pray to saints, their religion is not heavily dependent on the church. Precisely because their religion is "unorthodox" the Church-led counterrevolutionary movement in the 1920s proved unsuccessful: when priests closed down churches the "masses" tended not to rally to their cause.

[12] According to Michels, the "incompetence of the masses" reflects a social-psychological tendency of the masses more than a response to specific social conditions.

CONCLUSIONS AND IMPLICATIONS

Contrary to the situation during the 1920s counterrevolution and contrary to the widely held belief that today Church and state are structurally and functionally distinct, conditions within the three areas suggest that Church and state in Mexico are in fact intertwined and mutually reinforcing. Despite stringent legal, social, economic, political, and religious restrictions on the Church, local priests and leaders of lay groups have established ties with territorial based organs of the government and the dominant political party. However, while lay groups facilitate the Church's effort to extend its sociopolitical influence in an officially more acceptable form, they and their leaders generally are subordinate to the state and its representatives.

The institutional arrangements and processes illustrated above are not necessarily the only ones which link the Church with the PRI and the government in Mexico. Since parish priests and *políticos* in the areas under study sponsored different activities in accordance with their own background and the socioeconomic concerns of residents, different bases for interdependence possibly operate in other areas, depending on the backgrounds of leaders and rank-and-file members.[13] Such locally based extraorganizational linkages seem minimally to arise when groups have few internal resources of their own.

Despite such linkages, there is no reason to believe that close collusion between Church and state is inevitable. If either institution acts in a manner perceived to seriously challenge the status quo, if the population no longer needs or wants the goods and services that groups affiliated with these institutions now offer, if groups affiliated with the two institutions fail to adapt to newly developed wants of the people, or if other groups gain access to sizably more resources than they now command, the hegemony of the institutions may be seriously challenged and their structural links, as a consequence, diminished. Should existing bonds break down, leaders and their groups may come to publicly con-

[13] Although there are no studies of "middle-" and upper-class neighborhoods in Mexico, I am under the impression that territorial based political and administrative groups are less active in such neighborhoods than in low-income neighborhoods. The more well-to-do relate to the regime primarily through occupational, not territorial-based groups.

test for power, wealth, and prestige. At present it is questionable whether the Mexican government and hierarchy, foreign missionary orders, the Vatican, and the U.S. government will tolerate much opposition to the regime. The constraints imposed on priests in Latin America who advocate institutional changes is well demonstrated by the cases of Ivan Illich in Mexico and the revolutionary Camilo Torres in Colombia.[14]

Existing Church-state ties within the three areas produce seemingly contradictory consequences. On the one hand, affiliated organizations and their members are subject to external influences and are compelled to share symbolic if not actual power. On the other hand, since leaders of interlinked organizations may more readily achieve their goals than they could on their own, their power, wealth, and prestige seem to be strengthened at the same time that their groups lose their functional autonomy. Thus, interorganizational oligarchy may contribute both to the creation of societal elites and to the maintenance of intraorganizational leadership.

More generally, relations between Church- and state-linked groups within the three areas show that true organizational (and institutional) autonomy depends not merely on formal independence but also on the ability of organizations to resist the influence of forces in their social "environment." Since no organization is totally unaffected by such forces, organizational autonomy is relative, not absolute. However, the ties linking organizations may be formal or informal, direct or indirect, prescribed or proscribed. They may involve shared personnel, jointly sponsored activities, reciprocal exchanges of goods and services, or complementary activities.

The situation within the three areas also demonstrates that differentiation of religion and politics does not hinge on formal separation of the two institutions. This situation suggests that structural differentiation and formal organizational (or institutional) autonomy in general may not necessarily reflect actual organizational (or institutional) autonomy. If it is true that the structural exigencies of bureaucratic administration make for

[14] Because of Torres' commitment to revolutionary struggle the Cardinal forced him to abandon the priesthood; and military forces, advised by U.S. officers, subsequently killed him. Ric Edwards, "Religion in the Revolution?—A Look at Golconda," p. 2; Gerald Thiesen, "The Case of Camilo Torres Restrepo."

intraorganizational oligarchy and that power is increasingly concentrated in large-scale bureaucracies in "advanced" industrial
societies, interorganizational and interinstitutional linkages are
not likely to be limited to such "underdeveloped" societies as
Mexico.[15] Structural-functional modernization theory must be
modified to account both for the informal and indirect linkages
between formally autonomous organizations (and institutions)
and for the effects these have on organizations, institutions, and
the society at large.[16]

Thus, to fully understand the impact that religious, civic, and
political organizations—and, by implication, all organizations—
have on leaders and rank-and-file members one must examine
extraorganizational as well as intraorganizational relations.[17] The
more complete organizational analysis can help explain why
there is less overt conflict between Church and state and greater
religious hegemony of the Church in Mexico than, for example,
in Brazil, even though historically Church-state conflict has been
more severe and legal restrictions on the Church's secular and religious involvements more comprehensive in Mexico.[18] This type
of analysis can help account for mutual tolerance between organizations and institutions premised on apparently different values,
and for the greater success certain organizations have in recruit-
ing members and accomplishing goals than others publicly committed to the same set of objectives. Such elucidation also is
essential for comprehending mechanisms of social control and
potential avenues of social change.

The nature of local interorganizational ties depends largely on
the structure of opportunities for leaders to maintain and extend
their sphere of influence, not on the "needs," stated purpose, or

[15] Even in such a highly industrialized, so-called pluralist secular society
as the U.S., Church and state are much more intertwined than is commonly believed. Religious leaders, for example, played an important political
role in the civil rights movement. They also have helped legitimate the
state through public association with national political elites: Billy
Graham and the late Cardinal Spellman are cases in point.

[16] Talcott Parsons, *Societies.*

[17] A complete theory of organizations also requires analyzing the extraorganizational relations of rank-and-file group members and the effects of
such relations.

[18] On Church-state conflict in Brazil, see Thomas Bruneau, *The Political
Transformation of the Brazilian Catholic Church,* and Charles Antoine,
Church and Power in Brazil.

formal command structure of the organizations.[19] Since the local groups most interlinked are those with the greatest human and material resources within their institutional domain, there is no support for the widely held contention that interorganizational ties are established in response to organizational "needs." The local Catholic groups seem to be more directly and indirectly tied to the government than Protestant sects, *because* they have access to greater resources, not because they lack internal resources.

Extra- and intraorganizational forces, including formally defined interorganizational relations, shape the way in which leaders use their positions to enhance their interests, although these forces themselves do not determine actual interorganizational relations. Leaders are both "role-determined" and "role determining." When interorganizational linkages are proscribed, the leaders tend to establish ties indirectly and informally, rather than directly and formally.

The direct and indirect effect that the inter- and intraorganizational oligarchic tendencies described in this and the preceding chapter have on predisposing residents to support the status quo will be treated next.

[19] This analysis, therefore, adds a theoretical dimension to the growing body of studies dealing with interorganizational relations, such as (1) those by William Evan, "The Organization-Set," pp. 173-191, and Herman Turk, "Interorganizational Networks in Urban Society," pp. 1-18, which focus on the structure of relations between different kinds of organizations that are not by definition complementary; (2) those by Selznick, *TVA and the Grass Roots*; V. F. Ridgeway, "Administration of Manufacturer-Dealer Systems," pp. 464-83; William Dill, "The Impact of Environment on Organizational Development," pp. 94-109; S. Levine and Paul White, "Exchange as a Conceptual Framework"; Guetzkow, "Relations Among Organizations"; Eugene Litwak and Lydia Hylton, "Interorganizational Analysis: A Hypothesis on Coordinating Agencies," pp. 395-426; Thompson, "Organizations and Output Transactions," pp. 309-24; R. H. Elling and S. Halbsky, "Organizational Differentiation and Support," pp. 185-209, and Reid, "Interagency Coordination," which deal with interorganizational transactions, and (3) those by Thompson and William McEwen, "Organizational Goals and Environment," pp. 23-31; and Aiken and Hage, "Organizational Interdependence," which deal with the impact interorganizational relations have on internal organizational structures and processes.

CHAPTER FIVE

The Politics of Conformity

In capitalist societies with universal citizenship there is in theory a fundamental contradiction between the economy, premised on inequality, and the polity, premised on equality.[1] In such societies politicized electorates may impose demands which require governments to divert developmental resources to distributive programs.[2]

Since suffrage is universal in postrevolutionary Mexico, residents in principle could use the franchise to elect into office a party or group of people who above all defend their interests. Paradoxically, though, the very same forces which restrict the local residents' organizational effectiveness and contribute to Church-state oligarchy also predispose residents to support the PRI. Inhabitants are subject to political influences which shape their voting behavior, largely indirectly, through their involvement in nominally nonpolitical groups.[3] As a result, they support a political party and lend legitimacy to a regime which subordinates their social and economic interests to those of the numerical minority of capitalists, "middle-class" professionals and salaried employees, and organized industrial workers.

[1] T. H. Marshall, *Class, Citizenship and Social Development*.

[2] These assumptions are found, for example, in Deutsch, Lerner, and Almond and Verba. See Deutsch, "Social Mobilization"; Lerner, *Traditional Society*; and Almond and Verba, *Civic Culture*. Deutsch, for example, speaks of the burden "generated by the processes of social mobilization" (p. 221) and notes that "the growth in the numbers of these people produces mounting pressures for the transformation of political practices and institutions" (p. 211). Similarly, Almond and Verba talk of the "participation explosion" (p. 20) and of the necessity for the democratic citizen to "be active, yet passive; involved, yet not too involved; influential, yet deferential" (p. 343). In their view stability is more important than equality.

[3] I use the term "direct political involvements" in reference to groups which are formally or manifestly concerned with politics—groups with stated political objectives. I use the term "indirect political involvements" in reference to groups which sponsor activities which are politically consequential but not nominally engaged in politics—groups which do not espouse political or primarily political objectives.

FORMAL POLITICS

Residents rarely expressed interest in politics in their everyday life. Yet about 90 percent of the eligible voters interviewed said they voted in the 1964 presidential election,[4] a high percentage given that poverty, illiteracy, provincialism, and religious commitment often impede electoral participation.[5] Moreover, despite the regime's inegalitarian policies, 82 percent of the eligible electorate said they voted for the PRI in the last election. Only one person reported supporting the Popular Socialist Party (PPS). 11 percent said they cast their ballot for the conservative PAN, 7 percent that they did not vote, and 1 percent that they nullified their ballot.[6] Residents are not using the franchise, one of the few

[4] About 20-30 percent more persons interviewed reported voting in the 1964 presidential campaign than actually voted in the Federal District or the country as a whole (González Casanova, p. 233). The proportion of persons interviewed who reported voting also is greater than the proportion of residents who were recorded as having voted. Residents probably tend to over-report electoral participation because they tend to report prescribed behavior. The Constitution stipulates that all citizens must vote, although the regulation is not strictly enforced. In Almond and Verba's five-nation study fewer Mexicans (1 percent) than citizens of the other countries—particularly compared to Germans (16 percent) and Italians (32 percent)—refused to report electoral participation. The authors attribute the Mexican phenomenon to the "fact that the overwhelming majority of Mexicans vote for the Revolutionary party, which is the dominant party in the country. In other words, Mexicans unlike Italians of the extreme left, have nothing to conceal." Almond and Verba do not consider the degree to which their findings reflect *actual* voting behavior. See Almond and Verba, p. 81. Since residents in my sample, when asked about Church involvement, also tended to report the behavior expected of them rather than their actual behavior, they obviously are aware of prescribed behavior and feel reluctant to admit nonconformity.

[5] On the attributed relationship between economic status, education, place of residence, religion and voting, see Deutsch, "Social Mobilization"; Roger Vekemans and Jorge Giusti, "Marginality and Ideology in Latin American Development"; Betty Cabezas and Fernando Durán, "Orientaciones teóricas y operacionales de la marginalidad"; González Casanova, pp. 71-103; and Armand Mattelart and Manuel Garretón, *Integración nacional y marginalidad*. On the supposed relationship between these social and economic factors and democracy, see Seymour M. Lipset, *Political Man*, pp. 27-86.

[6] According to electoral statistics, approximately 2 percent of the electorate voted for the PPS. The percentage who reported voting for PRI in the three areas corresponds with the PRI's actual registered electoral strength on

benefits they gained from the revolution, to elect into office a party which primarily advances their interests; and the vast majority do not use blank ballots, as Peronistas formerly did in Argentina, to articulate dissatisfaction with their electoral options.

Not only does the PRI boast widespread electoral support but it also is the only party which claims a mass membership. According to local Party offices, approximately 90 percent of the people in the three areas belong to the PRI.

The PRI's local success may seem predictable since it is the only party with a grass-roots organization and local social service agencies.[7] District PRI offices offer classes in sewing, cooking, hairdressing, and typing, and medical and barber services. PRI functionaries also write job recommendations for residents, and periodically distribute such gifts as rice, *frijoles* (beans), and candy to residents. Furthermore, it is the only party which regularly solicits the government for social and urban facilities on behalf of residents. It thereby serves as an intermediary between the local communities and the municipal government.

Yet many of the low-level functionaries are not very active during electoral campaigns, much less in the interim,[8] and, according to the persons in charge of district PRI offices, only about two dozen people make use of most of the services offered at their headquarters. In addition, the PRI only intermittently allocates

---

the national level. According to official statistics, 88 percent of the people who voted in 1964 voted for Díaz Ordaz (González Casanova, p. 200). For analyses of voting patterns in Mexico, see, in addition, Barry Ames, "Bases of Support for Mexico's Dominant Party," and Cornelius, "Urbanization as an Agent in Latin American Political Instability," pp. 833-57. In support of my thesis, Ames's analysis of voting behavior between 1952 and 1967 shows an inverse relationship on the state level between economic development and receipt of government benefits, on the one hand, and support for the PRI, on the other hand: The more "advanced" states generally are better able to pressure the system to increase their benefits (p. 162). He also found that the PRI has gained in electoral strength with urbanization (pp. 165-66).

[7] The little political activity sponsored by the PAN and the PPS locally is organized primarily by nonlocal residents who are commissioned by the respective parties to work locally.

[8] In 1971 the district president of the PRI replaced local PRI functionaries. He attributed the decline in the PRI's local strength in the last election to the failure of incumbents to comply with their responsibilities. His own future political prospects, he believed, depended partly on his ability to maintain and increase the PRI's support base.

gifts locally, and merely a small proportion of the residents actually receive gifts. Moreover, while the PRI was the only party in which any interviewed residents claimed membership, only 10 percent said they belonged. Therefore, neither the activities of the formal PRI apparatus nor perceived membership in the PRI alone account for the PRI's widespread local electoral strength.

Nor can the PRI's local success be attributed to sympathy for the specific candidates running for office or to the Party's doctrine. The PRI candidates rarely are known locally before the campaigns. Although nationally the PRI is considered reformist and populist, because the Popular Socialist Party (PPS) also identifies itself with the urban lower and working classes, a publicly professed mass orientation in itself cannot account for residents' overwhelming support of the PRI. Moreover, the PRI gains electoral support despite local discontent with the corruptness of PRI—and only PRI—functionaries.

As presented locally, the party platforms are hardly distinguishable. One PAN congressman, for instance, defined the PAN to me as a party primarily concerned with "respect for human dignity, justice for the worker and peasant, and a decent salary for the worker." Another PAN congressman noted, "It's difficult to explain the psychology of PAN. It's concerned with respect and equality." And PRI functionaries rarely perceived the uniqueness of their party to be its program. Yet *políticos* associated with the PRI, unlike those associated with the PAN or other opposition parties, emphasized revolution-linked themes. The PRI politicians campaigned with such slogans as "Within our party all of us are servants to the revolutionary cause."

Undoubtedly, the PRI's ability to associate with the country's revolution contributes to its electoral success. However, when asked to name goals of the revolution only about half of the residents formally interviewed cited one, much less one associated specifically with the PRI. Moreover, those who mentioned a goal of the revolution spoke of such general economic concerns as "economic development" (24 percent) and such general political concerns as "liberty" (47 percent). Few of them (11 percent) viewed the regime as specifically concerned with problems of urban or rural poor. Accordingly, if the PRI support derives from its revolutionary mystique, residents vote on the basis of general, not class-defined, interests. Moreover, the association with the revolution is vague and not intense.

In addition, informal interviews suggest that residents' voting preference stems not from any identification with the PRI's unique political platform. People could not specify why they and their neighbors voted for the PRI. They mentioned that it was customary there to vote for the PRI, and depicted the main difference between the PRI and the other parties to be that "the PRI always wins," that it gets the most votes, and that it is the "most known." Although they did not regard the PRI as primarily committed to protecting their interests, they expressed no indication that any of the "opposition" parties might serve their interests better. The Party benefits from its populist image, from ignorance, political ritual, and lack of perceived viable alternatives.

Moreover, when the regime is openly challenged, as it was by the student-led protest in 1968, the government responds nationally and locally in such a way that residents do not as a consequence support opposition movements. According to interviews with local leaders and informal discussions with residents in 1971, Communists and foreign infiltrators—from the C.I.A. to Russian and Chinese agitators—were responsible for the protest movement. And youth themselves contributed to the impression that there was no viable alternative, as the number of youth in responsible local political and administrative positions increased markedly between 1968 and 1971.

Yet residents are unlikely to support the PRI merely out of default—because they see no reason to support "opposition" parties. Knowing in advance that the PRI will win they could choose to abstain. However, many of those interviewed in depth noted that they felt obliged to vote and that they feared reprisal if they did not. They generally regarded voting more as a duty than a right. Some feared that their children would not be allowed to register in school, that they might lose their job or pay, or that government functionaries would not tend to their problems if they were unable to present a voting certificate, verifying that they had voted. Although few of them know persons who actually experienced such recriminations, the fear in itself seems to drive many of them to the polls,[9] and once there, to vote for the PRI.

[9] Upon voting, citizens receive a voting certificate, which then enables employers and government functionaries to determine whether citizens voted. I am under the impression that "middle" and upper-class Mexicans are not induced to vote by such negative sanctions or fear of such sanctions. Since they can afford to send their children to private school and since they tend to enjoy greater job security than urban poor, such incentives probably would be ineffective.

"NONPOLITICAL" GROUPS

The PRI's electoral success stems not merely from the activities
and ideology of the formal political apparatus but also from the
politicizing effect of nominally nonpolitical groups. Many other
groups besides the Church-linked ones described in Chapter
Four expose members to political influences.

For many jobs membership in occupational groups is obligatory and automatic. Many of these economic associations are
formally affiliated with the PRI, as exemplified by the unions in
a few of the factories in *El Centro* and in the markets, schools,
and other government agencies in all three areas. Although these
associations are ostensibly concerned with the economic and social interests of their members, they are expected to engage occasionally in civic and political rallies. Center city area market
vendors, for example, were asked to participate in as many as
twenty or twenty-five manifestations per year. Union leaders do
not insist that all members of their groups attend all rallies. The
number they demand depends on the importance higher-ranking
government or PRI functionaries attribute to the specific event.
They induce participation in such events by fining or threatening
to fine workers. Heads of market associations generally get cooperation from at least some vendors by threatening to otherwise
close their stalls. Although workers also are given certain positive
inducements to partake in such activities—e.g., refreshments or a
prize contest—informal talks with them suggest that they generally collaborate to "avoid problems."

However, less than 10 percent of the residents interviewed
work in the area where they live. Thus, most of them are not subject to political mobilizations through local workplaces. But to
the extent that employed residents are members of PRI-affiliated
unions, they mainly partake in political and civic activities
through nonlocal economic groups. I have no data, though, on
the political activities of the nonlocal economic associations to
which local residents belong.

Despite membership in PRI-affiliated groups through work,
few people interviewed claimed membership in the PRI. They
obviously do not fully realize such indirect work-linked Party
ties. Unaware as they are, these indirect influences *are* real, as
confirmed by the leaders of local economic associations. These

leaders deliberately involved their rank and file in political and civic activities and oriented their groups according to the suggestions of their superiors in the political and administrative hierarchy.

In a similar manner, leaders of social groups affiliated with the PRI expect their members to participate periodically in civic and political activities and incline members to support the regime. For example, youth groups involve their members in manifestations and orient them toward voting for the PRI. Also, residents in *La Colonia* and *La Unidad* are reached for the same purposes through their association with local divisions of the PRI-affiliated FCP. The heads of the local affiliations, at the request of the person in charge of the organization for all of Mexico City, asked their followers to attend civic and PRI political manifestations, inaugurations of public works projects, and commemorations of legalizations of other squatter settlements. Although residents ceased to attend local FCP group meetings once they realized that their prospects of securing material benefits through the group were improbable, they had been exposed to PRI and government influence and encouraged to adopt a submissive form of political and civic involvement while active in the group.

Moreover, the effect of groups formally independent of the PRI on their members is not very different. The local administrative apparatus, in particular, has a politicizing effect on residents, as government and politics are closely intertwined. Leaders of various government organizations involve their members in PRI-related activities, even though such groups are supposed to be politically neutral. They technically avoid their legal restriction by claiming that they involve group members individually, not as a group. A similar political effect is produced when local government and PRI agencies at times use the same personnel and stress the same concerns. Persons affiliated with both institutions emphasize the importance of hierarchy, order, and the welfare of the poor, and occasionally encourage participation in the same civic and political events.

Many local government functionaries presently hold or previously held positions in the PRI. The highest-ranking local government functionary in *La Colonia* headed the district youth division of the PRI, and his predecessor had been secretary-general of the local PRI-affiliated association of market vendors and a local coordinator for the PRI. In *La Unidad* the heads of the PRI-affiliated FCP and two government-linked groups—the Promotion Committee for the new social center and one of the *sub-delegaciones* (the local unit of the geographically organized administrative apparatus of the DDF)—agreed to share the same personnel for their block representatives.

At times persons are selected for posts in the Party and government because of their affiliation with the other. In *El Centro* the head of the government social center intentionally invited the PRI district officer of youth affairs together with leaders of PRI-affiliated associations of market vendors both to help in a promotion campaign for the newly renovated center and to serve on the executive committee of the center. Moreover, on one occasion a government functionary organized a youth group which subsequently affiliated with the PRI.

Because of the PRI linkages, government-sponsored groups were politicized and the PRI at the same time extended its sphere of influence. Thus, a government functionary noted that he now receives orders which he transmits to his block chiefs not only from his immediate superior but also from the head of the local FCP; the head of the Promotion Committee claimed that the objectives of his group were identical to those of the FCP, even though, according to higher-level functionaries of the agency in charge of the center, their functions are quite distinct; and the youth group organized by a government functionary which subsequently affiliated with the PRI helped a congressman in his political campaign.

The PRI and the government also are interlinked through informal ties among leaders of groups affiliated with the two institutions. Personal bonds, which frequently crosscut institutional lines, generally have a more decisive bearing on patterns of interaction than formal institutional affiliation. For instance, one of the district government officers in 1968 had daily contact with the head of the city-wide division of the FCP but met the other district government bureaucrats of his rank at most once a month. Similarly, a government officer in one of the areas reported having daily contact with PRI functionaries at the district office but only weekly contact with his hierarchical superior. Through such ties leaders of the PRI and government groups influence one another's points of view and plan activities which they consider mutually beneficial.

PRI and government functionaries also seek each other's advice, and orient their groups accordingly. For example, a person sent by a government office to head a newly renovated sports center in *El Centro* mobilized interest in the center through the assistance of persons suggested by the local congressman. The congressman recommended persons who had been active in PRI-affiliated groups. Therefore, political considerations shaped this ostensibly nonpolitical group and the group served to reinforce and extend the existing PRI-affiliated leadership structure of the area.

Furthermore, government agents help subsidize the PRI and publicly associate with PRI politicians. They do not subsidize other political parties locally even though this is reputedly done on the national level. For instance, according to PRI functionaries in the district, some of the medicine for the PRI clinics is provided by government agencies. During the campaigns government functionaries tacitly lend their support to the PRI even if they do not directly engage in political activities. Government functionaries, for instance, welcomed PRI candidates at local political rallies and praised the candidates.

At times the political involvement of groups affiliated with the government is less explicit and direct. For instance, at the request of congressmen and other PRI district functionaries, school directors allow students to participate in inaugurations of public works projects and manifestations in commemoration of national holidays, the President's departures from and returns to Mexico, and other civic activities in which the PRI likewise is active. Such school activity may have a lasting effect in later life, and, most likely, educated residents in the three areas were involved in similar activities when in school.

The PRI and PRI-affiliated groups, as mentioned in earlier chapters, in turn help promote and organize administrative activities by directly collaborating with government functionaries, by complementing the work of the government, by serving as intermediary between residents and the government,[10] and by collaborating in civic celebrations. As the head of a PRI youth group

[10] Studies of provincial Mexican communities also reveal that the PRI serves as an intermediary to the government. See Fagen and Tuohy, pp. 30-31; Ugalde, pp. 139-49. Political parties in other Latin American countries serve similar functions. See, for example, Lisa Peattie, *The View from the Barrio*, p. 67; Leeds, pp. 78-79; and Epstein, pp. 113, 130-31.

commented to me: "We call a political reunion whenever there's an urgent need to prepare for a civic act—for example, for national fiestas and patriotic celebrations."

PRI-affiliated groups also assist the government in its tasks by administering such services as medical care, which supplement those provided by the government, and by helping to avert the development of local opposition to the regime. They even offer services which according to law are supposed to be provided by the government. For instance, a PRI district office houses an officially recognized closed-circuit educational program and, according to some residents of the area, a voting booth on election day. The PRI also provides awards for top athletes in sports competitions involving local school children and, according to some market administrators, distributes gifts to vendors on special holidays. Furthermore, a PRI-affiliated youth group and top boxers who held political posts collaborated with the government-sponsored beautification campaign in *El Centro*. The personal prestige of the athletes probably contributed more to the effectiveness of the campaign than their political status did, but their very involvement reinforces the blurred division between politics and government.

In general, there is little difference between the government and the PRI on the grass-roots level, largely because local groups affiliated with both institutions are formally powerless, and because overlapping leadership, informal ties, and common and complementary concerns among leaders of groups affiliated with the two institutions link the PRI with the government despite their formal separation. Low-level functionaries of groups affiliated with both institutions are limited financially in what they can do and are subject, ultimately, to similar hierarchical constraints. Consequently, groups affiliated with the two institutions reinforce each other's strength, even when this is not the primary intention of the leaders. Through civic groups people tend to be indirectly exposed to the PRI. Such exposure predisposes them to support the PRI at election time, particularly since the other political parties rarely are in any way intermeshed with the government. PRI-government linkages are so extensive that residents—judging from informal interviews—generally identify the PRI with the government. Even many local leaders could not readily differentiate between civic and political activities. The PRI and the government, they would say, "*es el mismo* (are identical)." This confusion of politics and administration is a key fact of political life in the areas studied.

Aside from government-affiliated groups, other nominally independent groups have a politicizing effect on members. I have previously reported pressures on persons affiliated with a Church-sponsored social group and a formally independent athletic group to be sympathetic to the PRI. Other nominally nonpolitical sports groups also involved members in political and civic celebrations. Paradoxically, while youth generally joined independent sports groups because of their aversion to politics, they were, often unknowingly, nonetheless exposed to similar civic and political influences as members of organizations openly affiliated with the Party and government.

In general, the leaders, through the positions they held, tended to be more aware of the political implications of group activities than rank-and-file members.[11] Aware or not, local poor have been exposed to a network of affiliations predisposing them to support the status quo.[12]

STRUCTURAL SOURCES OF INDIRECT POLITICIZATION

Why are group leaders more aware of the political consequences of group activities than the rank and file? Mainly because of the impact of national political structures: automatic, obligatory affiliations with politically linked groups that impose few readily identifiable political demands on members; little overt political competition on the national level; little concern on the part of national political elites with well-defined ideologies; a close

[11] As Mills noted: ". . . some men have the power to act with much structural relevance and are quite aware of the consequences of their actions; others have such power but are not aware of its effective scope; and there are many who cannot transcend their everyday milieu by their awareness of structure or effect structural change by any means of action available to them." Mills, *The Sociological Imagination*, p. 185.

[12] Accordingly, were the groups "leftist," we would expect members to vote leftist. On the radicalizing effect of group affiliations in other contexts see Alejandro Portes, "Political Primitivism, Differential Socialization, and Lower Class Radicalism," pp. 820-35; Joan Nelson, *Migrants, Urban Poverty and Instability in Developing Nations;* Robert Fried, "Urbanization and Italian Politics," pp. 509-30; and James Petras and Maurice Zeitlin, "Miners and Agrarian Radicalism." Portes, for example, found that leftist radicalism among Chilean slum dwellers rose with longer residence in communities where a left-radical political orientation predominated.

identification of a single political party with the government, but legal separation of politics and government; and centralized control of resources for public services.

These national institutional arrangements affect inter- and intragroup relations on the local level. As a consequence, politicians tend not to be concerned with politics qua politics and residents, in turn, neither fully realize the political implications of the activities in which they engage nor view formal political channels as a means by which to further their interests. Residents, as a result, knowingly or not, also become involved in politically consequential activities as an inevitable by-product of their involvement in nominally nonpolitical groups.

Moreover, because local groups lack economic resources they cannot readily generate political support in opposition to the status quo. Instead, leaders of local groups will structure their group so as to maximize their prospects of gaining access to resources. They believe they can enhance their chances by involving their group members in political and politically relevant activities.

Some functionaries structure their groups for political ends even when they themselves lack positive commitment to the regime. Fearing that their political careers will be terminated if they express their discontent with the regime, they privatize their feelings. In so doing they help legitimize the government despite their own reservations about it.

Other leaders of "nonpolitical" groups, as we already have seen, consider it expedient to play down their political involvement and to conceal the extent to which they expose members of their groups to political influences not because they personally are discontent with the regime but because their actual or potential constituents are. Conversely, PRI politicians in the districts under study considered it in their interests to engage in nominally nonpolitical activities in the interim between elections. They felt they could thereby maintain contact with the people in order to mobilize them readily at election time. Thus, they too were prompted to engage in activities which blur the distinction between political and nonpolitical activities.

Moreover, several local leaders engaged in political activities because they themselves did not differentiate between politics and administration. Some of them admitted to me that they did not clearly understand the difference between the two even though they knew, through hearsay, that the two were supposedly distinct. Other leaders defined the functions of their post to include ones which ostensibly did not fall within the realm of the institution with which they were affiliated.

As previously noted, the rank and file who actively participated in group meetings and activities—for example, in the FCP or local government-linked groups—in turn, have *indirect* political interests of their own: to seek material benefits. Thus, they ceased to attend meetings once they became convinced that they had nothing to gain. Only rarely did they attend group-sponsored political and administrative events because they were ideologically committed to the PRI or because they felt a civic commitment to participate.[13]

Co-optation of local leaders and incorporation of local groups contribute to the PRI's electoral strength, even though in the process the organizational effectiveness of residents is undermined. Since most local groups and movements, as they arise, are formally incorporated into national organizations and institutions, local groups tend not to develop in opposition to the status quo. The national organs do not clearly differentiate between political and civic activities, and they encourage passive involvement in the politico-administrative system; hence leaders of local affiliations encourage the same attitude in their rank and file.

As previously shown, in the process of securing goods and services from the regime residents are made to feel personally indebted either to the government as the bestower or to the PRI as the solicitor of the favors, and they are thereby encouraged to develop a personal rather than ideological conception of politics. In the process they become favorably disposed toward the PRI but they do not come to view politics as an institutional channel through which they can or should collectively defend common interests.

Indirect politicization also seems to be strengthened by the government's use of force and the ever-present threat of force. Periodic arrests of dissident leaders seem to have been sufficient —along with the other controlling pressures—to restrict at least "leftist" electoral opposition to the PRI. According to interviews with local heads of opposition parties, the government occasionally uses repression against active PPS members but not

[13] On the supposed relationship between participation and civic culture, see Almond and Verba, *The Civic Culture.*

against the PAN. Two active PPS members, both *comerciantes*, reported being arrested before elections. However, a PPS congressman who lives in a house in the housing development which · he received through political patronage reported no comparable experience. The government seems to treat PAN and PPS opposition differently, and PPS activists differently depending on their class and political importance.

CONCLUSIONS AND IMPLICATIONS

Local residents associate with groups that shape their political orientation in ways which they do not always realize. Their voting behavior is not primarily attributable to a well-defined party program. Politics is embedded in nonpolitical institutions and political activities are not clearly differentiated from other group activities, particularly from civic involvements. Especially through allocations of goods and services to local groups and through contacts on the grass-roots level the PRI and the administration secure support, even though residents thereby help elect into office a party and regime that subordinates their social and economic interests to those of capitalists (and, to a lesser extent, organized workers and salaried white-collar employees).

The situation within the areas suggests that as long as urban poor are not subjected to countervailing influences they are likely to support the status quo, even if their involvement in politics and exposure to political influences, directly and indirectly, is not very intensive. However, because residents, to varying degrees, are exposed to the media and because they engage in activities in other parts of the city and country, in order to determine conclusively the forces influencing local political preferences extralocal forces also would need to be examined.

Yet our findings suggest that the greater electoral support a pro-business party such as the PAN gets compared to a more ideologically "leftist" party such as the PPS is best understood in terms of party organization, repression, and the political influences to which urban poor are exposed through nominally nonpolitical institutions. While the Church is indirectly linked to the PRI and the government, it also is closely linked nationally with the PAN. Furthermore, backed by wealthy Catholics the PAN is able to run more effective political campaigns than the PPS, nationally as well as locally.[14] The PPS, in contrast, has no "non-political" institution such as the Church as an outside source of support.

When a political party is heavily intertwined with other institutions it can win electoral support. Mexican poor have gained formal but not real political equality through the extension of the franchise and formal incorporation into a mass-based political party. They have not, in the process, gained institutionalized influence on government decision-making. Electoral participation *is* important, but mainly because it contributes to the government's legitimacy. Elections serve this function even though voters do not necessarily either participate in politics with this end in mind or realize fully the political ramifications of the activities in which they engage.

Only if urban poor are made aware of the political consequences of their activities and have access to groups which they believe will resolve their problems better than the existing political-administrative apparatus, or if they cease to need or want the goods and services the Party and government offer and help them secure, are they likely to withdraw their support from the PRI. However, since in Mexico the PRI is so intertwined with the government a shift in voting would challenge the legitimacy of the regime. It would be unlikely to result in a smooth transference of power from one political party to another.

Differentiation of politics from other spheres of activity is not an inevitable evolutionary process, and it does not hinge on formal separation of political from nonpolitical institutions. A close intermeshing of a single political party with the government is not as likely to occur in "competitive-party" systems as in "one-party" or "dominant-party" systems. But even in competitive-party systems members of nominally nonpolitical groups, knowingly or not, may be subject to political influences.

This analysis also suggests that poor people in other parts of Mexico and elsewhere may support the status quo because they

[14] In the 1970 presidential election a smaller proportion of the electorate voted for the PRI than did in the preceding presidential election. This decline may be attributed to local corruption by PRI functionaries and to the few material benefits the Party and government allocated to the local community. However, while awareness of Party abuse or neglect may alienate residents from the PRI, it does not incline them to vote for ideologically leftist parties: rather, they nullify their ballot, abstain, or vote for the PAN.

are similarly exposed to political or governmental influences. In addition, because voting in Mexico involves little real choice and mainly serves a legitimating function, we now can understand why poverty and inequality persist in Mexico even as increasing numbers of poor people participate in the electoral process. For similar reasons we now can understand why wealth is not any better distributed in Mexico than in other Latin American capitalist countries with a limited franchise or none at all.[15]

However, the support resident poor give the regime is rather passive and not very intense. To the extent that this type of support is widespread in areas where relations have been routinized, the regime's legitimacy may be more problematic than it appears. The potential political crisis seems even more problematic since resident poor, as will be seen in the following chapters, contribute little to economic production.

[15] Several studies analyzing the politics of Latin American urban poor stress the importance of leadership and the relationship between dominant groups and the masses. See, for example, Weffort, "State and Mass," and Nelson Amaro Victoria, "Mass and Class in the Origins of the Cuban Revolution."

CHAPTER SIX

The Political Economy of the Local Communities

National and international capitalist forces, along with government policies, shape the local political economies: the array of
productive and distributive enterprises, patterns of ownership,
prospects of business success, and relations within and between
local businesses.[1] International oligopolies have absorbed the
most successful local businesses, and many of the other locally
operating businesses which appear—by local standards—to be
productive, profitable, and secure, are owned by nonresidents.
People who do not reside in the areas entered them with an
economic advantage over residents. Concerned above all with
advancing their own economic interests, the nonresidents neither
reinvest the income generated locally to upgrade the local communities nor employ many local residents. As a result, capitalist
forces limit the economic opportunities for residents in their own
communities.

Yet, there are locally run small and precarious businesses—in
the two newer areas in distribution more than in production—
persisting and proliferating, partly because of indirect government protection. The government, we see, does not always act in
the immediate interests of large-scale capital. In addition, residents have been able to assert some influence over the structure
of business activities, although rarely in very productive or financially rewarding ways.

Portions of Chapter Six were published in Susan Eckstein, "The Political
Economy of Lower-Class Areas in Mexico City: Societal Constraints on
Local Business Prospects," in Wayne A. Cornelius and Felicity M. True-
blood, eds., *Urbanization and Inequality: The Political Economy of Urban
and Rural Development in Latin America*. Latin American Urban Research,
Vol. 5. Sage Publications, Inc., Beverly Hills, California, 1975.

[1] This chapter focuses only on legitimate enterprises not directly controlled and regulated by the government. It therefore does not include a
discussion of economic conditions in the local government-administered markets, schools and public service institutions, and illicit activities.

PRODUCTION SECTOR

Local businesses, particularly in *La Colonia* and *La Unidad*, have not contributed to the country's impressive post-World War II economic expansion. Nonetheless, both the general structure of production within the three areas and differences in production activities among the three areas reflect national political and economic forces. The contrasting business production profiles of the three communities derive from the different historical epochs under which the areas have been in existence.[2] Since the colonial era the inner-city area has been a major center of craft production; since the industrialization of the country, the area, in addition, has become a center of small- and medium-scale industries.

Craft Production

While some residents in the two newer areas sew clothing, make parts of shoes, or do other piecework in their homes, there are few local sweatshops in either area which offer employment opportunities. In contrast, *El Centro* continues in its long-established tradition to be a major hub of artisanry, even though the types of crafts located there have changed over the years, in response to overall changes in the national economy. As previously noted, some of the new and to date more financially rewarding crafts in the center city area reflect technological developments introduced into Mexico during the course of the century: Auto mechanic work is a case in point. Other new local crafts, particularly shoemaking, have been transplanted from provincial communities. Artisans have relocated near the major market for their product, as the consumer population of Mexico City has grown.

Most of the sweatshops, operating in a highly competitive market, have low profit margins. As illustrated in the shoecraft sector in *El Centro*, the owners of artisan shops are exploited by their suppliers and distributors, but they may manage to stay in business and compete with shoe manufacturers by exploiting themselves and their employees, with tacit government support.

[2] Although I argue that the inner-city slum does not represent a "stage," which the other communities ultimately will replicate, the areas—as we see in this chapter—are not static: Small businesses are proliferating and experiencing high turnover.

El Centro Cobblers

The shoecraft sector in Mexico City in general and the center city area in particular has expanded markedly in the twentieth century.[3] Its expansion demonstrates that urbanization is not necessarily associated with the rise of industrial and the demise of artisan employment[4] and that small-scale labor-intensive enterprises may continue to contribute a sizable share to total production within at least certain spheres of manufacturing. In fact, more shoecraft enterprises are situated in Mexico City than in any other locale in the country and most shoe factories are located outside the capital. Forced to compete with manufacturers, artisans seem to find it propitious to locate near the main market for their product.[5]

Cobblers establshed themselves in the inner-city area because the area not only was residential but also a center of craft and commercial activity. Once the area became a center for shoecraft production, shoe artisans—mainly migrants and children of migrants from the provincial centers of shoe production—continued to locate there, because of the ready availability of materials and business contacts.

Although the local shoe artisan sector has expanded locally, the organization of production has changed little. The small *talleres* (sweatshops) produce only a few varieties of shoes. The *maestro* owns the shop, manages the production process, and sells the finished goods. One or more workers cut the leather. The others sew, glue, and adorn the shoes. If the *maestro* is poor he sends the leather out to be sewn and glued because he cannot afford to purchase the requisite machines. Workers learn the skills

[3] For a detailed discussion of artisans and industrial shoe production in Mexico, see Arturo Galindo Muñez, "Desarrollo e integración de la industria del Calzado en México." Approximately half the shoes produced in Mexico are made in small craft shops (p. 76).

[4] The literature on the occupational structure of Latin American cities emphasizes the expansion of the service ("tertiary"), not artisan sector. Fernando H. Cardoso and Reyna, "Industrialization, Occupational Structure, and Social Stratification in Latin America"; Glaucio Ary Dillon Soares, "The New Industrialization and the Brazilian Political System," pp. 186-201.

[5] According to a local priest, shoe artisans are migrating to Mexico City partly because they find it increasingly difficult to compete with the shoe factories in the provinces.

through an apprenticeship system. In contrast to most workers who learn only one skill, the *maestro* generally knows all the relevant ones so that he can substitute for any absent worker. The workers are paid on a piecework basis. Hence, when a cutter or sewing machine operator reports late to work, the others, unable to work, do not get paid for time lost.

Sweatshop owners often keep labor costs low by employing the cheapest labor: relatives, migrants, women, and, in violation of the labor law, children. They also minimize costs by expanding and contracting employment as their seasonal business fluctuates, which they can do since the Labor Code is not enforced in the artisan sector. As a consequence, shoecraftsmen do not enjoy job security or earnings comparable to those of workers in shoe factories, owing to employment policies and their weak bargaining position.

Despite such labor exploitation, the businesses are highly precarious. The reasons are structural. Since little capital and few skills are needed for most stages of the production process, and since artisans have not organized to limit the number of people in the craft, the number of shoe artisans has expanded over the years. And since these firms compete not only among themselves but also with the more efficient manufacturers, they cannot readily pass their costs on to consumers.

Formalized efforts to reduce costs have failed. A priest, for instance, tried to form a cooperative through which artisans could collectively purchase supplies more cheaply than when buying individually. While artisans liked the intent of the cooperative, they were reluctant to join, for fear that someone would run off with the group's money.

Kinship bonds are one of the few mechanisms which reduce competition among shoemakers. Relatives are expected to assist, not compete with one another. Thus, in one *vecindad* where several related artisans make shoes, there is a tacit agreement among them to cooperate and help one another in times of crisis. However, rather than organize an efficient, profit-generating collective enterprise, they engage in discreet noncompeting operations: the different households produce different types of shoes, find customers and occasionally buy materials for each other, and share the same car for delivering their products.

Taller owners are further victimized by their weak bargaining position at both the supply and distributive ends of the production process. They are exploited by the retailers and distributors to whom they sell their merchandise, and by the suppliers from whom they purchase materials. Distributors pay less for the shoes than retailers, and retailers often either pay shoecraftsmen with postdated checks or pay only part of the cost of the shoes upon delivery. As a consequence, shoemakers, in effect, supply retailers with credit. In addition, if the shoes, which are made to order, are delivered more than approximately two weeks late, retailers and distributors pay less than the agreed-upon price. Because of such abuse, owners of shoe *talleres* often find themselves with insufficient cash to buy equipment and supplies and pay workers. The capital shortage, in turn, impedes their ability to produce and make profits.

Taller owners attempt to resolve their financial problems by buying equipment and materials on credit, but because interest rates are high their production costs thereby increase. Tanners charge 5 to 20 percent interest on their loans and insist that their debtors buy leather exclusively at their tannery. Tanners can thereby minimize competition which would drive down the going market price for their merchandise. Since most tanners are located within the center city area they can watch their clients fairly easily. Should they catch shoemakers breaking the informal agreement, the tanners may refuse to loan the shoemakers additional money in the future.

Taller owners, however, are not completely at the mercy of suppliers. Even though they are reluctant to violate informal credit agreements, occasionally they do by discreetly sending relatives or persons they trust to tanners from whom they do not borrow money, in order to purchase less expensive materials. Moreover, *taller* owners have a certain hold over tanners in that they can threaten to transfer their business elsewhere if the tanners refuse to extend them credit.

The national association of shoe manufacturers further reduces the potential profits of sweatshop owners. All shoemakers are obliged to belong and pay dues to the national association, although some small producers have managed to stay out of it. In principle, the organization tends to the interests of all members, but because members' voting power depends on the amount of capital they invest in their business, in actual fact the association primarily looks after the interests of the large factories. For example, it promotes export trade.

The government, in turn, limits craft opportunities at the same time that it enables small business ventures to at least temporarily survive in the highly competitive market. For example, the government taxes shoe producers. Although local artisans evade business taxes, reputedly the large, nonlocal manufacturers benefit from tax loopholes for capital investments. Nonetheless, the government protects the small-scale labor-absorbing producers by insisting only that large firms pay workers the official minimum wage and provide workers with benefits outlined in the Constitution and Labor Code. In so doing the government enables the low-profit, labor-intensive handicraft shops to avoid additional labor costs which might force them out of business. Thus, even when the government is not directly involved in production it shapes local economic opportunities, including the competitive advantage local enterprises experience within the national economy.

Although there are plans to require sweatshop employers to provide their employees with social security benefits, to date differences between the social and economic benefits enjoyed by shoe artisans and blue-collar employees in shoe factories reflect differences in government protection, not differences in productivity. If the government enforces the social security regulation, the seemingly desirable and progressive plan may prove to work against the interests both of sweatshop owners, who will have to bear much of the cost of the social security coverage, and, paradoxically, employed artisans: Many of the *taller* owners who already operate on a small margin of profit may be forced out of business if they have to bear the additional labor cost, in which case artisans will lose their jobs.[6] The plan thereby would benefit

---

[6] The case of these shoe artisans demonstrates that developments within what economists call the "primary" market are related to developments within the "secondary" labor market, and that specific government policies affect the distribution of both employment and benefits within each labor market. On the notion of "primary" and "secondary" labor markets, see Michael Piore, "The Dual Labor Market," pp. 90-94. According to Piore, the "primary" market offers jobs which provide high wages, good working conditions, employment stability and job security, equality and due process in the administration of work rules, and chances for advancement. In contrast, the "secondary" labor market involves jobs which offer low wages, poor working conditions, variability in employment, harsh and often arbitrary discipline, and little opportunity to advance. On labor market stratification, see also David Gordon, *Theories of Poverty and Underdevelopment*; David Gordon, Richard Edwards, and Michael Reich, "Labor Market Segmenta-

indirectly the industrial shoe manufacturers, since they will not be subject to higher labor costs: They already provide workers with social security, and they can better afford the expense since labor constitutes a much smaller percentage of total production costs in the mechanized firms than in the labor-intensive craft shops. Capitalist expansion generates contradictions which the state cannot readily resolve. As a result, though, unlike workers in shoe factories, laborers employed in *talleres* do not enjoy job security and minimum wages, and not because their work necessarily differs.

Despite the large supply of labor *taller* owners have problems acquiring and maintaining a dependable work force.[7] They cannot attract the best and most reliable workers since they pay poorly. Production often is impeded because of absenteeism and tardiness, particularly after weekends. To minimize such problems some *taller* owners prefer hiring people who live near their shops, since they can thereby readily fetch those employees who fail to report to work.

Employers also are faced with the problem of finding workers they can trust. Workers tend to steal material from the shops, at least in part because they are paid poorly. Some *taller* owners attempt to resolve this problem by hiring relatives, who they feel are more trustworthy than non-kin. Or else they try to win workers' loyalty by providing such "noncontractual" benefits as shoes, loans, and medical assistance. The range of services offered partly depends on the contacts the *maestros* have. For instance, one *maestro* paid part of his employees' medical bills, but required that his workers use a specific doctor, a friend of his, who had agreed to charge a reduced rate in exchange for the patients the *maestro* sent him. Workers realize that they are

tion in American Capitalism"; Peter Doeringer and Piore, *Internal Labor Markets and Manpower Analysis*; for a critique of labor market analyses, see Glen Cain, *The Challenge of Dual and Radical Theories of the Labor Market to Orthodox Theory*, and the references therein.

[7] The problem of labor commitment in industrializing countries may well be economic more than cultural. If workers have sufficient inducement to work, they are likely to be dependable. Kazin, for example, shows that workers in the factory she studied in San Cristóbal, Mexico, reported early to work, for fear of losing the highly coveted factory jobs. Phyllis Kazin, "Socio-Cultural Aspects of Development." On the effect of paternalism in reducing labor turnover in Brazil, see Stanley Stein, "The Brazilian Cotton Textile Industry, 1850-1950."

expected to cooperate with and occasionally do favors for their employers to obtain such benefits. As a result, particularly during the busy Christmas season, artisans work very long hours, seven days a week. Thus, the paternalistic allocation of goods and services enables the *maestros* to control and exploit their workers.

While the various constraints limit the profits of shoe artisans, the small number of master craftsmen who, either by chance or adept business skill, succeed in generating a sizable profit rarely use their liquid reserves for further mechanization of the productive process. If they invest their profits in the business, they generally use it to extend the existing labor-intensive system: They hire more cutters, sewers, or other workers, on a piecework basis. They do not invest the capital in more productive machinery and alter the production process accordingly.

In sum, shoecraft production in *El Centro* has persisted and indeed expanded in the present century, partly because the government does not enforce the same labor policies in the artisan as in the capital-intensive sector. Yet local shoe production represents no mere continuation of the guild organization introduced in the colonial era. Currently the division of labor is more specialized in terms of both production and distribution, and the technology is more specialized. Since cobblers use imported machinery, local production is not replicating the independent pattern of development of shoe manufacturing as it evolved in the advanced capitalist countries.

Local Factories

Despite the expansion of craft production in spheres of the urban and national economy, in general the country's major growth stems from the expansion of more mechanized industries. Nonetheless, not only do *La Unidad* and *La Colonia* offer few artisan jobs, but owing to zoning restrictions they offer no industrial opportunities.[8]

The structure of local manufacturing illustrates still another way in which the local economies of the three areas are shaped by domestic and international market forces, and by government policies. Existing factories in *El Centro* mainly began during the

[8] Many of the new capital-intensive firms are located in the State of Mexico, on the periphery of the Federal District, due to zoning laws and tax incentives.

era of greatest industrial expansion under domestic ownership, in the immediate post-World War II era; although most firms have since changed hands, they initially located in the area because land at the time was cheap there and the locale was well-situated for business purposes.

While this area offers more industrial opportunities than the two newer areas, local factories, with one exception, contrast markedly with the profitable, productive, capital-intensive firms that dominate the national economy. Center city area factories therefore are not representative of current industrial trends in Mexico. Most goods manufactured locally are characteristic of early industries: there are firms manufacturing food products, textiles, paper bags, cardboard, furniture, curtains, mattresses, candles, and electrical signs. Furthermore, although imported, the machinery utilized locally—often purchased secondhand—tends to be antiquated, even in those firms which have "modernized" their production process in recent years.

The labor force is shaped by the technology employed. Since the firms are not heavily capitalized, they tend to be small and medium in size, and managed directly by owners. Only one factory employs more than one hundred workers. However, the number of employed workers reflects not only the degree of mechanization and capital accumulation, but also, at times, adaptations to the legal code. Employment in several firms dropped over the years, following increased mechanization of production. Yet the size of the paper bag factories demonstrates an industrialist's astute adaptation to the law. The same man owns the two local paper firms, as well as a third one in a different section of the city. He deliberately runs several different factories, each employing slightly fewer than one hundred workers, rather than a single large one, to circumvent the Constitutional stipulation that firms with more than one hundred employees provide their workers with housing and other benefits.

Owned by nonresidents, the profits generated in local factories leave the area. The monopolization of local industrial opportunities by nonresidents partly reflects the fact that residents possess few of the resources which are critical for successful competition in a capitalist economy. As is true nationally, the nonlocal owners are a select group, especially in comparison to residents. Several of them are children of immigrants, particularly of Eastern European Jews. They have a postprimary school education and useful kinship contacts,[9] and they received training relevant to their work before going into business for themselves. Since many parents and other relatives of the local industrialists had similar businesses, the local industrialists acquired business skills in their youth. From their kin they also acquired machinery, help in securing capital, and useful business connections. Such family background and personal experiences give them an advantage over local residents, even though few of them directly inherited their fathers' businesses. Partly because of these advantages they have not been faced with the same extensive competition as have owners of local sweatshops and, as we later shall see, owners of local distributive enterprises.

To illustrate how nonresidents establish successful factories locally, the biography of a center city Jewish manufacturer of cotton textiles is revealing. When he began his business he received help from relatives. Although he did not get along well with his father, who owned a similar factory in the State of Mexico, the father taught him useful business skills. Through his father he also acquired business contacts, including ones which enabled him to get financial backing, and access to suppliers and buyers. Moreover, his brother gave him the plant and the machinery. The brother had owned the business until he started to manufacture luxury fabrics. Since the present owner invested less than $100.00 of his own money when he took over the firm, personal accumulation of capital was one of the least important factors enabling him to become economically successful. Yet because of his family background he could readily borrow money and capital goods on credit. Since the family was of immigrant Jewish background such "particularism" does not reflect a cultural trait generally attributed to Latin Americans. Instead, it reflects an adaptive mechanism by which socioeconomic privileges are passed on from one generation to the next along family lines. This case also suggests that kin at times are prone to establish separate, but noncompeting businesses, as also was true among blood-related shoe artisans. The relatives pool their efforts in ways which, on the one hand, give them greater control over the

---

[9] In her study of Mexican firms, Derossi found that inheritance does not keep founders of Mexican businesses and their sons from recognizing the importance of acquiring specialized skills. The younger family members tend to be given specialized training before being put to work (p. 80).

market situation and, on the other hand, maximize their autonomy within their immediate work situation. However, they in
part employ this strategy to circumvent certain tax and labor
laws.

Because residents do not own the local firms, they cannot readily secure managerial and blue-collar jobs in the factories. The
managerial posts tend to be reserved for relatives or personal
acquaintances of the owners.[10] Thus, the Jewish paper bag manufacturer, who employed no relatives in his two local factories,
intentionally hired only Jews as plant managers. While the owners do not hire kin as manual laborers, several owners or managers deliberately discriminated against local residents, claiming
that they were drunkards and unreliable. Several owners also
preferred hiring docile migrants from rural areas to natives of
the city. Since most center city inhabitants were born in the capital, this management preference further limited residents' ability
to secure work in local industries.

Thus, even more than in the artisan sector, residents tend not
to be the main beneficiaries of the few industrial opportunities
which exist locally. And, as illustrated by the case of the one locally operating subsidiary of a foreign-owned corporation, international as well as domestic pressures have shaped local employment opportunities.

Denationalization of a Chocolate Factory

Reflecting the post-World War II trend toward transnational
ownership of large-scale domestically based industries, the two
biggest firms in *El Centro* in 1968—one manufacturing canned
goods, the other chocolate—were purchased by U.S. companies
by the time I returned to Mexico in 1971. These businesses
had been among the last major ones in the food industry to
remain in Mexican hands. Upon purchasing the canning company United Fruit moved the factory to Queretero. The other
firm, bought by Quaker Oats, still operates locally. These two
cases of denationalization suggest that international oligopolies

[10] Typically, Latin American enterprises represent an extension of the
family system, not a break with it. Stanley Davis, "United States vs. Latin
America," p. 60, and Derossi "Familism in Industry." According to Derossi, in Mexico, family-owned or controlled firms are most prevalent
among small firms and firms in traditional manufacturing activities.

absorb successful domestic ventures.[11] In so doing, they reduce the likelihood that Mexico will develop a strong autonomous capitalist class and capitalist production system, as the country continues industrializing.

The chocolate factory was the largest of its kind in Mexico. It had been owned primarily by one man who initially started the business in the state of Michoacan. He moved the firm to Mexico City in 1930, after fleeing to the capital to escape civil strife.

By the 1960s the firm employed about 350 people, mostly women from his town of origin, with little or no schooling.[12] He preferred hiring such workers because he believed them to be respectful, obedient, and willing to work for low wages. When he needed new workers he generally recruited through a few employees who were regarded by the other factory hands as "natural leaders."[13] These leaders were migrants from the hometown of the *patrón* who had worked many years for the firm. By hiring migrant women the *patrón* successfully kept workers both from affiliating with a national union and from forming their own informal organizations. For example, he blocked workers from establishing *cajas*,[14] a type of informal credit association. He thereby minimized not only labor costs but also labor's independence of him.

Yet the old man was not a complete tyrant. He permitted workers to have *tandas*, a rotating credit association much less

[11] Similarly, Evans found in his study of the pharmaceutical industry in Brazil that foreign companies almost without exception acquired leading, not faltering, domestic firms. Peter Evans, "The Latin American Entrepreneur," p. 197.

[12] Chaplin found that management in the textile industry in Lima also preferred hiring inexperienced Indian migrants to city born people. David Chaplin, "Industrial Labor Recruitment in Peru," p. 133.

[13] Roberts also discusses how success in the city may depend partly on the use of provincial contacts. Roberts, "Interrelationships of City and Provinces," pp. 207-35, and *Organizing Strangers*.

[14] Rotating credit associations are found in many preindustrial societies and have been instrumental in the mobility of certain ethnic groups in the contemporary United States. Ivan Light, *Ethnic Enterprise in America*, Chapter 2. Light argues that such associations were known to blacks in Africa but that U.S. slaves were forbidden to have them, and that U.S. blacks did not develop the associations after they were freed. In contrast, informal economic associations existed among Caribbean slaves. The author contends that American blacks have been less entrepreneurial than black immigrants from the Caribbean for this reason.

sophisticated than *cajas*, and lent money to workers upon request.[15] He also regularly donated money to the church in the provincial town from which he and most of his workers migrated; paid for the buses his workers took on their annual pilgrimage to the town, and for flowers and fireworks for the pilgrimage fiesta; and contributed money for a special mass associated with another annual pilgrimage workers made, in their native provincial costumes, to the Basílica of Guadalupe in Mexico City. In addition, he encouraged and institutionalized personal ties by serving as godparent to workers' children. In so doing, he helped reinforce a sense of subservience and loyalty which enhanced his paternalistic control over workers.

Nonetheless, the favors the *patrón* did for his employees never included extending opportunities for occupational advancement. The managerial posts were monopolized by the boss's sons, most of whom were college-educated, and by a few other relatives.

These kinship ties, however, did not keep family members from fighting among themselves. Because the relatives differed in their commitment to the business, their entrepreneurial skills, and their honesty, the aging founder of the business decided to sell the firm to an American corporation when faced with the problem of succession.[16] As one of the foreign executives phrased it: "Whom else was he to go to?"

The new owners still maintain certain aspects of the old business more or less intact. The few blue-collar workers who have been hired since ownership changed hands come from the same provincial town as most of the other employees, and were hired through the same "natural leaders" as the other employees. The new management also continues to subsidize the provincial community, by regularly donating money to the town church. They also pay costs associated with the annual pilgrimages. One of the foreign managers even accompanied workers on the Michoacan pilgrimage, and attended both a special Mass for the factory workers in the town and a lunch in the church for community

[15] According to a plant manager, 99 percent of the personnel owed money to the company in 1965. The average amount borrowed was $80.00. Davis, "Social Change in Mexican Enterprise" p. 171.

[16] The changeover in ownership reflects a transition from family to corporate industrial capitalism which also occurred in the U.S. historically. However, in the U.S. ownership remains in the hands of nationals, whereas in Latin America corporate ownership is denationalizing.

leaders. According to the manager, the priest spoke at the Mass of how fortunate the employees were to work for such a big company. Interestingly, the Americans have been more anxious to maintain socioreligious ties with the migrants' town of origin than with the local community in Mexico City: They no longer invite the local priest to celebrate an occasional Mass in the factory chapel, as the former *patrón* did. Their selective continuation of their predecessor's policies reflects their economic concerns. Since the new management continues to employ workers from the provincial town it does not wish to antagonize townsmen and employees in ways which would upset labor relations within the firm. Since they hire few local residents they feel little pressure to maintain the few community ties which the old *patrón* had established.

Certain changes, however, have been initiated since the takeover, and others are planned, in spheres more directly related to production than such socioreligious activities. First, only one son of the former owner, the one in charge of production, remains with the company. The rest of the managerial staff is foreign. Second, the new management has added several new departments, including sales and accounting departments, and a laboratory to help improve "quality control"—the "American way," to quote one of the foreign executives. Unlike the old *patrón* the new management is very concerned with regularly introducing new products. They were disturbed that the old *patrón* had not marketed a new product during the last five years he owned the firm.

In addition, the new management has attempted to restructure labor-management relations. Whereas formerly workers took their problems directly to the *patrón* or one of his sons, now authority is formally delegated. The Americans have introduced a hierarchical chain of command linking management to department heads, department heads to supervisors, and supervisors to workers, and they stress that decisions are to be made on the lowest level possible. However, these changes to date exist more in theory than in practice. Relations still tend to be personalized and centralized, as many workers continue to take their problems directly to "the top."[17]

[17] Studies of Latin American firms typically stress the particularistic and hierarchical nature of employer-employee relations and the unique way each worker is treated by management. In contrast, studies of U.S. firms emphasize that workers are group-oriented and that all workers of a given

The foreign staff also has attempted to make employer-employee relations more impersonal and efficient by introducing policies to treat workers categorically rather than individually. As a result, whereas workers formerly were not limited in the amount of money they could borrow from the firm, they now can borrow no more than the equivalent of one month's salary. Furthermore, while the old *patrón* had *compadrazgo* relations with many workers, the Americans do not. Only the son of the *patrón* who continues to work for the firm follows the tradition established by his father. He finds that those workers with whom he has *compadrazgo* relations are exceptionally cooperative and subservient, willing to work overtime, and sympathetic to management in labor disputes.[18] While the personalistic ties maintained by the former owner's son appear to conflict with the organizational blueprint and objectives of the Americans, in actual fact the son helps link the workers, accustomed to a paternalistic firm, with the new-style management. In the process, he helps to reduce tensions within the factory.

The new managers' limited success in "modernizing" relations within the factory reflects their being compelled to adapt to the environment in which they operate, in order not to antagonize labor. However, once they introduce new imported machinery

---

rank are treated similarly by management. The different patterns are attributed to general cultural differences between the U.S. and Latin America. Examples of this interpretation include Lawrence Williams, William Whyte, and Charles Green, "Do Cultural Differences Affect Workers' Attitudes?", pp. 17-24 and Davis, "U.S. Versus Latin America," p. 57. However, both the former and the present management of the chocolate factory believe that relations within the firm are a by-product of the structure of the organization, not the culture of the society. For this reason, in line with their different production strategies, the previous management deliberately encouraged personalistic relations with workers and the new management is deliberately attempting to make employer-employee relations more impersonal by reorganizing the firm. Workers' resistance to change suggests that once workers develop a set of expectations and behavioral patterns they do not readily forsake them. Davis, in another article ("Authority and Control in Mexican Enterprise," pp. 300-305), actually argues that the Latin American and North American patterns reflect adaptations to different social and economic conditions, not differences in culture.

[18] "Traditional" customs in Japanese factories also have been retained for expedient rather than cultural reasons. See John Bennett and Iwao Ishino, *Paternalism in the Japanese Economy*, p. 235. For a cultural argument, see James Abegglen, *The Japanese Factory*.

and a new system of production, as they intend to do, more of the now-established customs are likely to be curtailed, for the customs will conflict with the new technology and with management's new economic interests. Because the Americans will want a more skilled and experienced work force than they presently have and can recruit from the provincial town, undoubtedly many workers will be fired and ties with the provincial town severed. However, at that point management will feel less compelled to appease their present work force.

In sum, the case of this factory suggests that firms with a large labor force—indeed leading firms within a branch of industry—are not necessarily run impersonally, that formal schooling does not necessarily enhance workers' chances of securing factory jobs, and that personalistic criteria may be used in the selection of management as well as manual workers. Accordingly, this case also suggests that capital investments and patterns of ownership and control are more important than size of work force for understanding intrafirm relations and the significance of firms within the economy. Though obviously more stable than the craft enterprises previously described, even domestic manufacturers do not maintain a strong competitive position *vis-à-vis* foreign capital. And when locally initiated firms are acquired by multinationals, their structure of production, internal organization, and significance within the national economy may change while the firm itself remains intact.

DISTRIBUTIVE AND SERVICE SECTORS

While the more recently settled areas included in this study contain few production enterprises and none of any scale, all three areas contain commercial enterprises. This commerce represents an adaptation to a consumer-oriented industrializing society with a labor surplus. Both the abundance of nonproductive (or low productive) enterprises, and the organization and control of the shops, reveal once again how national economic forces shape the local communities. Because of the contrasting epochs in which the areas were settled, commercial as well as production opportunities in the old center city slum are better than in the two newer districts.

All three areas are dotted with stores, particularly small "mom and pop" type operations. The most typical ones are small retail operations, such as pharmacies, bakeries, grocery and furniture shops and, above all, *misceláneas*—small grocery shops that offer a limited supply of canned and bottled goods and pastas. The number and diversity of stores reflect the limited alternative economic options for the owners, more than the local demand for the goods marketed.

In addition, there are numerous repair shops, including, among others, those for shoes, watches, bicycles, metalwork, electrical appliances, and cars. In *El Centro* there also are a few businesses servicing buses, automobile generators and motors. At times service shops are combined with artisan operations or with small merchandising outfits if the owners have the capital.[19] For example, some cobblers both repair and make shoes, and some owners of stores selling handmade furniture are also cabinet-makers. However, most goods sold locally are not produced locally.

Although approximately two-thirds of the shops in the areas are owned by residents, nonresident businessmen increasingly are taking advantage of local economic opportunities. Consequently, as with factories, the largest stores, particularly in the two newer areas, are owned by nonresidents, including immigrants and children of immigrants. Several of these families are involved in a variety of business ventures, enabling them to buy merchandise wholesale and to get credit more easily than competing resident shop owners; for example, one Spaniard owns three bakeries in the center city area and another one elsewhere in the city; another Spaniard with local bakeries owns a chain of seventy in the capital; and a third Spaniard owns a real estate business in Acapulco, in addition to a large dry-cleaning establishment in *El Centro*. The shop owners of immigrant background generally began their local businesses with better skills and resources than native shopowners, especially in comparison with resident shopowners.[20] Of higher-class background, they

---

[19] The distinction between productive and distributive types of employment used here is an analytically, not empirically, derived distinction. Thus, the same individuals may be involved in both productive and distributive activities.

[20] The involvement of foreigners in commerce is not a specifically Mexican or Latin American phenomenon. Foreigners have played an important role in commerce in other countries as well, e.g., Chinese in Indonesia, and Indians in the West Indies and several African countries. While Hoselitz argues that foreign entrepreneurs generally are economi-

had better access to schooling and capital with which to begin
their stores; and because many of their parents were involved in
commerce, they acquired relevant business experiences before
opening their own businesses, locally and elsewhere in the city.
Commenting on economic advantages enjoyed by the shop owners of immigrant origin, the owner of a small furniture shop in
La Colonia noted to me that "about half the furniture stores here
are owned by foreigners—by Jews and Spaniards. . . . There's a
lot of competition among us. The only way I get any business
is by selling for less than the big stores. They began with more
capital. They therefore can offer better deals and can pay lawyers if they have problems collecting money. I have a lawyer
who helps me out a little, but it's difficult."

In contrast to the shops owned by children of immigrants and
other nonresidents, those owned by local inhabitants generally
are small. They tend to be run by spouses with the occasional assistance of children or other relatives. The shop owners rely on
kin because they feel kin can be trusted more and paid less than
non-kin.

Not only do the businesses generate few employment opportunities, particularly for non-kin, but they also tend not to be a
likely source of livelihood for the typical resident. The shops are
run by better-skilled and experienced persons. Shop owners tend
to have at least a primary school education. They also tend to be
offspring of men who either were independently employed, as
comerciantes, or enjoyed considerable autonomy in their work.
However, rarely did shop owners directly inherit their businesses
from their fathers, and some of those who did actually considered it a mixed blessing. An owner of an auto repair shop, for
example, complained that in inheriting the store he also inherited
large debts.

The shop owners rarely pulled themselves up by their own
bootstraps. Only about one-third of the store owners interviewed
financed their businesses themselves, and few of those who did
used money they had saved over the years: instead, they used

---

cally successful because they occupy a marginal status in host countries,
much of their success seems attributable to their atypically privileged
class background. Hoselitz does not consider the fact that foreigners frequently are a select group. Bert Hoselitz, "Economic Growth and Development," pp. 275-84.

money from land they had sold, indemnization they received when fired from previous jobs, or other one-time financial gains. Much more frequently, relatives—brothers, cousins, and uncles, more than parents—or former employers, loaned them money, or helped them get bank loans and merchandise on credit. Thus, a carpenter began his business with money that his brother borrowed from his employer, and the owner of a local stationery store established his own business with a loan from his former boss. Similarly, the daughter of a *colono* who owned a furniture store in another section of the city helped her father get merchandise on credit from her suppliers. With this merchandise he opened his own furniture store in *La Colonia*.

Although the shop owners typically are of higher socioeconomic background than the average resident, this is least true in *El Centro*. Nonetheless, resident shop owners in the center city area reported greater economic success than resident shop owners in either of the other areas. The success of center city area resident shop owners seems to derive mainly from the greater capital they initially invested in their businesses, their prior experience in related businesses, and the better sales opportunities in the long-established center of urban commerce.

In the two newer areas, and, to a lesser extent in the center city area, shopkeepers do not constitute a solidly established and integrated class. They live in similar conditions without entering into social relations with one another. Moreover, they move in and out of the stratum with great frequency. Although "petty" merchant employment has persisted and, indeed, increased over the years, most shop owners have had their businesses for only a brief portion of their working lives—for an average of five years in *El Centro*, less than four years in *La Colonia*, and about two years in *La Unidad*—and few of them have a history of entrepreneurial employment. The brevity of ownership seems in part to reflect the competition caused by the paucity of alternative business opportunities in the city, insufficient capital, and lack of merchandising skills.[21] However, the short life-span of

[21] The high turnover and failure rate of local shops and the low income of the many small shop owners suggests that Marx correctly argued that the *structural* importance of the petty bourgeoisie declines with the advancement of capitalism, because of the inability of the petty bourgeoisie to successfully compete with large-scale capitalists. Marx, *Capital*, I, and Marx and Engels, "Manifesto of the Communist Party," pp. 1-41. Although

stores in the two newer areas also reflects the recent proliferation of stores, in response to the growing local consumer market: the population has been expanding and residents' income improving.

As the following comments by shop owners reveal, their relevant training was largely indirect and informal:

> *Cabinet maker*: "I learned the trade from my father and from practice."
>
> *Owner of a plumbing shop*: "A friend of mine offered me a job in his shop. From him I learned to be a plumber."
>
> *Owner of an auto mechanic shop*: "I lived around auto mechanics since I was young. My father and relatives taught me how to do the work."
>
> *Owner of a barber shop*: "I used to work as an employee in a barber shop."
>
> *Owner of a stationery store*: "I'm acquiring experience little by little."
>
> *Owner of an upholstery shop*: "I once was an apprentice in a shop. Then I worked many years in shops, accumulating experience."
>
> *Owner of a shop which services electrical appliances*: "I was trained at Motorola, where I used to work."

The little prior experience shop owners had gained, particularly resident shop owners in *La Colonia* and the *La Unidad*, was mainly in trade rather than entrepreneurial skills. They generally opened their own stores either because they wanted to be their "own boss," in order to avoid the degradation and lack of freedom they suffered when working for others, or because they were too old or ill to find other jobs.

---

the petty bourgeoisie within the three areas are growing in number, few of them have established increasingly productive, profit-generating enterprises. Marx argued that the structural and the numerical significance of a class are not necessarily identical. From the point of view of employment, it is more accurate to speak of the petty bourgeoisification, not proletarianization, of Mexico City (and other major cities in industrializing semidependent capitalist economies). The Mexican government encourages such petty bourgeoisification through maintenance and regulation of markets and through legalization of squatter settlements, government-financed housing, and other urban-land distribution schemas. Home ownership is not identical to ownership of the means of production, but homes often are used to generate income.

Yet shop owners' perceptions of their own economic prospects have contributed to their business failure. Most of them view their situation as being determined by forces beyond their control. Seeing restricted opportunities, they respond in ways which make their prophecies come true. Many of them, particularly those who reside in the areas, see the demand for their goods and services as fixed and limited,[22] not expandable and changeable. Accordingly, they view their prospects in terms of the ratio of local buyers to sellers, and the buying power of customers. Comments which reflect this view include the following:

> *Owner of a beauty salon*: "Business is the same as two years ago because I have the same number of customers and equal profits."
>
> *Owner of a miscelánea*: "Sales are the same as they were a couple of years ago. Before there were fewer people and fewer *miscelánea* in the area. Now there are more people but there are also more *miscelánea*."
>
> *Owner of a photography studio*: "Business has been pretty good. I'm one of the few photographers in the area with a studio."
>
> *Owner of a small furniture store*: "Business has been bad. The large stores in the area monopolize the clients."
>
> *Owner of a miscelánea and a bicycle repair shop*: "There's too much competition here."

Other shop owners felt that they could not improve their businesses because they lacked sufficient capital with which to purchase equipment and merchandise or to hire personnel, or because they were victims of national economic trends and government policies. Thus, an auto mechanic and a plumber felt their businesses suffered because they had no money with which to buy

[22] Foster used the term "Limited Good" to characterize a similar attitude among peasants. According to him, peasants view their total environment as one in which all the desired things in life exist in finite quantity and in short supply. They feel that they cannot increase the available amount of "good things" ("Peasant Society and the Image of Limited Good," pp. 300-323). Actually, Foster seems to exaggerate the universality of the Limited Good in peasant societies for he associates fatalism with the Limited Good orientation. However, "voluntary" peasant migration to cities suggests that not all peasants are fatalistic: most peasants migrate because they feel their opportunities will be better in their place of destination than in their community of origin.

expensive materials and pay workers; a pharmacist complained
that his business was bad because he could not afford to stock his
store well; and an owner of a bakery felt his business failed because he could not afford quality bread. Those who saw their
problem as being linked to larger societal forces, spoke of general industrial developments, changing consumer preferences,
and specific government programs which discriminated against
them:

> *Metalworkers*: "People now prefer buying plastic rather
> than metal goods. Consequently I have less business than
> formerly."
> *Owner of a shop selling handmade furniture*: "People no
> longer order handmade furniture. It's out of fashion."
> *Barber*: "I have fewer customers than in the past because
> fashions have changed. Men don't go as frequently to barbers
> as they used to."
> *Shoe repairman*: "The new government controls capital.
> Therefore, there is no work now. Before people had money
> and I consequently had more work."
> *Tortilla maker*: "My profits are low because the government
> regulates the price of maiz."
> *Pharmacist*: "Now people rarely come to pharmacies. They
> all go to Social Security and ISSSTE."

Since they rarely evaluated their businesses in managerial or
marketing terms they tended not to consider how to restructure
their operations in ways which might enhance their profits. Even
those who realized that their businesses were poorly organized
did not know precisely the source of their difficulties. Because
they generally assessed their businesses in ways which did not encourage useful reorganization, they rarely exploited the limited
existing opportunities.

CONCLUSIONS AND IMPLICATIONS

The structure of the local economies has been significantly
shaped by political economic forces prevailing in the society at
large, presently and historically. Residents' local business opportunities are limited, largely through forces beyond their control.
Their problem is not one of lack of initiative or motivation, or
lack of creativity, as some proponents of cultural explanations of

"underdevelopment" lead one to believe.[23] They lack organizational skill and useful work experience.

While expansion of urban consumer demand has made possible the expansion of local production, service, and distributive enterprises, the proliferation of local enterprises goes beyond this demand. Most local businesses are in the distribution and service rather than production sectors, largely because the former require less capital investment and technical skill.

Residents suffer economically not merely from lack of local economic opportunities but also from an inability to make use of those local opportunities which exist. The most lucrative businesses are owned by nonresidents, mainly because their background gives them an advantage. Concerned as the nonresident entrepreneurs are with maximizing their personal profits, they have not taken a special interest in developing the local economies or in providing employment for local residents. Income generated locally accordingly leaves the areas.

Within the context of the national society, the small businesses help resolve a problem of capital-intensive development: capital-intensive firms displace labor at the same time that they increase production. The small-scale ventures absorb labor. In so doing, they serve certain economic and political functions, not merely for the persons so employed but also for the government and those with a vested interest in the status quo. These operations, at least temporarily, reduce unemployment and circulate money to people with little or no alternative sources of income; this income increases consumer demand which, in turn, stimulates production, although not necessarily for goods produced by nationally owned firms.

Nonetheless, at the same time that the multiplicity of small-scale local enterprises appears to serve such functions, not least through self-exploitation, the expansion of employment within

[23] David McClelland, *The Achieving Society*, and Everett Hagen, *On the Theory of Social Change*. Hagen argues that one of the main impediments to economic growth in "underdeveloped" countries is the "uncreative" personality complex. According to him, people with such personality types have a low need for achievement and a low need for autonomy, and believe that the world consists of arbitrary forces. While I did not learn whether shop owners in the three areas lack a "need to be independent" many of them indicated a *desire* to be independent. Furthermore, since the shop owners did not attribute their business success or failure to "arbitrary forces," Hagen's explanation is unsatisfactory.

the distributive and service sectors in part reflects an inability of dependent capitalist economies to absorb a growing proportion of the labor force very productively. Thus, the expansion of the ranks of such petty bourgeoisie actually contributes to the continued underdeveloped state of the country.

However, since most residents do not work within the areas where they live, the constraints operating locally are not necessarily the only ones shaping their job prospects. The next chapter focuses on the factors determining how residents gain access to jobs in other parts of the city, and whether the conditions residents face within the urban labor market reflect the same class forces as those impinging on the local economies.

CHAPTER SEVEN

Occupational Choice and Occupational Fate

Since Mexicans, as we saw in Chapter One, tend to enjoy economic and other prerogatives in accordance with their occupational group affiliation, the "life chances" of residents of the three areas are closely linked to the jobs they secure. Yet their opportunities are limited, the nation's revolution and rapid economic growth notwithstanding.[1] Although many local men initiate efforts to improve their economic standing, their occupational opportunities and the inter- and intragenerational occupational mobility they experience generally are limited by class forces that discriminate against them.[2] Their occupational "fate" is not

Portions of Chapter Seven were published in Susan Eckstein, "Occupational Inequality in Urban Mexico," in Willem Veehoven and Winifred Ewing, eds., *Case Studies on Human Rights and Fundamental Freedoms: A World Survey*. The Foundation for the Study of Plural Societies. Martinus Nijhoff, The Hague, 1974.

[1] According to Ossowski, a major factor creating opportunities for mobility is mass death, due to war, especially civil war. Cited in Lipset and Bendix, *Social Mobility in Industrial Society*, p. 14.

[2] The processes which determine the type of work men in the three areas under study do are not necessarily representative of the processes operating in Mexico City or Mexico as a whole, since the areas were not selected randomly. Thus, the upward mobility which in fact occurs at the bottom of the urban socioeconomic hierarchy does not signify that Mexico as a whole is a very "open" society, for excluded from our sample are *campesinos* and large-scale capitalists, the two groups which are most likely to be self-perpetuating—in one case by choice, in the other case partly by choice and partly by default. Furthermore, the sample, unfortunately, excludes people who have experienced marked upward or downward mobility within Mexico City. That is, it excludes those people who have been sufficiently successful to afford housing in more exclusive sections of Mexico City, and those who have been so unsuccessful that they have been compelled either to move to areas of the city with a lower cost of living or back to the provinces they initially migrated from. According to interviews with local elites and residents of the three areas, most families who moved away from *La Unidad* were ones unable to afford living there. In the area formed by squatters, few families moved away relative to the number who came to settle there subsequent to the invasion: the area presently is approximately twelve times larger than it

primarily determined by their cultural predispositions or by sociophysical environmental conditions.

For poverty and its persistence from one generation to the next along family lines to be structurally determined, the general nature of the production process must influence both the way in which labor is divided and the means by which people gain access to jobs. In principle, only capitalists can directly transfer their line of work to their children. However, most capitalists in Mexico—and other countries developing along similar economic lines—are "penny capitalists." Since they enjoy little social and economic security, such small-scale "capitalists" are not likely to wish their occupational fate on their children.

Because productivity depends on the uses to which capital is put, and because these uses depend largely on skill, education is likely to be a prerequisite for jobs, particularly in societies which stress productivity.[3] "Penny capitalists" therefore are likely to be motivated to educate their children to qualify for jobs offering more security than they themselves experience. In contrast, medium- and large-scale capitalists most likely want their children to inherit their businesses, but they probably also want to educate their children since profits largely depend on the way capital is used, and managerial skill generally is acquired through training. In comparison to "penny capitalists," though, these capitalists can afford to keep their children out of the work force, and thereby educate them better. Consequently, the more

---

was the first few years of settlement. As we know from Chapter Two, the people who moved into the area over the years have generally been of higher socioeconomic status than the earlier settlers. Those who left initially moved away primarily because they were unable or unwilling to pay for the land. Since then people have been moving away primarily because they could afford better housing. We also know from Chapter Two that the population in *El Centro* has remained relatively stable for the last few decades. The people who have moved away seem to have left mainly because they wanted and could afford better and more spacious housing. Hence, our findings probably underestimate the amount of upward mobility which center city dwellers have experienced over the years and overestimate the amount of upward mobility experienced by residents of the housing development and legalized squatter settlement.

[3] According to Daniel Bell, service-dominated "post-industrial" societies demand high education and training, but in comparison to capital-intensive industrial societies, they generate low rates of productivity (*Post-Industrial Society*).

successful parents are as capitalists, the more successful their children are likely to be.

Employees, on the other hand, usually cannot directly pass on their line of work to their children, even if they want to. Since wage earners vary greatly in terms of wealth, power, and prestige, employed persons, in addition, are likely to try to maximize their children's chances of job success by providing them with the best education possible. As with capitalists, their ability to afford keeping their children out of the work force is likely to depend heavily on their financial resources.

In sum, there is reason to believe that people differ in their ability and desire to have their children follow in their footsteps, and in their ability to give their children access to employment opportunities requiring schooling. There also is reason to believe that the quality and quantity of schooling people obtain depends on their class background, even though education, theoretically, is universally available to all.

However, people may be hired on the basis of so-called particularistic criteria as well, at least when jobs do not require great expertise and coveted jobs are scarce. As shown in the last chapter, among people equally qualified for jobs, employers may prefer to hire those known personally either to them or to someone working for them. Such workers are more likely to be loyal and cooperative when offered a job than workers hired through impersonal channels. To the extent that people's social contacts in general and job contacts in particular primarily are with persons of their own socioeconomic stratum this informal mechanism also serves to perpetuate differential access to jobs from one generation to the next along family lines.

Should we find that these formal and informal forces largely determine the job prospects of the men interviewed and that the effect of both sets of forces varies largely according to the men's class of origin, then the data would suggest that the men's job status is primarily determined by the structure of the economy and society. In contrast, if economic status stems primarily from the influence of cultural factors, then occupational differences among men residents should be associated more with cultural predispositions than with socioeconomic background. Accordingly, people should be able to alter their economic fate once they assimilate the values, norms, and attitudes appropriate for financially rewarding jobs. To perform "modern" jobs well one supposedly must be flexible, efficacious, rational, and able and willing to exert control over one's destiny, including one's work situation.[4] However, if the structural thesis is correct, socioeconomic factors limit the men's job prospects *irrespective* of how culturally predisposed persons are to assume well-paying and prestigious jobs, and to the extent that cultural orientations vary by socioeconomic class they are class adaptations—that is, "class-determined," not "class-determining." Thus, if a relationship between culture and class is found to exist, the strength of the structural explanation hinges on whether socioeconomic forces are the causal factor. The significance of rural-urban exposure, and more direct cultural measures—namely hopelessness, orientation toward the past and present rather than the future, and religion and religiosity—are examined below. These factors have been alleged to influence people's economic prospects, independently of socioeconomic forces.

Alternatively, people's job prospects might depend directly or indirectly on the type of neighborhood in which they live, particularly if the areas provide residents with an opportunity to own property which they can use to generate income. Their prospects also may vary depending on where they live if different dwelling environments differentially induce residents to be upwardly mobile. Accordingly, job differences between residents of the three areas should be greater than differences within each of the areas, and any correlation between residents' class background or cultural predispositions, on the one hand, and their occupational status, on the other hand, should in fact be attributable to the kind of dwelling environment in which they live or grew up.[5]

The actual applicability of each of these theses for explaining men residents' job status is examined, in turn, below.[6] The cri-

---

[4] Alex Inkeles, "The Modernization of Man."

[5] "Dwelling environment" is of a different order of abstraction than the socioeconomic and cultural attributes discussed here: it is a community-level or "contextual" variable, not an individual-level variable.

[6] No analysis is made here of the secondary sources of employment which some men have. If men had no job at the time of the interview, their most recently held job was considered. The fifty women interviewed in each of the three areas are not considered here, as men generally are the main breadwinners and employment conditions for women tend to be somewhat different than for men. Although omitted, they are at times either the main financial supporters of families or major contributors.

teria used for classifying the men's occupational status appears in the Appendix to Chapter Seven, and the questions used in the following analysis derive from the questionnaire contained in Appendix B of the book.

EDUCATION AND CLASS BACKGROUND

Among the sample of men, schooling generally is a necessary but not sufficient prerequisite for well-paying and prestigious jobs.[7] Schooling increases the men's chances of securing better-paying and prestigious jobs, but it does not in itself guarantee them such jobs.[8] The salaried white-collar employees generally have at least a primary school education (six or more years of schooling) (Table 1). Such education is less important for factory work than for white-collar work, but factory workers are more educated than artisans.

While almost as many independently employed men as factory workers have a primary school education, few of the former were sufficiently content to want their children to pursue their same line of work. When asked about the occupational aspirations they held for their children, only about 6 percent of them said they wanted their children to follow in their footsteps. Like the local shopkeepers discussed in the last chapter, these men prefer self-employment to the jobs available. Their options are limited because well-paying, secure blue- and white-collar jobs have not ex-

[7] Financially, for instance, whereas over three-fourths of the salaried white-collar workers interviewed reported earning $80.00 or more per month, only 30 percent, 35 percent, and 63 percent of the semi- and unskilled employed workers (in small-scale firms), independently employed and factory workers, respectively, reported earning that amount. In contrast, only 11 percent of the salaried white-collar workers said they earned $60.00 or less, whereas 39 percent, 35 percent, and 13 percent of the semi- and unskilled workers, the independently employed, and factory workers, respectively, said that they did. Other studies of stratification in Mexico show similar correlations between income and occupation. See Stern and Kahl, "Stratification," and the references therein.

[8] Educational prerequisites for certain jobs are determined less by the requirements of the job itself than by the general educational level prevailing in a particular society. For example, automobile workers in different countries will have different educational backgrounds even though they perform the same work. See Form, "Occupational and Social Integration of Automobile Workers in Four Countries."

TABLE 1

Relationship between Education and Occupation
(*percent*)

Education[a]	Occupation			
	semi-skilled and un-skilled in small enter-prise	*inde-pendently em-ployed*	*factory/ large enter-prise*	*salaried non-manual*
none	6	24	9[b]	8[b]
some primary	67	35	44	19
primary	28	42	47	72
Total %	101	101	100	99
Total No.	(36)	(46)	(32)	(36)

[a] Classification based on the question: "How much schooling have you had?" Primary school consists of six grades.
[b] "N" is less than 5.

panded as rapidly as the education level of the populace has upgraded.

Although the little overt conflict between workers and management conveys the impression that labor is satisfied with work conditions, local men speak of tension and hostility between employers and employees. As a metal worker noted:

> We realize that *patrones* try to convince us that we are not exploited. They tell us that they are personally helping us by giving us employment and helping us when we are sick. Yet we know that workers and *patrones* have always been in conflict; because the latter always have exploited the former. We are exploited because we earn little relative to the responsibilities we assume on the job, our knowledge, and experience. We're also exploited because we are pressured to do more work than we're really obliged to do. This unjust situation stems from the "egoism" of the *patrones* and occasionally also from the inefficiency of the unions.

It is precisely to avoid such exploitation and to enjoy the advantages of independence that some educated men have started their own small business, utilizing their limited capital and skills.

Not all independently employed men, however, have an education; in contrast to the others similarly employed, these men probably were unable to secure other work, for Table 1 shows that employers rarely hire uneducated men. Because these "penny capitalists" generally lack skills and capital, they have few options but to seek a means of subsistence on their own: They do not have access to any universal unemployment insurance. Yet even their self-employment opportunities are limited, owing not only to market conditions but to government policies. As a currently jobless ambulant vendor with two years of schooling explained to me, the only way he could subsist was by selling in the streets—toys when he had nearly no money, clothing when he had "a few *centavos* more." However, he noted that he no longer could afford selling in the streets as he was constantly arrested for selling illegally without a license. He noted that "one gets accustomed to going to prison. But whereas it used to be only for two to three days, one now is imprisoned for about a week. In fact, my wife and I never sell together, because we can't afford to be arrested at the same time."

Even though schooling provides the men with no guarantee of a job, it at times does seem to increase the men's success at small-scale business ventures. Educated shopkeepers generally can calculate and keep account of their expenses in a way which uneducated shopkeepers generally cannot, and many of them attribute their limited business success to this. Education at times is economically consequential for artisans as well. For example, a poorly educated owner of a shoe *taller* explained to me that his business had improved recently because his primary school-educated wife began assisting him. Before she started helping him he was constantly without cash and constantly in debt, as he never kept track of how he spent his money. If workers asked him for money, he loaned it to them. But then he in turn had to borrow cash when he needed it. Having little to offer in the way of collateral he rarely was able to borrow much money, and his business suffered as a consequence. When his wife took responsibility for the shop's accounting, she kept record of their expenses and receipts of payments. Now they no longer owe as much and they are able to get more credit since their finances are in better standing. They therefore rarely are short of capital any more, and they in turn can now afford more and better workers. Because the owners can guarantee more work, their employees, anxious to keep their jobs, are more accommodating.

In view of the potential payoffs of education and in view of the fact that primary school, according to the Mexican Constitution, is free and compulsory, why have over half of the men not completed six years of school? If they actually have failed to take advantage of facilities which permit upward mobility, their low occupational status might be their own fault. Yet in view of their personal regret that they themselves did not acquire more formal training, and the importance they attribute to education as a channel of mobility, they do not seem to be poorly educated by choice.[9] The following comments reveal the importance they attribute to education:

> *Owner of eight buses*: "An educated person has many open doors which an uneducated person doesn't have. My duty, therefore is to educate my children."
>
> *Building guard*: "If I had continued studying I would have a better job now."
>
> *Baker*: "It is crucial that children study. Owing to family circumstances I could not study. Fortunately, my son is getting educated. However, I must say, baking is a profession. Master bakers are chemists, and this should be recognized. You see, in order to make cakes one must know how much of each ingredient to use; one must know how to combine the ingredients, and this is pure chemistry."
>
> *Blacksmith*: "I work hard in order to be able to educate my children. They must progress."
>
> *Printer*: "All parents are obliged to teach their children to obey and study. I don't want my children to do the same type of work I do. I want the best for them—that they study a career."

[9] About half of the men consider education to be the most important requisite for success, and almost without exception the men wished they had received more formal education. Although the Constitution stipulates that primary school education is compulsory, the provision is not enforced, particularly since educational facilities are insufficient to school all the children. In fact, given Mexican standards, the men in our study are comparatively well educated. For instance, as many as one-third of the school-aged population in Mexico were not in school in 1960. Stern and Kahl, p. 11.

Class background appears to be a primary obstacle to schooling. Although the study did not investigate whether the inducement the men received from their parents to obtain an education varied in accordance with their parents' socioeconomic status, it did examine the relationship between the *actual* education the men received and the occupational status of their parents. The data show that the best educated men tend to come from the most economically successful families (Table 2).[10]

TABLE 2

Relationship between Respondent's and Father's Occupation
(*percent*)

Edu- ation f men	Campesino	semiskilled and un- skilled in small enterprise	inde- pendently employed	factory/ large enterprise	salaried nonmanual	Total
			Father's Occupation[a]			
one	34	7 [b]	3[b]	—[b]	4[b]	12
-5 years	37	50	53	46	30	43
+ years	29	43	44	54	67	45
otal %	100	100	100	100	101	100
otal No.	(38)	(28)	(34)	(13)	(27)	(140)

[a] Classification based on the question: "What type of work did your father do most of his fe?" The classification includes only those persons who knew their father and how their father arned a living.
[b] "N" is less than 5.

Moreover, school facilities—both in quality and quantity— reinforce the importance family background has on children's education, as facilities are not equally available to all socioeco-

[10] Other studies also show that the education Mexicans receive varies according to their class background. See Kahl, *Measurement of Modernism*, pp. 72-88; Martin Carnoy, "Rates of Return to Schooling in Latin America," pp. 359-74; *Anuario estadístico, 1964*; and Barkin, "Schooling and Social Distance in Mexico." Such unequal access to education is not, however, unique to Mexico, Latin America or capitalist regimes in general. On Latin America, see Arthur Liebman et al., *Latin American University Students*. For data illustrating unequal access to schooling in socialist countries see Joseph Fiszman, "Education and Social Mobility in People's Poland"; and Inkeles and R. Bauer, *Soviet Citizen: Daily Life in a Totalitarian Society*, p. 25.

nomic classes. In general, public school allocations are distributed differentially among rich and poor regions of the country,[11] rich and poor (urban and rural) communities,[12] and rich and poor sections within cities. However, without knowing the nature of school facilities in the communities where the men in the sample grew up, we cannot determine the extent to which the men interviewed were handicapped by the government's inegalitarian school policy. Nevertheless, given the national pattern, undoubtedly some of the men were accordingly jeopardized, particularly those of rural origin. To the extent that the limited availability of public education affected the level of schooling attained by the men, formal as well as informal pressures have restricted the education opportunities of the men. Certainly, the nature of school facilities within the three areas, described below, suggest that such forces seem to be impeding the educational prospects of the men's children.

THE LOCAL SCHOOLS

The class bias in government school allocations is evident from the number and kinds of facilities available in the three areas. For instance, in 1967-68 there was a shortage of school space in all three communities, although least so in *El Centro*. Consequently, despite parents' desire to educate their children, many children could not get into school. If rejected for two consecutive years, children generally are doomed to remain uneducated, for the schools do not like the age differential among first graders to be more than one or two years. When they are older, they can attend night school, but by then they have to work to support themselves and a family, making it difficult to study.

School facilities were particularly inadequate in *La Colonia*. There, over 2,000 children could not enter first grade in 1967-68, about three to four times as many as could enter. Consequently, the economic prospects of youth in *La Colonia* are less than those of youth in either of the other areas. The school problem would have been even more severe had there not been a few private schools, which opened in the area in response to the short-

[11] Charles Myers, *Education and National Development in Mexico.*
[12] Ibid.

age.[13] However, only one of the private schools offered the full six grades of primary school. Since public primary schools are reluctant to accept transfer students from the local private schools, even those families who are able and willing to pay private school tuition cannot guarantee their children sufficient schooling to qualify for most factory and white-collar jobs. The public school problem was further mitigated in 1971 when a new public primary school was built on land adjacent to *La Colonia*. The school was built mainly to serve a new housing development but because the school was completed before the houses, the *colonos* had the good fortune of being accepted in the school.

In *La Unidad* several thousand students were refused entry into school in 1967-68, four years after the area opened. Although the schools were designed to accommodate all the children, the planners assumed that only one family would live in each house and that families would be smaller than they actually were. By 1971 the crisis was partially alleviated as the government constructed a few new primary schools, but no additional schools were built in the poorest section which needed them the most.

Furthermore, there is reason to believe that the quality of teachers is poorer in the three areas than in schools in other sections of the city attended by more well-to-do children. Even within the three areas the quality of teachers seems to vary. To the extent that the quality of children's work depends on the motivation of teachers and administrators, children in *La Unidad* have an advantage over children in the other two areas, particularly over children in *El Centro*. When I asked teachers and administrators where they wanted to work they expressed a preference for schools with "middle-class" children, which is possible in certain sections of the development. Depending on years of service and contacts, faculty can be transferred to the school of their choice.

In terms of postprimary school education, of the three areas only the largely "middle-class" housing development has secondary schools.[14] It had one in 1968. Two more were built by 1971,

---

[13] The upper classes tend to send their children to private rather than public schools, and they enjoy long-term social and economic advantages as a consequence (Myers, *Education*). However, the quality and the prestige of those private schools are superior to local private schools.

[14] The secondary schools which the government built in *La Unidad* are indicative of the present-day government policy to allocate disproportionally

one of which was a vocational school.[15] Near *El Centro* there is a vocational school which some center city dwellers attend, but no secondary school which would channel children into white-collar rather than blue-collar jobs. Near *La Colonia* there is, since the mid-1960s, a secondary school. Therefore, those *colonos* who have been fortunate enough to get into local primary schools and finish six grades are able to get a postprimary school education, if they are not constrained to work full time to support their family.

In sum, education facilities are best in the most well-to-do area. However, even there they are not uniformly available to all residents. Schools vary in the different sections, according to the class composition of residents. Government allocation of formal education facilities seems to have the same effect as informal social forces. Both tend to reinforce the importance of class background.

PERSONAL CONTACTS AND CLASS BACKGROUND

In addition to schooling, personal contacts help men obtain jobs, even in the "modern" sector of the economy; and the men's range of contacts tend to be class-linked. About 38 percent of the men with factory and white-collar jobs said they obtained their work through a personal acquaintance, whereas only one-fourth of the men in small-scale enterprises said they obtained their jobs in that manner.

What contacts the men do have varies with their present class standing and their class of origin. Although the men are not entirely restricted in their close contacts to people of their own

---

more resources to secondary than to primary schools, even though primary school education is not universally available to all children. During the last twenty years inscription in primary school increased on the average of 3.7 percent per year, a rate no higher than the annual rate of population growth; inscription in secondary school, though, increased on the average of 16.9 percent per year (Navarrete, "La distribución del ingreso en México," p. 31). For data on returns to investment in primary and secondary schools in Mexico, in comparison to other Latin American countries, see Carnoy, "Rates of Return to Schooling."

[15] One of the new secondary schools is situated in a section of the development which opened in the interim between 1968 and 1971. However, children from other sections of the development attend the school, as secondary school districts are larger than primary school districts.

socioeconomic stratum, in comparison to people otherwise employed, salaried white-collar workers are friendlier with white-collar workers (Table 3). Some of the white-collar workers in the

TABLE 3

Relationship between Occupations of
Close Social Network and Occupations
of Men
(*percentaged on men's occupations*)

	Occupation of Men			
	semi-skilled and un-skilled in small enter-prise	*inde-pendently em-ployed*	*factory/ enter-prise*	*salaried non-manual*
% with any of 3 closest[a]				
Relatives who are nonmanual	26	26	31	57
	(35)	(43)	(29)	(35)
Fictive kin who are nonmanual	20	25	22	54
	(35)	(44)	(32)	(35)
Friends who are nonmanual	17	32	25	61
	(36)	(44)	(32)	(36)
Relatives, fictive kin, *or* friends who are nonmanual	47	60	52	85
	(34)	(40)	(29)	(34)

[a] Based on the question: "What type of work do they do?" (asked in reference to their three closest relatives, friends, and *compadres*).

sample may have become friendly with the persons similarly employed through their work, and not secured their work through such persons. However, since the men rely on relatives to help them obtain work and because kin tend to be of more or less similar socioeconomic background, personal contacts contribute to differential job access from one generation to the next along family lines, just as schooling does. Nevertheless, because the men's contacts are not entirely restricted to people of their own socioeconomic status, personal contacts undoubtedly facilitate some intergenerational mobility.

The men who intermingle with people of their own socioeconomic status do not all do so by choice. In-depth interviews with a small sample of men suggest that many men prefer to associate with people of higher status than their own. This preference is particularly true of the men who want to be upwardly mobile. They feel that people of higher status can teach and help them more. As the following comments reveal, such men feel they are unlikely to improve their socioeconomic status if, on the one hand, they do not first learn the appropriate behavior for positions of higher wealth, power, and prestige and, on the other hand, if they do not know people who can help them secure jobs.[16]

> *Worker in a shoe factory*: "It's better to have relations with families of higher status. One learns more that way. It's like in football. If one plays with a team of comparable strength, one doesn't budge, whereas if one plays with one that is stronger one has to exert oneself."

> *Worker in a shoe factory*: "It's preferable to have connections with families of a higher level, but it's very difficult. They always look down on someone of lower status. But it's good to have such contacts in order to improve one's experiences, perhaps to advance in one's work."

> *Building guard*: "I prefer having relations with persons of higher socioeconomic position because one needs to know influential people before new doors will be opened."

> *Blacksmith*: "It's better to be friendly with people who are better off because they can help you improve your situation."

In contrast, men who do not want or do not expect to be upwardly mobile consider contact with people of higher socioeconomic status to be less desirable and, in some cases, undesirable. For example, a fifty-eight-year-old baker, who has given up the idea of ever having a different occupation, mentioned that he prefers confining his contacts to his "own people," because in that way he avoids new expenses and new obligations. Similarly, a

---

[16] On the importance of "cue-searching" see Leeds, "Brazilian Careers and Social Structure," pp. 379-404.

printer who had no intention of being upwardly mobile noted that he preferred socializing with people of his own social category because he had the most confidence in them. He is proud of himself for never having received help from anyone.

The labor market, like politics, is particularistic. Yet *personalismo* does not necessarily work at cross-purposes to the demands of an industrializing society, for employers are not likely to give priority in hiring to persons known to them or their workers unless they think it propitious to do so. Probably favoritism induces worker loyalty.[17] Moreover, employers generally also take education into account when hiring workers. Employers, such as the former owner of the chocolate factory in the center city area, who deliberately hire poorly educated employees, do so because they believe such workers to be sufficiently competent and less demanding than educated workers. In either case, though, employers are acting in their perceived self-interest. Hence, once again we see that *personalismo* is important for socioeconomic, not cultural reasons[18]—here from the viewpoint both of the employer and the prospective employee. If people have contacts they obviously make use of them, for labor unions, employment agencies, political parties, advertisements, and other impersonal market mechanisms have proved to be of little use to men in search of work.[19]

[17] Although labor commitment is becoming a serious problem in such advanced industrial countries as the U.S., the literature on contemporary developing countries attributes it to be a particularly severe problem when countries first industrialized. See especially Wilbert Moore and Arnold Feldman (eds.), *Labor Commitment and Social Change in Developing Areas.*

[18] *Personalismo*, however, is frequently said to be culturally-determined. Gillin, for example, considers *personalismo* to be a distinctively Latin American cultural trait, as does Parsons. John Gillin, "The Middle Segments and Their Values," pp. 24-40; and Parsons, *The Social System*, pp. 198-200. Since a 1960 study shows that 38 percent of Americans aged 21-45 obtained their most recent job through a member of their family or a friend, *personalismo* is not unique to Latin American culture or to semi-industrialized countries. See Robert Crain, "School Integration and Occupational Achievement of Negroes," pp. 593-606.

[19] To get unionized jobs one needs union consent. However, in many cases workers find jobs on their own and subsequently get union approval. Local district offices of the PRI help residents secure employment in exchange for political support, but generally only by providing letters of recommendation. Much less frequently does the Party locate jobs for residents.

PRIOR JOB EXPERIENCE, AGE, AND PRESENT
OCCUPATIONAL SUCCESS

An analysis which focuses on channels of recruitment at a single
point in time overlooks the mobility that people make within the
course of their lifetime. Both the degree of mobility into and out
of the petty bourgeois sector and the high turnover rate of shoe
talleres, and employment within *talleres*, described in Chapter
Six, suggest that people in urban low-income areas may experience considerable job mobility. If indeed people do move significantly up or down the occupational hierarchy within their
working careers, the apparent importance of class of origin could
merely be a function of the particular time at which the investigation was done.

The men seem to experience some vertical intragenerational
mobility, although least so into the salaried white-collar
stratum.[20] The limited movement into salaried nonmanual jobs
perhaps is a result of the high birthrate among Mexican professionals and white-collar employees,[21] combined with the tendency of job status, as shown below, to be indirectly passed on
from one generation to the next. It may also be because men
white-collar employees choose to live in more well-to-do sections
of the city. While we do not have data on their entire work histories, a comparison of the men's last two jobs reveals that even
though most men experience mobility, they are more likely to be
"horizontally" mobile, moving from one job to another within
their same occupational category, than mobile into any single
other occupation; that men who secure white-collar status tend

[20] In the industrial city of Monterrey, Mexico, intragenerational job and
occupational mobility also is limited. The mobility which men do experience
tends to be before age twenty-five. See Browning and Waltraut Feindt,
"Diferencias entre la población nativa y la migrante en Monterrey," pp. 183-
204. Limited intragenerational manual/nonmanual mobility tends to be characteristic of advanced capitalist industrial societies as well. Lipset and Bendix, pp. 156-81.

[21] While the salaried white-collar stratum is expanding more rapidly than
the working class, it may be that the sector is not expanding sufficiently rapidly, given the high rate of population growth, to absorb many persons from
other class backgrounds. The average number of children of different occupational groupings in Mexico in the 1960s was as follows: *campesinos*, 4.9;
workers, 5.32; service workers, 5.15; white-collar employees, 4.53; and professionals, 4.58. See Maria de Lourdes Ortiz Reyes, *Manfestaciones demográficas a nivel familiar.*

not to forsake it; and—though the number of cases is small—that factory workers who are vertically mobile are more often downwardly mobile than upwardly mobile (Table 4).

TABLE 4

Intragenerational Mobility: Relationship
between Last Job and Present Job
(*percent*)

Present Job	no previous job	semi-skilled and un-skilled in small enterprises	independently employed	factory/large enterprise	salaried non-manual
			Last Job[a]		
semiskilled and unskilled in small enterprise	46	41[b]	14[c]	—[c]	7[c]
independently employed	23	20	36[b]	39	14
factory/large enterprise	16	20	27	46[b]	7[c]
salaried nonmanual	14	18	23	15	71[b]
Total %	99	99	100	100	99
	(43)	(49)	(22)	(13)	(14)

[a] Based on the question: "What type of job did you have before your present job?"

[b] These figures refer to nonmobile persons.

[c] "N" is less than 5.

The men at times change jobs, even when they do not in the process change occupations because the businesses which employ them go bankrupt or because they have problems with their employers. More frequently, though, they change jobs because they succeed in finding slightly better paying positions. In these cases they shift work more out of a determination to improve their economic situation than a lack of commitment to work. At the same time, though, many of them see their possibilities limited to ones within their own occupational category (*oficio*), as they consider the skills they acquire over the years to be nontransferable from one type of occupation to another. Such a perception contributes to their occupational fate's becoming a self-fulfilling prophesy: men who think accordingly do not seek out other types of jobs. To the extent that this occurs, cultural forces are economically consequential, but they are shaped by socioeconomic forces. The interviews also suggest that when the men do seek out different work it generally is because they cannot find a job within their own *oficio*; because they acquired additional schooling; because they befriended someone who helped them get a new type of employment; or because they wanted and were able to go into business for themselves. The biographical accounts below illustrate some of these forces:

> *Metalworker*: "At age 15 I worked making scaffolds in a meat-packing plant. The factory closed, at which point I found a job as a worker in a factory manufacturing aluminum products. I did not initially intend to continue at this new line of work, but I found that I liked it better. So I decided to continue at it."

> *Printer*: "All my life I have worked in small printing shops. I have worked in many shops, shifting from one to another in order to earn more money. Occasionally, however, I changed jobs because I had problems with my boss or because the shop closed. But I have never considered jobs in any field besides printmaking because I don't know any other. I would be tempted to change only if I could thereby get a better paying job."

> *Blacksmith*: "I don't want another type of job because this is my vocation. I am, however, considering the possibility of opening my own shop. It's actually pretty easy since one does not need a large outlay of capital to install a shop. The machinery and the tools which one needs are cheap. I have an architect friend who is helping me find a locale for my shop. He also has promised to give me sufficient financial assistance to begin the business."

> *Public accountant*: "I worked as a mechanic for various years while studying at night for a career as a public accountant. I held many jobs, changing whenever I found a shop which would pay me more. That way I could continue my studies and support my family. I never tried to find jobs other

than as a mechanic because I felt I knew mechanic work best. I never liked working as a mechanic but it was a way to finance my studies. Once I finished studying I became a public accountant. What I like best about my new career is that it enables me to make decisions. I want very badly to have a high position which allows me to exercise control."

22-year-old shoe artisan: "At age 15 I was already working as a shoe artisan. I have been doing the same ever since, although I have worked in many sweatshops over the years. I mainly changed jobs because I could thereby earn more money. I had wanted to study but was not able to do so for financial reasons. Now I'm too old to change professions, unless I come across some very good opportunity. . . . My father also was a shoe artisan. He influenced me, but he never helped me."

Shoe artisan: "I wanted to study engineering but I never was able to do so. I then thought of following in my father's footsteps—becoming a textile worker. But when I realized how difficult it was for textile workers to find jobs I decided to become a shoemaker."

Since the men in fact do not experience much upward occupational mobility, particularly into the salaried white-collar class, the jobs available at the time they enter the labor force may have a long-term effect on their future job prospects. Given the country's high rate of economic growth since World War II one might expect the men who have entered the work force in recent decades to be more successful occupationally than the older workers. Yet the younger generation of men in the three areas does not appear to have an advantage over the older generation. Interestingly, the men under forty seem no more likely than those over forty to hold salaried white-collar jobs: They are more likely to hold factory jobs, because factory employers discriminate against persons over forty. Either the recently employed salaried white-collar employees are not recruited from this stratum of the population or they tend not to settle in areas such as these.

INTERGENERATIONAL OCCUPATIONAL MOBILITY

Family background limits the men's job prospects, but not because the men directly inherit their father's line of work. The sons of salaried white-collar workers were most likely to be white-collar workers even though they could not directly inherit the jobs,[22] and most of the men interviewed whose fathers were self-employed did not continue in their father's business even though independently owned businesses are inheritable (Table 5). In fact, of the men interviewed, the sons of independently

TABLE 5

Intergenerational Mobility

		Father's Occupation[a]			
Respondent's Occupation	Campesino	semi-skilled and un-skilled in small enter-prises	inde-pendently employed	factory/large enter-prise	salaried non-manual
semiskilled and un-skilled in small enterprise	21	43[b]	21	33[c]	11
independently employed	34	32	35[b]	17[c]	19
factory/large enterprise	24	11	21	42[b]	22
salaried nonmanual	21	14	24	8[c]	48[b]
Total	100 (38)	100 (28)	101 (34)	100 (12)	100 (27)

[a] Based on the question: "What type of work did your father do most of his life?" The classification includes only those persons who knew their father and how he earned a living.

[b] These figures refer to nonmobile persons.

[c] "N" is less than 5.

employed men were *least* likely to pursue careers similar to their

[22] Since both in the Soviet Union, where individuals do not own the means of production, and in advanced capitalist societies family background largely determines a person's "life chances," there is added reason to believe that informal class-linked mechanisms serve to perpetuate socioeconomic inequalities from one generation to the next along family lines, independently of ownership of the means of production. On the Soviet Union, see Inkeles and Bauer, p. 89; on advanced capitalist countries, see Lipset and Bendix, pp. 11-75.

father's. Family wealth and prestige seem to influence sons' occupational fate more than ownership of the "means of production."

Nonetheless, sons of certain class backgrounds tend to be more mobile than others,[23] and not all sons who have been mobile have moved up the socioeconomic hierarchy. For instance, although the number of cases is small, workers' sons are more likely to be employed artisans or peons than salaried white-collar employees.[24] As to those persons who have been fortunate enough to be upwardly mobile, many do not come from what has been conventionally labeled "adjacent" strata. Recruits into the working class are not necessarily from artisan backgrounds,[25] and most white-collar recruits have not come from working class backgrounds.[26]

[23] The intergenerational mobility pattern described here appears to hold even when education is taken into account (introduced as a "control"). However, the small sample makes it difficult to estimate accurately the importance of class background in determining the individual's occupational fate, independently of schooling.

[24] According to Reyna's study of intergenerational mobility in Mexico, artisans and workers experience the most downward mobility of any sector of the population. Reyna, "Occupational Mobility," p. 117. Lipset and Bendix more optimistically conclude in their analysis of advanced capitalist countries (in *Social Mobility in Industrial Society*), that there has been considerable mobility from the manual to the nonmanual sector. In contrast, S. M. Miller, in his "Comparative Social Mobility," pp. 1-89, argues that about 25-30 percent of the people in most industrial societies experience upward or downward mobility between the blue- and white-collar strata. J. H. Goldthorpe, "Social Stratification in Industrial Society," pp. 648-60, makes a similar argument to Miller.

[25] There also is evidence that in nineteenth century America factory workers were not primarily declassé artisans either. Stephen Thernstrom, *Poverty and Progress.*

[26] Kahl argues (p. 175) that the low blue- white-collar mobility in Mexico stems from the country's still being in an early stage of industrialization. To substantiate his argument he compares mobility rates in Mexico, Brazil, and Puerto Rico with rates in such industrialized societies as the United States, Denmark, and France. Similarly, Lipset and Bendix (esp. pp. 11-75), argue that the "requisites" of industrialization are such that countries at a comparable level of economic development have comparable rates of mobility, independently of the cultural emphasis on mobility. If this were true, the pattern of mobility in Mexico would reflect the stage of industrialization and not the pattern of industrialization. However, this interpretation is questionable in light of the data reviewed by S. M. Miller in his "Comparative Social Mobility" and the findings reported by Thernstrom and Rogoff. In *Poverty and*

Whereas in Chapter Six we saw that the most upwardly mobile
group of shopkeepers were offspring of independently employed
men, among our sample of men residents, sons of *campesinos* as
well as "penny capitalists" have tended to experience the most
mobility into the white-collar stratum.[27] Their relative success
may be an indirect consequence of the autonomy which their fathers enjoyed in their work situation, or it may stem from a preference some employers have for workers of rural origin, the
types of families who migrate, or the impact the experience of
migration has on families.

Work experience may indirectly serve to perpetuate inequality
from one generation to the next because of the economic and cultural impact work has on family life. Economic constraints prevent the children of manual workers from enjoying much upward
mobility. For instance, fathers who are artisans either have their
sons assist them for financial reasons, particularly if they are paid
on a piecework basis, or have their sons apprenticed to someone
else at an early age. Consequently, the sons get absorbed into
craft activities before they are old enough to select a career on
their own. In addition, parents who exercise independence and

---

Progress, Thernstrom notes that the amount of mobility in the United States
has remained more or less constant since the nineteenth century and that the
amount never was very great. Similarly, Natalie Rogoff, in *Recent Trends in
Occupational Mobility,* argues that the growth of the nonmanual sector in
twentieth century America reflects an upward movement of the entire occupational structure and not individual mobility. Moreover, owing to the way
Mexico is developing it is doubtful whether mobility in the country will ever
approximate that of the highly industrialized countries.

[27] Other studies also report similar mobility patterns: Zeitlin, *Revolutionary
Politics and the Cuban Working Class,* p. 142; Perlman, pp. 214, 219;
Bertram Hutchinson, et al., *Mobilidade e trabalho*; Lipset and Bendix,
Social Mobility; Rogoff, p. 45; and Bowles, "Unequal Education and the
Reproduction of the Social Division of Labor." Zeitlin notes that among
Cuban workers the children of *petty bourgeois* background are more likely
to hold "skilled" jobs, even though their "life chances," as measured by
education, theoretically put them at a disadvantage in comparison to workers of other class backgrounds. Lipset and Bendix find in all countries
they studied except the United States that sons of farmers in nonfarm occupations had a better chance of attaining non-manual work than did sons of
manual workers. Similarly, Bowles finds in his study of occupational mobility in the United States that children whose fathers are self-employed
are more likely to attain white-collar positions than children of fathers who
are otherwise employed.

assume a position of dominance within their work situation may, consciously or not, raise children who take initiative. In contrast, "peons," employed artisans and workers, particularly workers in small, old paternalistic factories—in which most of the workers interviewed are employed—may extend the hierarchical and paternalistic cultural and behavioral patterns learned at work and reinforced at work to relations within their homes. They may assume within the family the dominant role denied them in the firm, and, consequently, raise their children to be dependent. The explanation, however, cannot account for the fact that some sons of employed manual workers *are* independent "penny capitalists," unless such sons pursue the work by default, because they are unable to secure other employment.

As to migrant families, they undoubtedly are a select group.[28] Compared to the average person they leave behind in the provinces, they are better educated. They probably also are more self-confident and more willing to take initiative and risks, or they would not have moved. Moreover, at least some *campesinos* in the provinces have considerable autonomy in their work situation, just as the independently employed do. Should these *campesinos* be the most likely to migrate, their prior experience possibly helps them adapt to life in the capital.[29] Furthermore, relative to families native to Mexico City, they may be more determined to succeed, in order to justify their move.

Social-psychological studies, at least of Americans, lend credence to these interpretations, as they show that persons trained

---

[28] Migrants are particularly likely to be a select group in areas with a low proportion of recent migrants. Studies of migrants suggest that those who leave the countryside increasingly are more representative of the education level of provincial people. On the selectivity of migrants in Mexico see Robert Kemper, "Family and Household Organization Among Tzintzuntzan Migrants in Mexico City," pp. 25-26; Browning and Feindt, "Selectivity of Migrants to a Metropolis in a Developing Country," pp. 347-57; Balán, "Migrant-Native Socio-Economic Differences in Latin American Cities," p. 4. On the selectivity of migrants in other Latin American countries see Morse, "Internal Migrants and the Urban Ethos in Latin America"; Glenn Beyer, *The Urban Explosion in Latin America*, p. 98; and Gideon Sjoberg, "Rural-Urban Balance and Models of Economic Development," and Gino Germani, "Social and Political Consequences of Mobility."

[29] Fromm and Maccoby discuss social, psychological, and economic differences among *campesinos*. Our data, unfortunately, is not sufficiently detailed to test whether *campesinos* of diverse backgrounds have adjusted differently to the city. Erich Fromm and Maccoby, *Social Character in a Mexican Village*.

early in life to be independent are more motivated to achieve and assume responsibilities than those who are brought up protected.[30] In contemporary America, training in independence is generally restricted to the "middle class"—particularly to the self-employed "middle class."[31] Those Americans who exercise greatest independence in their work situation employ child-rearing techniques which result in their offspring learning both to be independent and flexible and to exercise control over their environment.

Although these studies attribute the training in independence to "middle-class" upbringing, other socioeconomic strata or family experiences could conceivably induce people to employ similar child-rearing practices. Should other occupations and experiences—particularly in societies stratified along different lines than the U.S.—demand workers also to be independent and responsible, the autonomy in the work situation might have a similar effect on family relations as independently employed "middle-class" jobs apparently have in the U.S. If this line of argument is correct, it is not surprising that the children of independently employed men and *campesinos* in our sample have been more upwardly mobile than sons of employed workers. It too would suggest that the class structure is transmitted from one generation to the next not merely directly through differential class-linked access to schooling and contacts but indirectly through class-linked cultural forces.

PROVINCIALISM

One of the culturally linked forces which allegedly shape people's economic prospects independently of class-linked forces is urbanism. Rural and urban communities are generally depicted as culturally distinct and people brought up in the two types of

[30] In making comparisons between child-rearing practices in the United States and Mexico I do not wish to imply that people holding comparable positions in the two countries have been trained equally to be independent, but that in comparison to other workers in the respective countries they perhaps have been. In general, I would expect Mexicans of all socioeconomic strata to be trained to be more submissive than their American counterparts and more reluctant to take risks.

[31] For a comprehensive summary of psychological studies of socialization in the United States, see Urie Bronfenbrenner, "Socialization and Social Class through Time and Space," pp. 362-76, and the references therein.

communities as therefore different.[32] For instance, people raised in small towns and villages are said to have different and much lower expectations and fewer skills to do other than agricultural work than people brought up in urban centers.[33] Although the mass exodus to capital cities in Mexico and other Latin American countries demonstrates that provincial people may acquire aspirations which cannot be satisfied within the confines of their place of origin, the size of the community in which migrants are born or grow up possibly influences their aspirations and expectations, even in the cities.

The size of community in which people are born and raised may be important not only because of the different cultural ethos said to prevail in different-sized communities, but also because of the education and occupational opportunities which different-sized communities offer. Objective opportunities may affect people's perceptions of possible careers, their career orientations, and, in turn, the actual careers they pursue.[34] Whether viewed in cultural or structural terms, if the type or size of community in which people grow up sets limits to their "life chances," then the earlier in life people are exposed to large metropoles, the more successful they should be in the long run. They thereby would have more time to acquire the values and skills which would drive them and enable them to take advantage of urban economic opportunities.

More recently, however, studies have suggested that social contacts have a greater impact on people's values, norms and attitudes, and "life chances" than the physically delineated community in which they live or are raised.[35] For example, city dwellers who maintain close contact with fellow villagers in the provinces or cities are said to be less likely to forget values and customs generally regarded as provincial than those who break such ties. Accordingly, if rural people ascribe to a cultural orientation which is not conducive to economic mobility, then city

[32] Emile Durkheim, *The Division of Labor in Society*; Ferdinand Tönnies, *Community and Society*; Robert Redfield, "The Folk Society," pp. 293-308; and Louis Wirth, "Urbanism as a Way of Life," pp. 1-24.

[33] Foster, "Peasant Society," pp. 302-23.

[34] See Lipset and Bendix, pp. 203-26, and Balán, Browning, and Jelin, *Men in a Developing Society*.

[35] Lewis, "Urbanization Without Breakdown," pp. 424-37, and Gans, *Urban Villagers*, pp. 197-226.

dwellers would have to abandon ties with provincial people before they could prosper in the city.

However, the experiences of the men living in the three areas under study disprove each of these theses (Table 6). In fact, so far as jobs are concerned, the migrants from small towns compete favorably with those who have been living all their lives in the capital. If a different cultural ethos prevails in communities of different sizes, the cultural forces have no lasting impact on the men who either were born or raised in a particular community but subsequently moved, at least not in job-related ways. Moreover, the men raised in areas which afford few occupational opportunities seem not necessarily to be jeopardized in their chances of securing factory or white-collar work once they move to a community offering more opportunities.[36]

In addition, the men who maintain close contact with the hinterland are as likely to be salaried white-collar employees as they are to be unskilled laborers. While migrants might possibly have experienced more occupational mobility if they had confined their contacts to Mexico City, periodic exposure to rural society has not had the negative economic effect assumed by some. The one rural-urban factor which apparently has a decisive bearing on the men's job prospects is the age at which they migrate. Men over thirty who move to the capital do not secure salaried and wage work. Yet it is undoubtedly their age, not their rural origin, which puts them at a disadvantage in the employment market, for employers—as previously noted—discriminate against middle-aged people, particularly those over forty, be they of urban or rural origin.[37]

---

[36] Other studies of Mexicans also show that occupationally migrants compare favorably with urban-born people within the cities. See Cornelius, "Urbanization as an Agent in Latin American Instability," p. 840; Browning and Feindt, "Diferencias entre la población nativa y la migrante en Monterrey"; Balán, "Are Farmers' Sons Handicapped in the City?" pp. 3-29; and Kahl, pp. 175-82. However, migrants seem not to compare as favorably with city-born people at the top echelons of the socioeconomic hierarchy in Mexico. Vernon, p. 157. In the United States, Peter Blau and Otis D. Duncan, in the *American Occupational Structure*, found that migrants on the whole were more successful than people born in cities with comparable levels of schooling.

[37] The apparent success of migrants in comparison to nonmigrants may be exaggerated, for unsuccessful migrants are less likely to stay in the city than successful migrants. Little is known about migrants who return to their town of origin or to other parts of Mexico because of economic failure in the

TABLE 6

Occupation of Men according to Provincialism
(*percent*)

	Occupation				
	semi-skilled and un-skilled in small enter-prises	*inde-pendently employed*	*factory/ large enter-prise*	*salaried non-manual*	*Total*
Size town when 15[a]					
less than 10,000	24[f]	35	12[f]	29	100 (17)
10,000/less than Federal District	13[f]	38	25	25	101 (24)
Federal District	26	29	21	25	101 (94)
Age migrated[b]					
didn't migrate	26	26	22	26	100 (77)
1-15 years old	22[f]	39	17[f]	22[f]	100 (18)
16-29	24	29	22	24	99 (41)
30 or over	14	50	21[f]	14[f]	99 (14)
Time lived in Federal District[c]					
5 years or less	33[f]	33[f]	33[f]	—	99 (6)
6-15 years	22	22	33	22	99 (18)
16-29 years	28	27	20	26	101 (51)
30 or more years	27	28	19	26	100 (74)
If ever see people who live in provinces[d]	27	28	19	26	100 (96)
If ever go to provinces[e]	21	26	24	29	100 (110)

Based on the Questions:
  [a] "Where did you live when you were fifteen?"
  [b] "How old were you when you came to Mexico City?"
  [c] "What is your age?" and "How old were you when you came to Mexico City?"
  [d] "Do you have close relatives or friends who live in the provinces?" If YES: "How frequently do you see them?"
  [e] "How frequently do you go to the provinces?"
  [f] "N" is less than 5.

Again, there is reason to believe that the selectivity of migrants (including the fact that most migrants come when young), the migrant experience, and the preference some employers have for employees of provincial origin may account for migrants' relatively successful adaptation to Mexico City—at least during a period of economic expansion[38]—just as it seems to contribute to the successful adaptation of sons of *campesinos* relative to children whose parents are otherwise employed. Rural-urban cultural forces are shaped by socioeconomic forces.

PESSIMISM AND PRESENT-ORIENTATION

The lower classes are typically depicted as "present-oriented"— as pessimistic and unwilling and unable to sacrifice immediate for future pleasure.[39] Proponents of cultural interpretations of poverty accordingly argue that if impoverished people want to improve their economic lot and if they are willing to forego instant rewards, they are likely to be economically mobile.

The interest that interviewed men expressed in changing jobs

---

city. "Out-migration" probably does not occur very frequently since migration to the capital is greater than migration from the capital, but it nevertheless does occur. Furthermore, Balán, Browning, and Jelin report in *Men in a Developing Society* that recent urban migrants appear to be less successful than earlier migrants, not because they have lived less long in the city but because they are less skilled in urban occupations and less educated and because some of the economic failures, not strongly rooted in the city, may have moved away shortly after arrival. None of the three areas house a large proportion of recent migrants. Therefore, mobility profiles of residents are not necessarily indicative of the less educated and skilled recent migrants who live in more peripheral sections of the capital.

[38] There is some evidence from Mexican and Argentine studies which suggests that migrants economically adapt well to cities mainly during periods of economic expansion but that their background does not otherwise necessarily inevitably predispose them to fare well in cities. See Balán, Browning, and Jelin, *Men in a Developing Society* and Germani, "Inquiry into the Social Effects of Urbanization in a Working Class Sector of Buenos Aires." In a declining economy, the point at which people enter the urban work force may be more important than in an expanding economy.

[39] Edward Banfield, in his *Unheavenly City*, defines socioeconomic classes by such cultural criterion. For critiques of the deferred gratification thesis see Harry Beilin, "The Pattern of Postponability and Its Relation to Social Class Mobility," pp. 33-48, and Miller, Frank Reissman, and Arthur Segull, "Poverty and Self-Indulgence: A Critique of the Non-Deferred Gratification Pattern," pp. 416-32.

and, above all, the aspirations they entertain for their children (e.g., 87 percent of the men want their children to be professionals or salaried white-collar workers) suggest that they are hopeful, particularly for their children's prospects. Their outlook is reflected in comments such as these:

> *Worker in a shoe factory*: "There is no reason why children should do the same type of work as their fathers. The obligation of fathers is to help children get ahead, to assure that they study so that they are better off than their parents by the time they marry."
>
> *Shoe artisan*: "I make shoes, just as my father did. But I want my children to do something better."
>
> *Metalworker*: "Children must learn something better than the *oficio* of their fathers."
>
> *Printer*: "I don't want my children to do the same type of work as I do. I want the best for them, that they study a career."
>
> *Baker*: "Children must live better than their parents. . . . It is the obligation of fathers to help their children to get ahead. For this reason I tell my son to study."

The optimism they entertain for their children stems from the faith they have in education as a channel of mobility, not from skills or capital that they intend to bequeath them. Given the limited effects education had on improving their own occupational prospects, their faith in education seems unrealistic: They themselves experienced little intergenerational occupational mobility relative to their intergenerational increase in education.

In contrast to their aspirations, their expectations seem pessimistic, particularly regarding their own job prospects. Apparently they have adjusted their own aspirations to what they more or less realistically can expect to attain.[40] They settle for displaced and vicarious gratification—through their children. If their pessimism about their own prospects is a *consequence*, not

---

[40] The tendency for people to resign themselves to their occupational fate at an early age seems to be a fairly universal response, at least in societies without "militant" political or labor groups. Eli Chinoy, in *Automobile Workers and the American Dream,* for example, points out that before age forty the automobile workers he studied realized how limited their opportunities were to climb the occupational ladder and they adjusted their hopes and expectations accordingly.

a cause of their immobility, we can conjecture that cultural influences tend to be structurally induced and that socio-economic forces assume the primary role in determining how labor is divided. Comments by workers reflect the way in which their perception of the economic situation affects their outlook:

Blacksmith: "It's difficult to change occupations. I see this in the blacksmith shop where I work. People come by looking for work, but they're not hired because they do not know the *oficio*. A friend of mine said that the same problem exists in the construction field."

Building guard: "It's especially difficult for older people like myself to find work. There is an age limit, after which it is very difficult to secure jobs. But it's also hard for young people to find work, because of 'favoritism.' One has to have good contacts."

Metalworker: "It's difficult to find work now because there are few jobs in the *oficio* in which I was trained."

Printer: "The main difficulty in finding work now stems from the fact that there are too many people and too few jobs, and that increasingly one needs to be more qualified to find work. At least one needs to have gone to school for increasingly more years in order to secure work. Yet there are many people like me who are not skilled and who have not gone to school."

Public accountant: "There are too many people with my type of training. Since we want to work, most of us have to work for little remuneration, thereby driving down the income one with such training should be able to earn."

Worker in a shoe factory: "The field of shoes is not my vocation. Due to family circumstances I had to work since I was young. I had wanted to study engineering. When one can't, one must accept the situation. Now I can't change *oficios*. . . . It's difficult to find work. The *patrones* are exploiters, thieves. They are concerned only with their own profits. It's particularly difficult for skilled workers, because there are few factories and the *patrones* don't want to pay more."

Construction worker: "Before there used to be many more jobs. The country has progressed over the years, but by means of industrialization. For example, whereas before each family used to make their own tortillas, now no one does. There are few mills where everyone buys their tortillas. And before I worked as a bricklayer on projects hiring more than 100 people. Now, if I am lucky enough to get a job, I am employed on projects with only about 10 people."

Several other manual workers mentioned that economic prospects were very limited for people like themselves because of the competitive labor market. As they see it, the problem stems from the changing nature of the economy and the growing pool of laborers in search of work. To the extent that they see the problem as an individual rather than a structural one, they see it as a problem of inadequate training.

While they are pessimistic about their own occupational prospects, other economic views they hold reflect optimism. The men believe that at least individually their families can rise within the system and want them to do so.[41] They also believe that they can improve their material level of well-being, independently of their occupational status, and hope to do so. Such optimism prevails even without a Mexican equivalent to the Horatio Alger myth. It seems to be generated by the economic system, an expanding economy, and political propaganda.[42] Furthermore, the migrants must have been optimistic and future-oriented or they would not have moved to the capital. Clearly, their low socioeconomic status is not attributable to feelings of despair.

However, low occupational status might instead derive from an inability or unwillingness to defer gratification. In particular, if the men have a proclivity to spend rather than save they are likely to use money which they could otherwise invest in educating their children or in building up a small family business. Interview questions dealing with consumerism suggest that herein lies their problem. They buy material goods which, in light of their income, they can ill-afford. For instance, more than 80 percent of the men have radios and more than half of them have

[41] Since countries such as Russia generate similar aspirations among different socioeconomic strata, hopes for individual mobility seem not to be linked specifically to private capitalism but to an economy expanding within a system of differential rewards. On Russia, see Inkeles and Bauer, p. 89. Independently of actual prospects for mobility, expanding production, together with government propaganda, apparently generates certain optimism.

[42] According to residents interviewed (see *supra* p. 128) economic development is a primary goal of the Mexican revolution.

television sets. Since only about 10 percent of them have savings, most of them are dependent on credit buying, making purchases all the more costly. Since, in addition, almost without exception the families felt it important to save money (91 percent), their spending habits seem to reflect a system which discourages them from saving and drives them to want such goods. The life-style of the "middle" and upper classes, the advertisements of the mass media, and the persuasion of door-to-door salesmen all seem to induce them to consume beyond their ability to pay. Industrial expansion—except that which is export-oriented—requires an ever-larger consumer market. Again, though, to the extent that cultural forces are important in shaping the men's economic life they are by-products of structural arrangements.

CUSTOM AND SUPERSTITION

Similarly, people oriented to the past are said to be less likely to accept work discipline, more likely to be fatalistic, and more likely to feel that they have little control over their environment than people who are future-oriented.[43] As a consequence, they supposedly are not motivated economically in a manner conducive to occupational mobility.

According to this line of argument, the men in the sample who hold the most coveted jobs should be, for example, the least superstitious and the most likely to adhere to scientific explanations of sickness and death. The data show that in comparison to the men partaking in traditional socioreligious activities—i.e., commemoration of deceased relatives on the Day of the Dead in a "folkloric" manner and use of herbs for medicinal purposes[44]—those who do not are more likely to be salaried nonmanual workers. Since, however, there is no consistent relationship among the men between their orientation toward sickness and death (as measured here), custom and superstition at most influence only certain "life chances" (Table 7).

[43] Inkeles, "Modernization of Man"; Walter Miller, in "Lower Class Culture as a Generating Milieu of Gang Delinquency," pp. 5-19.

[44] In using these indicators of "traditionalism" I do not wish to imply that the original meaning of these customs remains unchanged. Lewis, in "Urbanization Without Breakdown," for example, notes that although Tepoztecans in Mexico City continue to use herbs, they use herbs less for medicinal purposes and more for cooking than they did in Tepoztlan.

TABLE 7

Occupation of Men according to Traditionalism and Religiosity
(*percent*)

	Occupation				
	semi-skilled and un-skilled in small enter-prise	*inde-pendently employed*	*factory/ large enter-prise*	*salaried non-manual*	*Total*
What do Day of Dead[a]					
Traditional					
Activity	27	32	25	16	100 (100)
Nothing	18	28	15	39	100 (39)
Other	22	22	11	44	99 (9)
Use herbs for[b]					
Medicinal cure	25	31	25	19	100 (32)
Cooking	25[e]	33[e]	8[e]	33	99 (12)
Tea or No use	24	31	21	24	100 (95)
Frequency attend church (Catholics)[c]					
weekly	27	34	27	13	101 (64)
annually (not weekly)	27	21	23	29	100 (52)
rarely/never	14	41	14	32	101 (22)
Frequency confess[d]					
2+ times a year	27	31	23	19	100 (26)
Annually	26	13	45	16	100 (31)
Less than once a year	24	34	14	28	100 (85)

Based on the Questions:
  [a] "Did you celebrate the Day of the Dead last November?" If yes: "How did you celebrate it?"
  [b] "For what purposes do you use herbs?"
  [c] "How frequently do you attend religious services?"
  [d] "How frequently do you confess?"
  [e] "N" is less than 5.

RELIGION AND RELIGIOSITY

Historically, the rise of capitalism was closely associated with the rise of Protestantism. According to Max Weber, Protestants tended to be more successful economically, more involved in capitalist activities, and more inclined to accumulate savings than Catholics. Should religion in Mexico assume the same role it did in the past, differences among the two religious groups should exist, and Catholics should vary in their economic success depending on how religious they are.[45]

The Protestants in the sample are too few in number to permit safe generalizations. However, their job profiles suggest that conversion in itself did not cause them to be "upwardly mobile." Their job status did not generally improve after they changed religions.

Since the least religious Catholics, as measured by frequency of church attendance and confession, are the most likely to hold salaried jobs, religiosity if not religion may have some bearing on occupational success.[46] However, since religiosity bears no relationship to the likelihood that the men hold factory jobs, and since religious men are as likely to be factory workers as employed unskilled laborers, religiosity too at best is economically consequential only with respect to certain types of employment (Table 7).

Because most "penny" and medium-scale capitalists in an economy such as Mexico enjoy little social and economic security, if religion and religiosity motivate people economically, it seems to motivate them *not* to become small-scale "entrepreneurs" but to seek out the more rewarding white-collar jobs. Economic motivation is perhaps channeled into different career patterns in contemporary industrializing capitalist countries than in the countries which first industrialized, because financial and other rewards associated with the jobs in the two sets of countries differ.

[45] It should be kept in mind that Max Weber, in the *Protestant Ethic and the Spirit of Capitalism*, addressed himself to the conditions which initially gave rise to capitalism. He did not argue that the same relationship between religion and economic behavior necessarily held at later points in time.

[46] Gerhard Lenski suggests, in the *Religious Factor*, that people's degree of religious interest may have a greater bearing on economic advancement than their religious affiliation per se, at least in the United States.

There probably is greater competition among small-scale "capitalists" in the contemporary Third World than there was historically in the countries where capitalism originated, owing to the failure of capital-intensive industry to absorb a large proportion of the work force, including rural labor displaced by the capitalization of agriculture.

Not only does there seem to be no consistent relationship between religion, religiosity, and economic success, but the men themselves see no relationship between the two. In discussing the subject some of them commented as follows:

Metallurgist: "One learns religion from the time one is a child, but work is different. When I go to Mass I ask redemption for my sins. I don't go to ask for work."

Office worker: "Whether or not one is religious in no way affects one's work."

Baker: "The situation of the poor depends not on the will of God, but on what the head of each family does. The misery of the people stems more than anything from lack of good administration on the part of the head of the family."

Shoe artisan: "If God would hear us we wouldn't be as we are. Our situation primarily depends on our personal force. There are additional causes, like the lack of job opportunities. The religious fiestas, the pilgrimages and other religious activities are primarily a pretext to rest and go drink (*parranda*). People's faith is only momentary, nothing more. All is a question of luck and commitment."

Even those men who believe that their religion helps them economically generally recognize that it is not the only factor, and not necessarily the most important factor. According to a retired soldier, for example, "religion helps one feel better when faced with problems, but it doesn't help one resolve the problems." And a church-attending printer noted that "the ministers of the church do not help us resolve our economic problems."

Thus, biographical data on men in the three areas suggest that cultural factors are not the decisive influence determining the men's job success. To the extent that culture-linked attributes bear any relationship to economic status, they tend to be shaped by socioeconomic forces.

THE IMPACT OF PHYSICAL AND
SOCIAL ENVIRONMENT

The type of dwelling environment in which the men live, in addition, may shape their occupational prospects. Because the center city area physically most closely corresponds to an "area of blight" and the housing development to a "middle-class" residential community, if there is any relationship between physical or social environment and individual well-being, then people in *El Centro* should be least successful economically,[47] and residents of *La Unidad* the most successful. Because *La Colonia* is neither as deteriorated as *El Centro* nor as posh as *La Unidad colonos* should occupy a post in between.[48]

In the last chapter we saw that there were more businesses in *El Centro* than in either of the other areas. However, the most lucrative businesses there are owned and controlled by people who reside in other parts of the city and the employees of such businesses, particularly the factory employees, are for the most part not local residents. Moreover, the interviews with men residents reveal that center city dwellers are least likely to secure factory and white-collar employment (Table 8). Since there are no factories and few places hiring white-collar workers in either of the other areas, proximity to centers of employment is not the major factor determining accessibility to jobs.

Center city dwellers' low occupational status is particularly striking, given their educational credentials relative to those of residents of the two other areas: although 40 percent of the *colonos* and 46 percent of the residents of *La Unidad* with six or more years of schooling hold salaried white-collar jobs, only 27 percent of the center city dwellers with comparable education hold such jobs. Businessmen have not located their enterprises in *El Centro* because they find it propitious to be situated near a qualified pool of workers. Rather, as stated previously, factories are situated there for historical reasons: They were established at a time when the city was smaller, when land in the center city

47 Burgess, *The City*; and Perry, "The Neighborhood Unit." In reference to contemporary Latin America, see Portes, "The Urban Slum in Chile."

48 Charles Stokes, in "A Theory of Slums," calls such squatter settlements "slums of hope."

TABLE 8

Occupation of Men in Each of the Three Areas
(*percent*)

	Area of Residence		
	El Centro	La Unidad	La Colonia
semiskilled and unskilled in small enterprise	28	20	25
independently employed	45	22	27
factory/large enterprise	9	33	21
salaried nonmanual	19	26	27
TOTAL	101	101	100
	(47)	(51)	(52)

area was less expensive, and when it was legally easier to locate firms in residential areas than it is now.

Center city dwellers' failure to get jobs for which they are qualified, according to current Mexican standards, seems largely attributable to a combination of socioeconomic and community-linked forces. Their class backgrounds partially seem to account for the preponderance of local "penny capitalists," as more center city dwellers (33 percent) than residents of *La Unidad* (21 percent) or *La Colonia* (20 percent) had fathers who were independently employed. As previously shown, sons are more likely to pursue the same type of work as their father's than any other single type of work, although this is least true of sons of independently employed men.

Perhaps of greater significance, opportunities, exposure, experience, inherited equipment, and job contacts seem to predispose center city resident men, when young, to pursue artisan and commercial occupations. Economic opportunities for "penny capitalists" and small businessmen tend to be better in *El Centro* than in either of the other areas because historically the section has been a major commercial center, attracting customers from diverse parts of the city. As a consequence, people there have greater economic incentive to go into business for themselves than they do in either of the other areas. And because the area has long been an important center of cottage industry and small-scale commerce, children raised locally have been exposed to craft and "penny" commercial work since they were young. They often helped their parents and, in the case of artisans, even at times inherited tools from their fathers.

Furthermore, more men in *El Centro* than in either of the other areas tend to be employed in commercial ventures—and, to a lesser extent, craft production—probably because persons so employed there are not anxious to move. They enjoy the convenience of living near where they work. Ever since trades were established locally by the Franciscans in the colonial era many residents have worked in their homes or in neighborhood shops.

In addition, although the number of cases is too few to conclude with certainty, semi- and unskilled laborers and independently employed men in *El Centro* seem to have fewer factory and white-collar workers among their network of close relatives, *compadres*, and friends than do men similarly employed in the other areas, particularly in comparison to residents of *La Unidad*. Since contacts are critical for securing jobs, network ties also probably contribute to the apparently low rate of occupational mobility in *El Centro*.

Yet this seemingly small movement of educated center city dwellers into factory and white-collar jobs may well be characteristic mainly only of artisans and "penny capitalists," not of all residents of the area. According to discussions with residents and local leaders, white-collar inhabitants have been much more inclined to move away than artisans and "penny merchants," partly because their work is more separated from their living, but largely because their values and life-style are at odds with those of most center city dwellers. As noted in Chapter Two, "middle-class" residents tend to be the most critical and ashamed of the community. Since, in addition, informal interviews suggest that white-collar workers in *El Centro* are more likely to move to other parts of the city than residents of the other two areas who are similarly employed, center city area residents seem to have experienced more upward mobility than is apparent from the present-day composition of the area and the type of work interviewed men reported doing. Of the three areas, the center city area is most stigmatized by Mexicans as an immoral, vice-ridden, and unhealthy locale.

Thus, immobility among center city dwellers stems not primarily from subjection to a slum environment, nor from lack of schooling or distance from sources of employment. It stems mainly from class-linked tendencies.

Nevertheless, since residents of *La Unidad* have been more successful than residents of the other two areas, "middle-class" housing appears to have a positive economic effect on inhabitants. Yet upon closer examination their success is attributable not to their housing but to their socioeconomic background and status before moving to the area. Many more residents of *La Unidad* (32 percent) than center city dwellers (19 percent) or *colonos* (8 percent) had fathers who were white-collar workers; as we previously have seen, sons of salaried white-collar employees are more likely than sons of other occupational backgrounds to secure white-collar jobs. Moreover, recent arrivals to the development are of *higher* occupational status than the original settlers, even though they have been less exposed to the "middle-class" ambience of the area, and almost all of the factory and white-collar residents of the housing development had their jobs *before* moving to the area. They actually moved to the area *because* they held such jobs, even though the development, theoretically, was designed for persons displaced by public works and for impoverished persons living in areas the government wished to demolish. As we previously have seen, some families secured houses through the white-collar and industrial associations to which they belong and some workers and salaried white-collar employees obtained their homes through political contacts. Still others, because they had the means to do so, illegally paid off someone who officially had been allotted a house by the government. In moving to the area such persons merely consolidated their overall socioeconomic status;[49] they did not in the process improve their occupational standing. The main group of people who improved their job status in response to moving to the development were a group of men involuntarily moved by the government. Because they were unable to pay the rent, they were offered unskilled jobs in government agencies. But because they had to wait three months to get their first paycheck, only a small number of those offered the jobs were able to take advantage of the opportunity for job mobility.

[49] Similarly, Turner argues that movement from inner-city to peripheral urban areas reflects status "consolidation." See Turner, "Housing Priorities."

HOME OWNERSHIP AND CAPITAL ACCUMULATION

Since the value of urban land tends to rise over the years, the property owned by many families in *La Colonia* and *La Unidad* serves as a long-term investment. Furthermore, since rooms can be sublet or used as a shop or work place, since animals and vegetables can be raised on the land either for business or subsistence purposes, and since homes can be used as collateral for credit purposes, private property can be used for generating short-term economic gains as well. For such reasons, the "life chances" of the men could depend not on community of residence per se but on home ownership. In contrast to property owners, tenants can use their quarters as a workshop, but for little else economically.

Yet the low occupational status of center city dwellers stems *not* from their being tenants. Center city dwellers are the most likely to work in the area where they live and the most likely to be self-employed. Moreover, self-employed center city dwellers report higher earnings than men similarly employed in the other two areas.

Consequently, even though government housing and land programs have created favorable dwelling environments and provided men residents with a modicum of social and economic security, the programs have not generated "favorable investment climates" or access to new jobs. The programs have contributed to the formation of a propertied poor stratum, a stratum which we previously saw to be exposed to political regulation in the process of formation.

CONCLUSIONS AND IMPLICATIONS

The residents' job-"fate" is largely a by-product of class forces. Inequality linked to occupation tends to be perpetuated from one generation to the next along family lines mainly because of socioeconomic reasons. To the extent that cultural factors are important they tend to reflect adaptations to structural arrangements. Children whose fathers hold positions of dominance over their immediate work situation, even if not over the general market situation, have an advantage over other children. They tend to receive the best education and have the best network of contacts to help them secure jobs. Consequently, they also expect to do better, and probably strive accordingly.

These mechanisms operate on an individual level to perpetuate an inequality which originally stems from the father's occupational group affiliation, since it is this affiliation which largely determines his ability to provide his children with an education and useful job contacts.[50] Yet while most jobs related to industrial development are not directly inheritable, the labor force can be adapted to technological changes in a way which was not possible in guild or estate societies, and without loss of productivity. Furthermore, because employers generally take education or skill level into account in hiring workers, there is little contradiction between the desire of economic and political elites to maximize productivity and the formal and informal social mechanisms which tend to keep the labor force in self-perpetuating socioeconomic groups.

Nonetheless, despite the effect family background has on the men's occupational prospects, inter- and intragenerational job changes are considerable. However, these shifts tend more often than not to be between jobs differing little in the rewards they offer.

To the extent that social forces operating within the three areas reflect national forces, the data have policy implications. Schooling, adherence to values commonly labeled "modern," and dwelling environment do little in themselves to alter the men's "life chances." The best educated have access to the most economically and socially rewarding jobs, but because such jobs are not expanding as rapidly as schooling, education in itself provides no guaranteed job. Hence, programs aimed at expanding the education system are unlikely to alter significantly the socioeconomic position of persons of humble origin within the socioeconomic hierarchy in these areas or elsewhere in the city, unless education facilities for wealthier Mexicans are not commensurately expanded and new economic opportunities develop. Similarly, urban renewal and legalization of squatter settlements may resolve housing concerns of urban poor, but rarely their more pressing employment problem.

[50] In the case of sons brought up fatherless, their "life chances" probably depend on the socioeconomic status of their mothers or some father surrogate. Whether in fact the same processes operate in such cases is beyond the scope of our concern, but the problem merits systematic attention.

As evidenced in the three areas, the government thus far has done little to resolve the *most* fundamental problem plaguing Mexican urban poor: access to well-paying, secure employment and the social and economic benefits which are linked to occupation. To expand the number of such jobs the government would have to rely more heavily on labor-intensive industrialization. Yet, unless Mexico reduces its dependency on U.S. capital and unless government policies are altered to favor small- and medium- over large-scale enterprises, labor-intensive industries are unlikely to be able to compete effectively with capital-intensive ones, except through great labor exploitation. In order to equalize access to jobs for all persons, the government would have to provide social services such as child-care centers, so that children of diverse family backgrounds would be exposed to similar socialization experiences and similar opportunities from the time they were born. To the extent that schooling is a major criterion by which the labor force is divided—recently disputed by Jencks with respect to the U.S.[51]—the government would also have to develop an educational system that provided all students with the same quality and quantity of education.

To conclude, many of the same socioeconomic forces which tend to perpetuate occupation-linked inequality in advanced capitalist countries restrict the opportunities of men within the three areas. Most likely, they also restrict the opportunities of men within other parts of Mexico City, since the constraining influences operating locally are rooted in Mexico's political economy. Yet the job opportunities available in Mexico differ somewhat from those in the more highly industrialized capitalist economies, owing to the introduction of capital-intensive technology into a nation with a large supply of labor.

APPENDIX TO CHAPTER SEVEN:
OCCUPATION CLASSIFICATION

The criteria used in the classificatory schema are: (1) skill and technology; (2) scale of enterprise; and (3) ownership/nonownership of the means of production. The criteria were selected because they were assumed to measure the following phenomena:

Skill: the complexity of the work an individual performs;

[51] Christopher Jencks et al., *Inequality*.

Scale: the complexity of the administrative or production process in which an individual is involved;

Ownership/nonownership: control exercised by an individual within his immediate work setting.

The logically distinct occupational categories used in the analysis are based on the following combinations of these three factors:

1. *Peon, unskilled, semiskilled worker*: a person employed by someone else in a place employing less than twenty persons; the work done by such a person is generally believed to require little skill in comparison to the skills demanded of factory and white-collar jobs; examples include a gardener, domestic servant, artisan employed in a small shop, janitor, and night watchman;

2. *Factory worker or unskilled worker in large enterprise*: a person employed in an enterprise with twenty or more employees, as a factory hand or in some other manual capacity; the work he does generally requires skill and coordination of labor with other workers;

3. *Salaried white-collar employee*: a person not independently employed; the work he does generally offers job security, requires some formal training, and is defined as nonmanual; examples include a bureaucrat, secretary, and shop clerk;

4. *Independently employed*

a. *"penny capitalist"*: a person self-employed without hired assistance; he lacks resources, and possibly also training requisite for jobs in industry and administration; examples include an independent artisan and a market vendor;

b. *small businessman or professional with little specialized training*: a person who is self-employed, with sufficient skill and resources (e.g., hired employees, capital, technology) to define himself as a proprietor, e.g., a proprietor of an artisan shop or store; noncertified or minimally qualified professionals, e.g., a noncertified doctor or lawyer; since few persons in the sample fall within this category, they are considered in the following analysis together with the "penny capitalists."

The men interviewed are classified according to their principal occupation only.

CHAPTER EIGHT

The Poverty of Revolution: Mexican Urban Poor in Cross-National Perspective

Conditions within the three areas suggest that poverty and responses to poverty are largely shaped by the structure of the society at large, and that similarities and differences between urban poor cross-nationally therefore should be understood within the context of national institutional arrangements. Despite conditions unique to the three areas, residents are constrained by similar economic forces as are other urban poor in Mexico and other capitalist societies, particularly other semidependent Latin American capitalist societies. Some broad cross-national comparisons are made below, necessarily precluding specific national variations.

The postrevolutionary Mexican economy operates predominately according to capitalist principles, but it is not following the same path of development as northwest Europe and the United States. Mexico is not merely farther behind the advanced capitalist countries but dependent on those countries for technology, capital, and trade. Furthermore, it is developing within a vertically structured corporately organized social order, rooted in its Indian and Spanish colonial heritage but reinforced by the structure of the contemporary political economy. The corporate order contains both geographic and occupation-based groups, but the groups wield political influence mainly on the basis of their importance to capitalist production and the nature of their ties to the government.

As groups emerge, they tend to be formally incorporated into the state apparatus through the PRI when they involve lower, working, and certain "middle-class" persons, and through direct but not publicly obvious ties to the government when they involve capitalists. In the process the government opportunistically attempts to gain the support of all groups by acting and promising to act in their interests.

Because group interests conflict, the government initiates contradictory policies. Although the formal political structure, the populist revolution-linked ideology, and the responsiveness of the government to demands of urban poor for land and social services, all convey the impression that the government primarily identifies with "popular" forces, its economic policies unequivocally favor capitalists over other groups. The benefits extended to capital often are indirect, in the form of tax benefits and tariff protection, but they generate much more income than the direct material benefits extended to "popular" PRI-affiliated groups. Not merely unregulated market forces but also specific government policies serve the interests of the numerically small economic group that wields no official political power.

Since the real bases of societal power do not rest in the formal political apparatus and since decision-making power is concentrated in the executive, formal political incorporation provides no guaranteed influence on government policy formation or law enforcement. Primarily, formal political incorporation contributes to the legitimation of the government. At the same time it makes groups share responsibility for government policies which they do not help make, policies which in effect often discriminate against them. As a consequence, those formally co-opted can neither effectively organize to defend their own interests nor be readily available for demagogic manipulation by dissatisfied members of the elite. Formal incorporation into the political-administrative apparatus generates these effects even though the people involved may be unaware of their political affiliations and the political ramifications of these affiliations.

These national forces shaped political life in the urban areas I studied. They influenced group formation, structure, and concerns, and relations between groups. Informal constraints—hierarchical, class and corporate-group pressures, and the government's co-optative and repressive resources—rooted in the general political economy, in turn, inhibited local poor from using those groups to which they gained access principally for their own ends. Consequently, even though groups helped establish institutionalized ties between the community and its inhabitants, on the one hand, and authoritative national groups, on the other, they led neither to increased pluralistic pressure group politics nor to class polarization.

Local leaders established ties with regional and national functionaries because they wished both to secure benefits for their constituents and to maintain and extend their own spheres of influence. They felt that the ties would serve these ends, although they did not necessarily realize that thereby their political effectiveness would diminish and that their interests would be subordinated to those of higher-ranking functionaries and the economic interests the state protects. Paradoxically, local groups became less politically effective when they affiliated with revolution-linked national organizations and institutions. Also paradoxically, the groups' political effectiveness was undermined precisely when they seemed to be most effective: when they received land, public facilities, and other benefits from the state. This situation developed because they were at that point subjected to political and social deterrents and controls, regulating local demand-making and political participation. As a consequence, the local groups, organized along territorial lines, were exposed to nonlocal influences which subordinated their interests indirectly to those of the well-to-do, organized along occupational lines, and directly to those in command of the state apparatus. Hence, local trends reflect general post-revolutionary trends: i.e., the centralization of territorial politics and the increased importance of corporate-occupational group politics with lower-status groups being subordinated to privileged groups.

As local associations established ties with national political and administrative institutions they became more alike, even when they initially were founded for different reasons. This tended to be equally true of autonomous groups as of groups formally affiliated with the PRI and the government. Generally, organizations were subordinated to higher-ranking functionaries, de facto if not de jure, both because they could not independently accomplish their goals since they had few resources of their own, and because ambitious group leaders otherwise could not advance.

Although differences between groups diminished once relations within the areas were routinized, they never entirely disappeared. Neither those organizations which were formed at the initiative of nonlocal authorities nor those which were formed independently were rigidly synchronized and subordinated to the goals of national authorities. Current differences reflect contrasting "clientelistic" contacts cultivated by local residents, contacts without which groups could not easily procure goods and services from the government and individuals could not easily move ahead politically and economically. Above all, though, differences have come to reflect the socioeconomic status of group members and leaders, independent either of the conditions which initially gave rise to the groups or of their stated objectives. These class biases reflect those operating in the society at large, linked to the dynamics of Mexican capitalism and to the governmental policies which favor capitalists—and, to a lesser extent, salaried "middle-class" and organized workers—over urban and rural poor.

However, not only have inter- and intragroup relations generally served to reproduce the bases of stratification prevailing in the society at large, but so have government-allocated benefits. The government benefits rarely reduced inequities in the national distribution of wealth and power, and the administration took little from the well-to-do to give to the poor. Such political reforms as the extension of the franchise, formal inclusion of opposition parties in Congress, and the government's proclaimed concern with *apertura democrática* convey the impression that the state is becoming more responsive to popular and divergent interests. However, the reforms in fact strengthen the stability of the government since they enable the state to incorporate and thereby control a larger proportion of the population. Because the formal political apparatus wields no autonomous political power these reforms reflect merely the extension of the symbols of power, not power itself.

Similarly, the increased access of urban poor to public schooling, to government housing subsidies, and urban services has had little effect on reducing economic inequality. Schooling often is an important prerequisite for well-paying and prestigious jobs, but the quality and quantity of education children receive depends largely on their socioeconomic background. Thus, as urban poor have become better educated so, too, have the more prosperous stratum. Furthermore, as the general educational level of the population has risen, many employers have raised educational prerequisites for jobs. Job opportunities for the poor have not concomitantly increased, because the job structure is shaped primarily by economic exigencies, not by schooling. On the other hand, low-cost government-financed housing, government-enforced rent control, and legalization of squatters' land claims provide urban poor with a solution to their housing problem, an indirect subsidy providing a modicum of security cushioning the impact of economic crises, but these subsidies provide no guaranteed minimum subsistence income.[1]

Undoubtedly because the government is financially dependent on capital it tends not to initiate economic redistribution programs. It probably will continue to act accordingly unless either the economic importance of capitalism declines, owing, for example, to a crisis in international capitalism, or capitalists come to feel that redistributive measures serve their interests. Should they, for example, come to believe that a more equitable allocation of national wealth will stimulate consumer demand, and, in turn, production and profits, or that it will mute civil disorder, they may well support redistributive schemas which appear to conflict with their immediate class interests.

Politics and administration do not provide resident poor with institutionalized bases for protecting their own interests; likewise, the structure of the local and national economies is such that the poor rarely are effective in securely improving their social and economic standing through market mechanisms. This is at least true of residents who by choice or default remain in the three areas. The dynamics of Mexican capitalism, and the corporate structure associated with it, shape business opportunities within the areas, and residents' limited job contacts, capital, and skills put them at a disadvantage relative to those nonresidents who enjoy such resources. As a result, nonresident petty bourgeoisie and capitalists tend to benefit at the expense of local inhabitants. However, a small proportion of residents successfully either establish businesses or find work in the areas where they live, particularly in *El Centro* with its unique socioeconomic history.

The same forces which limit the employment opportunities for residents in the areas where they live also restrict their opportunities in other parts of the capital. Consequently, the economic success of resident men depends largely on their class background, even though they rarely inherit their fathers' line of work directly through property transference. The economically most successful are sons of salaried white-collar workers, persons who could not automatically follow in their father's "footsteps."

[1] In other sections of the capital, especially in the State of Mexico, the government has indirectly or directly extended other housing benefits: for example, *de facto* recognition of squatters claims to housing and government-sponsored self-help site-and-services projects.

Furthermore, the men who occupationally are most upwardly mobile are sons of independently employed "penny capitalists," precisely those who could have inherited their fathers' businesses.

However, the men's job opportunities throughout the city have been determined not merely by socioeconomic forces. They also have been shaped by government policies, directly and indirectly. Zoning restrictions, the Labor Code, and other laws influence where businesses locate, the size of enterprises, and the benefits workers receive. Similarly, nonenforcement of laws, like those dealing with minimum wages and social security, affect residents' job opportunities; if such laws were implemented, low-profit, labor-absorbing enterprises would be forced out of business, in which case fewer jobs would be available for residents. Direct employment by the state and government regulation of neighborhood markets influence still other economic opportunities for residents. Through the Division of Markets the government controls work conditions among vendors, facilitating the survival of small-scale ventures which otherwise might not be able to compete with better capitalized and better organized commercial enterprises.

The government and market forces have enabled certain local poor to acquire property (or low-rent housing) and jobs at the same time that it nationally favors large-scale capitalists. Its pro-labor-absorbing stance actually helps resolve contradictions generated by dependent capitalist development, although it creates other problems in the process. The small businesses absorb some of the labor which large-scale capital-intensive businesses do not, thereby mitigating unemployment and the political crisis which long-term unemployment might generate.[2] However, because their labor is not very productive the state, in supporting labor-intensive enterprises, not only acts against the immediate interests of capital but also fails to maximize production and state revenues. Thus, while such policies may help the state maintain "popular" legitimacy they simultaneously contribute to the country's continued dependent world economic status.

Accordingly, class and political forces contribute to the per-

[2] Evidence from other Third World countries indicates that anti-government protest behavior among urban poor is potentially greatest under conditions of high unemployment. Hobsbawm, "Peasants and Rural Migrants in Politics," p. 67; Portes, "Urbanization and Politics in Latin America"; Cohen, *Urban Policy and Political Conflict in Africa*.

petuation and expansion of small-scale craft and commercial enterprises, not to their disappearance. Capitalism has created within its interstices a stratum which identifies with the margins of "bourgeois" life: a petty bourgeoisie who will not and wish not be proletarianized. As domestic capitalism advances this stratum may grow in number, but through the addition of homologous units, not a more complex division of labor. The work of the petty bourgeoisie isolates them from one another and forces them into indirect competition. As a result they are weak politically. While many of them formally belong to politically affiliated economic associations the associations are, for the most part, politically ineffectual. The structure both of economic and of political relations is such that their interests are, at best, represented through the executive. They do not represent themselves. Much like the peasantry in the aftermath of the French Revolution who for similar structural reasons found their representative in Bonaparte, this urban stratum finds its representative in a more institutionalized authoritarian politico-administrative apparatus. They do not provide a political base for a liberal democratic capitalist regime.

Because many urban poor in Mexico and other Latin American countries with no comparable revolutionary history have for more than four centuries been exposed to similar international capitalist constraints, their "fates" tend to be similar, even if not identical. Under colonial rule Latin American nations were organized along corporatist lines and integrated into the international mercantile system in a subordinate position. Since Independence the societies have industrialized, to different degrees, within an adapted corporatist-capitalist framework, with heavy reliance on foreign capital and technology. In these countries, particularly in the semidependent ones, capitalist forces have produced more or less parallel effects on the structure of economic opportunities and access to those opportunities as in Mexico.

In Chile, under Allende, urban poor acquired a marked increase in social, urban, and housing benefits and their relative economic standing improved somewhat, as a result of top-level government policies. But as in Mexico, they never attained institutional power on the national level, despite "popular" grassroots political participation. The foreign pressures which debilitated the regime economically and politically and the repressive pro-capitalist, anti- lower- and working-class *junta* which later

illegitimately assumed power suggest that Latin American regimes supporting redistributive policies are unlikely to succeed
within the current world capitalist order.

Similar cross-national inequities in income and land distribution give added credence to the thesis advanced here that Mexico's ostensibly democratic political institutions—its mass-based
party, multiple party system, regularly scheduled elections, and
universal franchise—do not serve as means by which urban and
rural poor, on the basis of their numerical strength and legitimate political organizations, can effectively advance their own
interests. Otherwise, Mexican urban poor would be better off
than their economic counterparts in nondemocratic Latin American countries.

The nominally different governments similarly subordinate interests of urban poor to capital,[3] although those with a less effective revolution-linked hegemonic formal political apparatus, such
as Brazil, have had to use more repressive regulatory controls.
Institutions, such as the PRI, which regulate urban poor in Mexico are unique to the country, but the hierarchical personalistic,
clientelistic, and class-based relations and the types of largely
non-redistributive economic benefits extended to urban poor in
Mexico are found in other Latin American countries as well.

The urban poor portrayed here share common experiences not
merely with urban poor in other semidependent capitalist countries but also with those in advanced capitalist countries. Although the stratum is numerically larger in the former set of
countries, irrespective of the degree of industrialization all urban
poor in capitalist economies are handicapped by their class background: persons of lower status origins have restricted access to
jobs and opportunities to exert political influence through legitimate political channels. Even in the U.S., where political power
is officially more decentralized than in Mexico, urban poor are
unable to effectively pressure for a reduction in income inequality through the ostensibly pluralistic, democratic party apparatus. As in Mexico, most effective initiatives in the U.S. for elimi-
nating poverty and improving conditions associated with poverty

[3] Similarly, Schmitter argues that Latin American regimes have much
greater historical continuity than is apparent from the official forms of government. In particular, he discusses the underlying continuities in the Brazilian *sistema*, despite shifts from civilian to military rule. Schmitter, "The
'Portugalization' of Brazil?," pp. 179-232.

come from the federal government, and those initiatives have been negligible except when the U.S. government has been threatened by major domestic economic and political crises.[4]

Despite these similarities, the Mexican and U.S. urban poor differ in important ways, owing to variations in the structure of the Mexican and U.S. capitalist economies. These variations are linked to the contrasting conditions under which the societies have been developing historically, not to different stages in a single unilinear development process. In the U.S., urban poor enjoy a higher standard of living, and the percentage of the population living at a subsistence level is less. Yet there are proportionally more *propertied* poor in Mexico: that is, persons who own the "means of production" or urban land.[5] Mexico also has fewer unemployed poor, mainly because it has no public unemployment relief system comparable to that of the U.S., and because the Mexican government has deliberately protected certain small-scale commercial and productive enterprises. Moreover, although individuals in both countries have experienced inter- and intra-generational occupational mobility—both "up" and "down" the socioeconomic hierarchy—proportionally fewer Mexicans have experienced mobility into the working class; despite industrial expansion the working class is barely increasing in the proportion of the labor force it absorbs, owing to the capital-intensive nature of much industry, particularly foreign-financed industry.

Even the nature and location of housing available to urban poor in the two countries differ: in lieu of the centrifugal, "invasion and succession" pattern of tenant residency found in many early industrial cities in the U.S., in Mexico urban poor increasingly live in vertically integrated new areas on the periphery of metropolitan centers, frequently in small owner-occupied homes established through an aggregative process. Such housing in

[4] For example, increased welfare benefits and the "Great Society" programs of the 1960s were established under the initiative of the Federal Government, undercutting both state and local government. The extension of these federal benefits was largely a response to the disorder caused by ghetto riots. See Frances Piven and Richard Cloward, *Regulating the Poor*.

[5] Other Latin American governments also deliberately allocate small property to urban poor. See Collier, *Squatters and Oligarchs*, and Mauricio Solaún, Fernando Cepeda and Bruce Bagley, "Urban Reform in Colombia," pp. 97-130. The authors of the latter article argue that all proposed urban programs designed to meet the urban crisis in Colombia envision the creation of an environment in which each family owns its dwelling.

Mexico is legally or informally recognized and at times encouraged by the state.

Furthermore, both the economic subsidies extended to urban poor and the manner in which the benefits are distributed contrast in Mexico and the U.S. Mexico offers its urban poor no direct economic assistance. It extends no direct income benefits comparable to those provided in the U.S. through the Aid to Families with Dependent Children Program, and no work incentive schemas. In Mexico economic assistance, at best, is indirect. Furthermore, it consists mainly of de jure recognition of de facto illegal land claims by urban poor, and access to competitive, nonprofitable small-scale enterprises.

While the benefits in the U.S. are allocated through impersonal bureaucratic channels, in Mexico they are allocated through paternalistic institutions. The different distributive methods reflect —in Weberian terms—the U.S.'s more rational legal government administration and Mexico's more patrimonial-populist government administration. Since Mexico's patrimonial-like system is deliberately re-created in new areas and in new groups in already existing areas, as they emerge, the cross-national differences reflect different authoritative principles upon which the two governments are premised, not merely the persistence of long-established political institutions. The continued patrimonialism helps the government gain and maintain the support of the ever-increasing number of urban poor. The urban poor, in turn, contribute to the government's stability and its modicum of independence from capital.

The level of well-being of Mexican urban poor differs not only from that of urban poor in the U.S. and other advanced capitalist countries but also from that of urban poor in such socialist countries as Cuba. The differences in the two types of "underdeveloped" societies are rooted, above all, in the differing structures of their economies and government policies.[6] To the extent that the Castro government regulates its urban poor in the process of extending benefits to them, it does so for different ends: to institute a contrasting type of political economy. Schooling and health care are more available to Cuban than to Mexican urban poor.

[6] For data on the expansion and distribution of goods and services and rural-urban trends since the Cuban revolution, see Jorge Domínguez, "The Performance of the Cuban Revolution"; Barkin and Manitzas (eds.), *Cuba*; and Rolando Bonachea and Nelson Valdés (eds.), *Cuba in Revolution*.

Furthermore, income is more equitably distributed in Cuba than in Mexico, and the poorest city-dwellers in Cuba also are not faced with the same housing problems as are urban poor in Mexico and other dependent capitalist countries. Although there still are shortages of housing and deteriorated buildings in Cuba, rent there never exceeds 10 percent of workers' salaries. New housing is planned and distributed through work groups on the basis of need and work contributions, not market forces and manipulation of private property by corrupt *políticos* and land speculators. Moreover, because the government is deliberately expanding social and economic opportunities in the provinces, urbanization—and associated urban plight—is not increasing as rapidly in Cuba as in Latin American capitalist countries. Above all, though, Cuban men, unlike their counterparts in capitalist economies, have guaranteed employment, and rarely as "penny capitalists," since small businesses were nationalized in 1968. Consequently, the lower socioeconomic stratum is not subject to the same degradation, unstable income, and job insecurity in Cuba as in countries with a market economy. Mainly because the Cuban state identifies above all with proletariat interests state power is used for different ends there than in capitalist countries where the state protects above all the interests of capital.

While nationalization of the "means of production" might reduce urban squalor and improve the living conditions of urban poor in Mexico, only if the government allocated the resources it thereby acquired primarily to urban poor would the conditions presently associated with city poverty be improved and social and economic inequality in the society at large be reduced. As long as capitalism remains the dominant economic force, nationalization of certain segments of the economy, which has increased since the Cardenas era, is unlikely to do much to improve urban plight.

Because the prospects of socialism and other political movements mainly committed to the interests of the poor presently are meager in Mexico,[7] the "life chances" of the poor are not likely to improve greatly in the three areas or elsewhere in the country. If the economy continues to expand, the standard of living of the

[7] Many of those who participated in the 1968 protest were not Marxists but critics of specific government policies. They focused on the lack of civil liberties, not economic inequities.

poor may rise. The decline in the rate of economic and job expansion, the rise in inflation and consumer prices, and soaring
population growth suggest that the economic prospects for the
poor are not great. In 1974 an estimated 5.7 percent of Mexico
City's economically active population were unemployed and 35.3
percent were underemployed,[8] while consumer prices increased
at an annual rate of 23.3 percent nationally and even more rapidly in the capital.[9] And in the 1965-70 interim Mexico had the
highest population growth rate not only in its history but in the
history of Latin America.[10]

Moreover, as long as existing class and power relations remain
intact, the standing of urban poor relative to the well-to-do is unlikely to improve. The one economic benefit increasingly available to urban poor, land, has a conservatizing effect: in the process of securing land recipients develop a stake in the status quo
and they are subjected to social and political controls.

To date, the main organized opposition to the government has
been pro-capital and linked with the PAN. On the few occasions
when leftist or anti-status quo opposition has been articulated it
generally has been either co-opted or repressed, as exemplified
by the massacre and imprisonment of student protestors in 1968.
Rebel peasants are more concerned with limited access to land
than with basic political and economic change, and the government has responded to their aggressiveness mainly by co-opting
and repressing them, or by extending limited land, capital, and
technology to them in such a way as to reestablish political order.
Thus, the main challenge to the regime currently is, in Barrington Moore's words, "capitalist and reactionary."[11]

[8] *Excélsior*, June 21, 1975, 10A, cited in Cornelius, *Politics and the Migrant Poor*, p. 231.

[9] *Latin America*, May 30, 1975, p. 163.

[10] *Economic Bulletin for Latin America* 18 (1973), p. 97.

[11] Moore argues that there are three possible modernization paths: (1)
capitalism and the gradual evolution of democracy; (2) fascism and "revolutions from above," when countries try to modernize "without changing their
social structure"; and (3) Communism and peasant revolutions (Barrington Moore, *Social Origins of Dictatorship and Democracy*). Although
the Mexican government does not glorify militarism and stress violence, it
has other characteristics generally associated with fascism: it emphasizes hierarchy, authority and order, and it has a corporatist-capitalist political economy. Since the Mexican regime contains such "fascistic" elements, despite
the violent peasant-fought upheaval in the early part of the century, "capitalist and reactionary" regimes arise not only in the absence of revolutions.

As a result, even though many of the *campesino* forbears of today's urban poor fought a violent social revolution, partly in *opposition* to capitalist penetration of the countryside, today's urban poor experience negative as well as positive benefits from the country's capitalist expansion. The regional and class contradictions generated by the country's pattern of economic growth, exacerbated by the country's high rate of population growth, may ultimately precipitate new revolutionary pressures for a more egalitarian society, but the foreseeable future of these poor looks bleak. "Revolutionary" institutions are being used to regulate the poor.

Contrary to Moore's contention, the Mexican case suggests that a peasant-fought revolution may facilitate the institutionalization of capitalism as the *dominant* mode of production in all sectors of the economy when (1) Communists neither constitute a leading political force in the revolution nor gain control of the government in the course of the revolution; (2) the power of the domestic commercial and industrial elite increases and the power of the landed oligarchy collapses or weakens; and (3) the absolute power of the urban elite remains sufficiently weak so that it cannot gain and maintain power without the support of the peasantry (and the urban poor, as the country becomes increasingly urbanized).

Methods and Ethics

Findings of any study are intrinsically related to the theoretical paradigms scholars use, and these paradigms, in turn, reflect scholars' implicit if not explicit ideological biases. My conceptual framework, subject of study, and time and financial constraints in part influenced my choice of methods. However, while I tried to conform with the established criteria of "scientific" inquiry both by maximizing the reliability and validity of my data and by doing quantifiable sample survey research, my work has convinced me that researchers' findings are shaped above all by their ideological presuppositions. No large funded survey of urban poor in itself would have enabled me to adequately comprehend the importance structurally rooted forces have on shaping urban poverty. As I delineate below, in the process of doing my research I clarified my theoretical understanding of my problem of inquiry, and shifted my methodological priorities accordingly. I describe the sources I used; how and why I modified my perspective, and my research design accordingly; and some of the ethical dilemmas my field work, willy-nilly, raised.

APPROACHES USED

For my in-depth study of the three areas of Mexico city I relied on a multi-approach method to get different types of information and to check the accuracy of the data secured from any one source. In describing the methods I discuss their utility for the book.

Formal and Informal Interviews with Residents

1. *Survey of Residents.* The quantitative data dealing with inhabitants of the three areas, contained primarily in Chapters Two, Five, and Seven, derive from formal interviews in 1967-68 with 300 residents. Since no detailed household census of the areas was available from which to draw a sample, I made a door-to-door census of a select number of blocks from diverse sections

of the communities. From this census I selected one hundred households in each of the three areas for the sample: in half the cases men were to be interviewed, in the other half women. I substituted neighboring households in the thirteen cases (twelve male and one female) when there was no one of the designated sex in the households selected for the sample and in the four instances when respondents (two male and two female) refused to be interviewed.

To secure information on the social, economic, and political behavior, attitudes, and perceptions of residents, in line with my original theoretical perspective, I designed a questionnaire for this sample which included questions pertaining to respondents' social and economic background; their informal social contacts; their integration into and attitudes toward their community of residence; their perceptions of the local communities; their assessment of how the local area changed over the years and how they would like it to change; their work and general economic situation; the economic mobility they experienced and aspired to; their class identification; their material level of well-being and mass media exposure; their participation in "voluntary associations" and other groups; the social and economic aspirations and expectations they hold for their children; their evaluation of the general social and economic situation in Mexico; their involvement in, knowlege of, and attitude toward politics, civic matters, and the Church; and their view of the role of the U.S. in Mexico. Before I finalized the questionnaire I interviewed inhabitants informally about the topics related to my subject of inquiry and read studies of Mexican urban poor. After approximately three months of field work I developed a formal interview schedule with the assistance of Mexicans. Where possible I included questions previously contained in studies made by other social scientists so that the findings could be systematically compared. After a pretest I partially revised the questionnaire. I then had social work and sociology students with interview experience administer the questionnaire, under my close supervision. The interviewers met with few problems, although in a number of cases they had to make several visits to locate the people selected for the sample, gain the confidence of the interviewees, or complete the interviews. The questionnaire appears in Appendix B.

2. *Survey of Protestants.* In 1971 the Instituto Mexicano de

Estudios Sociales (IMES) administered a modified version of the above questionnaire, together with additional questions dealing with religious behavior and attitudes, to a sample of Protestants in the two areas with Protestant congregations—*El Centro* and *La Colonia*. I drew the sample from membership lists provided by the ministers of the congregations.

I added this "purposive" sample to learn more about the types of people who convert to Protestantism and what effect, if any, Protestantism has on residents' economic life. My analysis of the original survey showed interesting differences in occupational mobility among Protestants and Catholics, but because I had only a small number of Protestants I was uncertain whether the differences were statistically significant.

Although I had the backing of local ministers I encountered more difficulties administering this questionnaire than the first one. Interviewers had to spend considerable time convincing the Protestants that the study was not going to be used to persecute them for their religious beliefs. Some interviewers even went so far as to attend church in order to win the confidence of the Protestants. However, once the Protestants trusted the interviewers the difficulties subsided and the interviews frequently ended with the Protestants giving the interviewers Bibles, extending invitations to attend church, or saying prayers on behalf of the interviewers. Because of the research difficulties and marginal importance of these interviews to the study, I limited this sample to twenty. Textual data from this survey appear in Chapter Seven.

3. *In-depth Interviews with Male Residents.* In 1971 I also had university students with interview experience conduct "in-depth open-ended" interviews with two dozen men in the three areas who differed occupationally. These interviews provided me with a better understanding of the experiences and attitudes male residents differently employed had than did the formal questionnaires. I include material from these inquiries primarily in Chapter Seven.

4. *Informal Interviews with Residents and Group Members.* In addition, I regularly spoke informally with residents, including with diverse, locally employed persons, local group members, and other residents to learn about their perceptions of social, economic, and political life in the communities and Mexico in general. During these interviews I always had questions firmly

in mind. From these informal discussions I learned about local businesses, and about informal and formal group life, from the point of view of rank-and-file residents. However, since they, for the most part, had only a limited understanding both about the groups and about the history of the local communities, I used this information mainly to supplement and help me assess the validity of the information I obtained through the interviews with local leaders. Such interview materials proved particularly useful for the three chapters on politics and the one on the political econo-mies of the local areas.

Formal and Informal Interviews with Community Leaders

Chapters Two-Five contain information from interviews with local leaders. I did most of these interviews in 1967-68, although in 1971 I reinterviewed local leaders. The leaders with whom I spoke were mainly persons in charge of formally chartered groups or divisions of institutions operating locally, that is, "positional elites."[1] I located them by visiting all visible local in-stitutions and group headquarters, asking persons in charge of those facilities for names and addresses of other formal groups active in the areas, speaking with personnel at the places they named, and asking those personnel, in turn, the same question. I continued this procedure until I learned of no new groups.

In the case of subunits of city-wide or national groups, I inter-viewed not only the heads of the local units, but also their non-local superiors to whom they were formally responsible in their organizational hierarchy. I also spoke with persons affiliated with groups working in the three areas which had no local headquar-ters. Such nonlocal persons were interviewed because they as well as locally based leaders shaped relations within the commu-nities, and because I could cross-check their responses with those of their local subordinates.

The "positional" leaders interviewed included all parish priests (7); all leaders of parish-wide lay groups (4); all local ministers (9); directors of all local parochial schools and church-linked hospitals (3); nonresident religious personnel who worked lo-cally (4); local administrators of government-run facilities, i.e., directors of at least one shift of all public primary and secondary

[1] On the "positional" approach see Robert Schulze and Leonard Blumberg, "The Determination of Local Power Elites," pp. 216-22; and Robert Dahl, *Who Governs?* pp. 63-71.

schools (20), and directors of all medical and other social service agencies (6), all sports facilities (6), and all markets (10) in the areas; all *subdelegados* (the highest-ranking local functionaries of the territorial based organization of the municipal government (4) and their nonlocal hierarchical superior; the administrator of the housing development; personnel in government agencies concerned with the areas, e.g., the agencies which designed the housing development and handled problems in the squatter settlement relating to legalization of land claims and provision of basic social services; six of the ten highest-level local representatives of political parties; all heads of territorial based politically affiliated social groups (2); local officers of the association of market vendors (10 of 15); and all formally organized nominally autonomous social groups (3).

The interviewed leaders generally were asked open-ended questions about the following issues:

1. *The group (organization, institution) they headed*: the nature of organizational tasks their group undertook; the objectives of their group; accomplishments of their group; the activities in which they were empowered to engage; budgetary resources and sources of material assistance; how their group changed since they assumed leadership of it; how their group differed from other local groups and (when applicable) other divisions of their same parent organization; the frequency of and reasons for contact with other local and nonlocal groups; and the internal formal and actual structuring of their group.

2. *Biographical data*: the way in which they obtained their post; other positions they previously held and presently hold, and how they obtained them; their future ambitions.

3. *General questions about the local communities*: how the areas have changed over the years; who was responsible for the changes and when the changes occurred; names of other groups presently and previously operating locally (including groups with no local headquarters), the names of the heads of the groups, and the accomplishments of the groups; incidences of conflict and disharmony within the areas; and general information about residents.

Because of their positions and socioeconomic background "positional" leaders tended to be more knowledgeable about the local areas and more skillful observers than "ordinary" residents, although many of the nonresident ones who were commissioned to work locally had only limited familiarity with the communities and only limited contact with persons in the communities.

Through information I elicited from these positional leaders I tried to chart the social structure of each of the communities. However, owing to time limitations my analysis necessarily focused more on reported interaction patterns than on observations of actual operations of local groups and the activities of local leaders over time. Since I not only used other sources of information but also interviewed most local leaders several times, I could compare and therefore check the accuracy of each of their reports. When the leaders reported contradictory information, I, in subsequent interviews, asked questions to uncover inconsistencies.

I further learned about the communities through interviews with leaders located by the "reputational" approach sometimes employed in "community power" studies.[2] Each time I spoke with positional leaders I asked them to name the three persons in the community who had the greatest wealth, power, and prestige, and when "common" residents were interviewed they were asked to name the persons whom they considered most important locally.[3] I made contact with the three other-than-positional leaders who were cited two or more times, one of whom no longer lived locally. I also spoke with persons who positional leaders said formerly were important. From them I learned about previous conditions in the areas and why they now are inactive locally.

Since in the course of interviews with the leaders located by these two techniques it became evident to me that local leaders lacked institutionalized authoritative power, I relied on them largely as informants about the local communities, not as a total or representative sample of the local community power structures.

A few of the leaders I interviewed served as key informants. They were persons with whom I established especially close rap-

[2] Floyd Hunter, *Community Power Structure*, pp. 262-71.

[3] In the pre-test, residents were asked to name the three wealthiest, most powerful, and most prestigeful local persons. Because most respondents were unable to name persons in the three categories, in the final questionnaire I revised the question to read: "What are the names of the three most important persons in the *colonia* (*la unidad*)?"

port and talked regularly. They generally confided in me and informed me about local conflicts and aspects of community life which they thought would interest me. They also invited me to civic and political activities, within the areas and in other parts of the city. Since I used these informants only as one of several sources of information, my findings were not biased by what to me is a basic limitation of the key informant approach: that informants, however honest they may be, portray the community only through their own "lenses."

Participant-observation

In general, I observed as much of local life as possible while I worked within the areas, to get a feeling for the local communities, to sensitize me to local issues and styles of interaction, and to establish a contextual framework within which I could evaluate and comprehend the material I obtained through other research techniques. By attending meetings of the different social and political groups that convened locally during the period I was there I could discern the degree to which leaders and rank-and-file members accurately portrayed their groups to me. However, because some groups rarely if ever met during my stay in Mexico, and because transactions at meetings reveal only limited aspects of groups, these observations served primarily to supplement and validate other information I obtained.

While I also engaged in participant-observation by socializing with residents, this information was not central since my study focuses on the relationship between local and national political, economic, religious, and social institutions, not on individuals and families. I mixed informally with residents largely because I felt both a desire and a commitment to respond to their hospitality, a reluctance to limit my local contacts merely to those serving my specific research interests, and because I was enjoying, and often learning a lot on such occasions. In calculating the amount of time necessary for my study I regretfully did not take this human dimension sufficiently into account. On a number of occasions, I am afraid, I offended residents by not spending more time with them socially, for many of them either regarded me or wanted me as a friend.

Whenever I did partake in local activities, though, I never entirely shed my role as an observer, and despite local residents' receptivity to me I always was somewhat of an outsider. I at times geared conversations to subjects of interest to me, and the people with whom I socialized at times asked me questions which they would not have otherwise discussed among themselves. Several residents also held parties specifically in my honor or invited me to parties or gatherings in part because they felt that being seen in my presence would enhance their prestige.

Self-conscious as I was at the time, I underestimated the effect my very presence unwittingly had on people in the three communities and on events which took place while I was there. To the extent that I had such an effect I was not a neutral observer, even though I considered myself to be. Rather, I was a participant, though an "outsider." In Gans's words, I was never a "real" participant.[4]

Survey of Shopkeepers

In line with my new concern with the economics of poverty, in 1971 I added a survey of local shops. Accordingly, I made a census of all businesses or signs of businesses visible from the streets. Since families may run businesses in their homes without advertising them on building fronts, the census is only an approximation of the total number in each area. It most underestimates the number of businesses in *El Centro*, the area with the most densely populated multifamily housing units and the most cottage industries. The Instituto Mexicano de Estudios Sociales administered the survey to seventy randomly selected shops from this census. The questionnaire included questions dealing with the size of the enterprise, the number of kin and other persons employed, business conditions, and perceptions of factors affecting business; the social and economic background of the owner and (if relevant) manager, e.g., his or her place of birth, area of residence, prior and other present employment, education, and religion; the occupation of the owner's father; and business financing. Because of financial constraints this sample, too, was necessarily exploratory. Chapter Six contains material from this survey.

Written Documents

Finally, I read articles dealing with the three communities in local and nationally circulated newspapers and magazines; documents dealing with the local communities and local institutions,

---

[4] Gans, *Urban Villagers*, p. 339.

e.g., concerning the legal status of the areas, and groups within the areas; letters of correspondence between local individuals and groups, on the one hand, and district, city-wide, and national political and government agencies, on the other hand; and records kept by local groups. This material proved useful particularly in conjunction with the analysis contained in Chapters Two-Five. Since records mainly only contain formal communications, this source of information also had limitations.

Except when inquiring about sensitive issues I generally took notes during interviews which, at the end of each work day, I typed up along with my field observations and the information I obtained by other means. On the basis of the data I daily accumulated I wrote new interview schedules and determined what additional information I needed to verify my findings and test new ideas generated by the field work.

Because the generalizations contained in the book derive from a limited number of observations, they necessarily have what Merton calls "low evidential value."[5] However, the "evidential" value of the interpretations is greater than it would have been had I not used an array of research techniques and had I not continually tested ideas that came to mind in the process of doing the field work. Nevertheless, the strength of the study is closely linked to the basic assumptions on which my work is premised and, accordingly, the data I collected, the reliability of my interpretation of the data, and the material I selected to report. To assess the universality of my findings ultimately requires additional research.

While studies generally present only "positive" findings, that is, data which support hypotheses developed in advance or *post factum*, below I discuss how and why I adjusted my conceptual framework in the course of doing my research and how I consequently adjusted my methodological emphasis. The discussion reveals the limitations of the widely upheld "scientific" procedures to which I tried to adhere by subjecting my data to frequent checks of consistency, reliability, and validity and by attempting to do objective value-free research. Perfecting my sources of information within an "individualistic" paradigm in itself never would have led me to my present understanding of sources and consequences of urban poverty.

[5] Merton, *Social Theory and Social Structure*, pp. 93-95.

THE FIELD WORK: INTERPLAY OF THEORY
AND METHODS

When I first designed my study I assumed that the poor differ
from other socioeconomic strata in their level of institutional participation and knowledge of national and international affairs.[6]
Although always concerned with community and national institutional arrangements, I viewed poverty primarily from an individualistic perspective; above all, I considered attitudinal and
behavioral integration of marginal groups into the dominant, national society to be of critical importance. Once integrated into
national society I thought such groups would cease to be poor.
Furthermore, I envisioned the poor to be deprived, frustrated,
and alienated, and to use the franchise and political parties to
articulate their dissatisfaction.

As is obvious from the text, I came to find these notions to be
ethnocentric and empirically incorrect. My field work increasingly convinced me that the "fate" of urban poor is primarily,
though not entirely, shaped by structural forces rooted in the
national political economy. Accordingly, I came to understand
that the persistence of Mexican poverty stems mainly from the
way the society is structured, not from poor people's failure to
participate actively in the national society. Only by abandoning
my initial conceptualization, which assumed that conditions associated with poverty were determined by people's social, economic, and political predispositions, and by substituting a framework that took into account the country's semidependent
capitalist economy and corporatist polity could I correctly understand why so many migrants and city-born are poor, and why
they do not pressure for more social and economic benefits. I
retrace the major steps in my intellectual development below, in
hopes that other people interested in urban poverty in Mexico
and other parts of the world will benefit from my own intial mis-
conceptions and naiveté.

Stage 1 / Original Hypotheses and Design of Study:
Participation and Dwelling Environment as Important
Determinants of Poverty and the Politics of Poverty

First, I hypothesized that the following factors would incline

[6] See, for example, Deutsch, "Social Mobilization," and Lerner; *Traditional
Society.*

people to be informed about politics, as purportedly occurred in
the countries which industrialized first:

1. exposure to metropolitan life—as measured by longevity
of residence in the city, size of community of birth and early
socialization, and age at time of migration to the city:
2. exposure to the mass media;
3. education, and
4. employment in the "modern" sector of the economy, i.e.,
employment as factory worker or non-manual employee.

Second, I hypothesized that dwelling environments have a decisive impact on residents. I thought that different types of sub-
urban communities facilitate or hinder the "integration" of residents into local urban and national life, and that they affect the
extent to which residents are content with metropolitan living.
I expected, for instance, that the intensity and extensity of neighboring would vary from one type of community to another, and
that their feelings of political alienation and political radicalism
would vary accordingly. In line with Kornhauser's thesis, I assumed that informal integration prevented anomie and alienation.[7]

Thirdly, I hypothesized that people would articulate their
satisfaction or dissatisfaction with their social and economic situation politically.

The first hypothesis implied that as the social, economic, and
cultural background of Mexicans became more "modern," Mexican politics would increasingly come to resemble Anglo-Ameri-
can politics. It also implied that so-called social, cultural,
economic, and political participation are interrelated phenomena. The second hypothesis implied either that people with different socioeconomic backgrounds tend to settle in different
types of housing environments or that different housing environments offer different opportunities and experiences to residents.
The third hypotheses implied that people use the franchise to
express their sense of deprivation and their frustrations.

To test these hypotheses I designed a study which enabled me
to compare individuals in diverse lower-class dwelling environments on the basis of quantifiable data obtained from formal interviews. I decided to focus on an old center city slum with a
large proportion of people who lived most if not all their life in

[7] Kornhauser, *Politics of Mass Society.*

Mexico City, a newer area (one formed initially by squatters) with a large proportion of migrants, and a low-cost housing project, also with a large proportion of residents who lived most if not all their life in the capital. I expected to find the following differences between the three areas:

1. *In the Center City area*

a. level of social-economic participation—as measured by education, occupation, participation in secondary associations, style of living, use of institutional services, exposure to the mass media—and therefore political participation—as measured by party membership and voting—which would be relatively high, owing to the urban background of residents;

b. a local subculture, due to values and attitudes reinforced through extensive and intensive friendship and kinship ties among neighbors, despite the seemingly disorganized nature of the area;[8] and

c. minimal alienation from the regime despite the deteriorated environment and pervasive poverty, since people's rich network of friends and relatives would compensate for their material deprivation;

2. *In the Area Formed by Squatters*

a. the extent of social and economic, and therefore, political integration into the society at large would be less than in the center city area, primarily because residents there would tend to be more provincial;

b. life within the community would be more rural-like and less disorganized than in the center city and consequently neighbors would be more friendly;[9]

c. a low level of alienation would incline people to support the status quo;

3. *In the Housing Project*

a. in comparison to the other two areas, widespread social, economic, cultural, and political integration into the national society due to the urban background of residents;

b. negligible integration into the local community since

[8] I derived this assumption from ethnographic accounts of ethnic "villagers" and slum dwellers in Mexico and in other countries. See Gans, *Urban Villagers*; William F. Whyte, *Street Corner Society*; Lewis, *Five Families* and *The Children of Sanchez*.

[9] Tonnies, *Community and Society*.

such projects are impersonal and not suited for low-income life-styles;

    c. extensive dissatisfaction and alienation, due to the impersonal environment of the project.

Schematically, the similarities and differences I expected to find in the three areas are summarized below:

	participation in modern activities	close network	national awareness	political orientation
squatter settlement	—	+	—	indifferent
housing project	+	—	+	alienated
center city area	+	+	+	positive

Note: (+) and (−) are used relatively.

I anticipated not only aggregate differences between the three areas but also differences within each of the areas. In particular, I expected that the community of residence would serve as an important frame of reference for residents and that consequently people with similar backgrounds would respond differently to their objective situation, depending on the type of community in which they lived. For example, I thought that in areas with extensive neighboring (e.g., in the center city area), socially isolated individuals would feel more lonely and discontent than people with equally few social contacts who lived in areas where neighbors tended not to intermingle (e.g., in the housing development) and that their different social-psychological states of mind would affect their respective political orientation. That is, I expected the former to be more supportive of movements and political parties which challenged the status quo. Alternatively, I thought that people who are wealthier than the majority of their neighbors (e.g., in the area founded by squatters) would be more satisfied with their level of living and therefore more supportive of the status quo than people of comparable economic status who lived in a more well-to-do community (e.g., in the housing project). I deduced such hypotheses from reference group theory and the logic of contextual analysis.[10]

[10] Merton, esp. pp. 225-386.

*Stage 2 / Additional Hypotheses and Expansion of Research
Design: The Importance of Community Elites*

Before beginning my actual field work I decided to focus my
study not only on residents within each of the three areas but
also on community elites. Through interviews with local elites
I thought I would be able to learn about:

1. the community power structure, i.e., about the types of
persons who tend to hold positions of wealth, power, and
prestige;

2. attributes which distinguish elites from the typical
resident;

3. patterns of interaction between local elites, between local
elites and persons outside the communities, and between local
elites and local residents; and

4. the groups which operate within the areas and how the
groups in particular and the communities in general have
changed over the years.

I did not initially understand how to systematically link such
community level data with the individual data I intended to obtain from interviews with residents. Nor did I understand how
sub-urban communities and institutions within such communities
were structured in a society such as Mexico. On the one hand, I
recognized a similarity between the Mexican political system and
authoritarian or fascist-like regimes. On the other hand, I seemed
to assume that the local elites potentially could function independently of national elites, as is implied in most of the literature
on "community power" in the United States.[11] The local versus national origin and orientation of the elites seemed to me to be the
most crucial dimension for understanding the elites, the groups
they headed, and the community in general. As indicators of
local-national orientation I intended to measure the degree of
fiscal autonomy and decision-making power heads of groups had,

[11] Such local autonomy is implicit both in the pluralist and in the elitist
models of community power structure. See, for example, Dahl, "A Critique
of Ruling Elite Model," pp. 463-69; Raymond Wolfinger, "Reputation and
Reality in the Study of 'Community Power,'" pp. 241-50; Hunter, *Community Power Structure*; Nelson Polsby, *Community Power and Political
Theory*. The few American social scientists who emphasize the centralization
of power in the United States—e.g., Mills in *The Power Elite*, and Domhoff
in *Who Rules America?*—concentrate on national, not local, politics.

the nature of their contacts with nonlocal persons, and the procedure by which they obtained office. I conjectured that in comparison with nationally oriented elites, locally oriented elites would be:

1. less prestigeful and powerful;

2. less oriented to change, i.e., more conservative and traditional;

3. more cliquish, i.e., more informally bound to one another through ties of friendship and kinship;

4. more aware of community problems; and

5. more particularistic versus universalistic in the way they conducted their groups and related to their constituencies.

Furthermore, I seemed to assume that the more locally oriented elites were, the less integrated local groups and residents would be into urban and national society. For example, I expected elites in the squatter settlement, on the city's periphery, to be the most locally oriented, just as I expected inhabitants of that area to be the most marginal to national society. Nevertheless, I did recognize the possibility of an elite-mass "gap" and anticipated that the "width" of the gap would have significant social consequences. For instance, I thought that the more locally oriented the elites were, the more informed and concerned they would be about local problems, and the more likely they would be to have interests similar to those of residents. Accordingly, I expected residents of the area to be less alienated and politically opposed to the status quo.

Stage 3 / Field Work

Once I arrived in Mexico and selected the three areas I intended to study, I informally interviewed persons in elite positions and "common" citizens. I also pretested the formal questionnaire I designed in light of the hypotheses I initially set out to study. On the basis of this field work I modified the questionnaire which I planned to administer both to local elites and to a sample of residents within each of the areas in the following ways:

1. I shortened the length of the questionnaire, as I found the quality of responses deteriorated markedly after approximately one hour; generally adults could not leave their children unattended for more time and they had to tend to other family responsibilities;

2. I eliminated a number of questions which were intended to reveal respondents' level of knowledge of local and national political and government affairs, as many residents resented having to constantly reveal their ignorance;

3. I rephrased open-ended questions dealing with socioeconomic class and class consciousness since I discovered that the poor did not perceive the social structure and their position within the social structure in terms of clearly defined classes.

In addition, I modified the procedure I planned to use for selecting my sample of elites and the purpose for which I used the elite interviews, largely because the communities were structured differently than I had initially imagined. I discovered that by none of the methods conventionally used for deciphering the power structure of American communities could I delineate an identifiable group of locally powerful elites.

Many persons occupying top positions within local institutions —e.g., school directors, priests and ministers, government functionaries, administrators of social services, local officeholders of political parties and groups affiliated with parties—tended to be ill-informed about the local communities (though more informed than "ordinary" residents), minimally involved in the local communities, and limited in the activities they initiated except as intermediary "brokers" between the local communities and non-local institutions. Most institutional elites primarily oriented their activities toward higher-ranking functionaries within their own institutional realm outside the areas. To consider them members of a local "power structure" therefore seemed ill-founded and ethnocentric.

Similarly, the "reputational" technique did not enable me to uncover a locally based power structure in each of the areas. While persons holding offices locally were better able than most residents to name local individuals whom they perceived to have power, wealth, or prestige, many of them could name few, if any. Furthermore, in *La Colonia* ordinary residents, when asked, mentioned one of the early leaders following the land invasion, a person who neither lives nor is active in the area anymore: he formerly held formal political posts locally and wielded informal political influence, but ever since relations within the community were routinized and he was promoted by nonlocal government and Party authorities, his actual local importance has dwindled.

The residents who continued to refer to him as a local leader no longer were active or very interested in local activities. In addition, the institutional elite who were most knowledgeable—the priests—were not the institutional elite formally vested with the greatest power, and they were not perceived either by other elites or by the residents to be the most important persons within the local communities. Were priests de facto if not de jure powerful or influential persons within the local communities, the "reputational" technique—which relies on people's reported perceptions of the power structure—did not make this self-evident. The official anti-clerical bias of the regime blinded people from recognizing whatever influence local priests wielded. Most people believed that the government was the most authoritative institution, but it was the national government that assumed formal responsibility for local administrative activities. Authoritative decisions were not made locally. Therefore, I also decided against using the "decision-making" approach sometimes used in "community power" studies.[12] The forces which affected the lives of people within the three areas were, for the most part, not rooted in the local communities.

The inadequacy of these various approaches convinced me that:

1. Mexico is hierarchically structured;
2. groups form the basic unit of the Mexican regime, but

    a. these groups tend not to function as autonomous units, particularly on the local level; and

    b. generally, the lower the socioeconomic status of group leaders and, secondarily, the lower the socioeconomic status of rank-and-file members, the less influence they can exert on the government through their own institutional hierarchy.

Furthermore, since the elites within each area were of diverse social, economic, and political status, and since there was no autonomous local power structure, I abandoned the idea of doing a systematic, quantifiable analysis of the local leaders. I decided, instead, to focus my analysis on existing and previously existing groups operating within the communities, and changes in the groups over the years.

Upon recognizing how little institutional autonomy the communities, the groups within the communities, and the heads of

[12] Polsby, "How to Study Community Power," pp. 297-304.

the groups had, I came also to realize the impact nonlocal forces had on residents as well as local elites. At this point I finally concluded that the "life chances" of persons in low-income areas were largely determined by structural forces external to the communities. The shift in my theoretical orientation also stemmed from the following observations:

1. despite marked differences in the physical and social environment of each of the areas, most residents supported the official party;

2. residents tended to support the party independently of whether they thought the regime was responsive to their interests, independently of whether they felt their personal situation had improved over the years, and independently of whether they had a rich network of friends and relatives;

3. residents over the years became increasingly less involved in territorially based politics, and local groups became incorporated into the official political-administrative apparatus, but their involvement in local and nonlocal occupational groups did not simultaneously decline;

4. the extent of variation in economic status among residents, i.e., in occupation, income, and style of living, within each area was greater than the variation in economic status of residents from one area to the next, and that therefore the type of community in which people lived had little bearing on residents' social and economic fate.

These observations, in sum, convinced me that in order to understand conditions which give rise to urban poverty and the politics of poverty in Mexico I *above all* had to understand the nature of the Mexican "development" process—presently and historically—and how the urban settlements, leaders, and residents were linked to this process. The analysis contained in this book is premised on this perspective.[13]

RESEARCH PROBLEMS

Even after I decided which research techniques to use, the actual field work raised a series of dilemmas. First, I had to decide which communities to study. Second, I had to gain entry into the

[13] For an excellent example of a Marixst analysis of urbanization and the structure and culture of cities, see Manuel Castells, *La question urbaine.*

communities, a problem compounded by the fact that I was both
a foreigner and a young single female. Third, the research raised
several ethical issues, not all of which I realized at the time.
These problems are discussed, in turn, below.

Selection of the Three Areas

As previously stated, initially I wanted to study the effect
dwelling environments had on the social, economic, and political
life of poor people. Since I wanted to examine the formal and
informal organization within communities I studied and since I
thought that they both might vary according to community size
(that is, population), as much of the rural-urban literature suggested, I decided to focus my study on areas housing roughly
comparable numbers of people. Since I thought people of similar
socioeconomic status would differ politically depending not only
on the type of neighborhood in which they lived but also on their
rural-urban background, I decided to select areas housing popula-
tions differing in the degree to which they were born or raised in
the capital. Once I decided to focus my study on the above types
of dwelling areas and to concentrate on areas housing roughly
comparable numbers of people, but people differing in their rural-
urban background, I had little difficulty selecting two of the
three areas. Few areas remain in the center city which continue
both to be primarily residential and to house people in old, deteriorated dwellings. Many sections of the center city have become heavily commercial or they have been physically transformed through "urban renewal-type" projects. There also are
few low-cost government developments housing urban poor, particularly ones housing approximately as many people as are
found in the center city area I considered most appropriate to
study. I had more difficulty deciding which squatter settlement
to study since there are many more from which to choose: however, most such settlements are in the State of Mexico, not in the
Federal District to which I limited my investigation. I made my
final selection partly on unscientific grounds. I chose an area
which fitted my image of what I believed a legalized settlement
still inhabited by original squatters would look like. I did not
want an area that was too "urban" looking, with well-constructed
multifamily housing units. Yet, before I finally decided which
three communities to study I personally visited several dozen
areas in the city, consulted leading urban experts—architects,

engineers, anthropologists, sociologists and government employees, and examined demographic statistics of the city.

Entry into the Communities

Self-conscious and scared as I initially was to do my study, particularly since I was a young single female alone among poor
people in a foreign country, I overcame my inhibitions in the
following ways:

1. *Walking Through the Areas and Informally Talking with
People in the Streets*: I used this approach especially when I
first began my study. Initially I tended to talk to residents only
if they looked at me and I at them to the point that I felt I
needed to explain my presence. I remember full well the first
person with whom I brought myself to speak; someone wear-
ing an identical sweater to mine, for I felt we shared something
in common![14]

2. *Formal Interviews with Residents*: Since I had a draft of
a questionnaire prepared when I began my field research I
used it as a means to establish contact with local residents and
overcome my inhibitions to speak with them. Given the dis-
comfort many residents felt when subjected to formal ques-
tioning by a stranger, I found this tactic of limited use.

3. *Block Census*: The census of blocks from which I drew
my sample for the formal interviews with residents provided
me with an additional means to establish contact with local
residents. Generally when I visited the *vecindades* or other
housing quarters I inquired not only about the number of
households living there but also about residents' experiences
in the community.

4. *Interviews with Local Elites*: I personally contacted local
institutions which were readily noticeable from the street almost immediately after I decided to study the communities.
The only letter of introduction I had was from the Ministry of
Education: to get access to the schools. Persons at the local
institutions with whom I spoke usually suggested names of

[14] Clothing assumed an important psychological function to me in my field
research. I wore only a few "slum outfits" the entire time. The skirt and
sweater outfits that I wore were casual and slightly out-of-fashion, as was the
clothing most residents wore. I tried to "go native" in this way less to deceive
inhabitants about my socioeconomic status than to help myself overcome the
class and national barriers which I felt differentiated me from them.

other elites who they thought might be of interest to me and, either then or after subsequent interviews, invited me to meetings of their groups, to local public gatherings, and to private fiestas. I thereby gradually established contact in the communities and became a familiar face locally. Once seen in the presence of local elites I generally had no difficulty establishing rapport with their subordinates, either because the elites told their subordinates to collaborate with me or because the lower-ranking functionaries assumed they could and should follow the example of their hierarchical superior and talk with me if I approached them. The prestige hierarchy in the community, in sum, had a "halo" effect which readily facilitated my research. Whenever I introduced myself to people I told them, minimally, that I was making a study of the people and organizations in their and a few other sections of Mexico City. I also mentioned that the study was for the thesis I was preparing at the university in the U.S. where I was studying. Generally, however, the nature of my explanation had little to do with people's receptivity to me. Much more important was the personal rapport I established with them.

The "Marginal" Status of the Researcher

My nationality and my sex proved both advantageous and disadvantageous in my research. On the one hand, as a foreigner I stood outside the status system. The generally accepted standards of who talks to whom and what one talks about applied less to me than to Mexicans. I was excused if I did not conform to the norms which customarily regulate interpersonal relationships. As a consequence, I could investigate matters which would be sensitive ground for an "insider." Since I stood outside the local status structure people often felt safe talking to me. I could act interested and ignorant and ask questions that a "middle-class" Mexican could less readily ask. The poor people interviewed would assume either that their "middle-class" compatriots are more knowledgeable than they themselves are or that revealed information might be used against them.[15] Most of the people in the areas, I am afraid, were flattered that I, an American, took interest in them and their problems.

[15] Since I frequently asked persons I interviewed questions even when I knew the factual answer, to learn about their perceptions and beliefs, I was not as ignorant as I appeared frequently to be.

On the other hand, however, my nationality created certain difficulties, particularly in interviews with nationalistic "middle-class" functionaries who hold ambivalent views toward the United States. Defensive about Mexico, they at times told me what they thought would impress me, not what they honestly believed. They were particularly inclined to present a good image of Mexico in view of the widely publicized work of Oscar Lewis (*The Children of Sanchez*) which Mexicans considered to be highly critical of their country. A few of them were particularly hostile toward and suspicious of my formal questionnaire. Fortunately, I minimized such antagonism by administering the questionnaire to elites only at the end of my stay in Mexico, when I had established rapport with them.

My sex facilitated my field work as people I interviewed generally viewed the political intent of women less suspiciously than men, in line with prevailing sex stereotypes. Furthermore, the people I met seemed to find me compassionate and concerned. Prompted by *machismo*, men in particular took interest in me. They were attracted by my fair skin and—by Mexican standards —light-colored hair. Thus, they took pleasure in explaining things to me and showing me around.

Yet because I was a single female I never felt entirely relaxed, particularly in the evenings. I also felt uneasy participating in certain activities, such as drinking in local bars. Being a foreigner at times enabled me to violate the usual sexual barriers without being suspect sexually by men. At a few fiestas, for example, I talked for a while with the men who sat separately from the women, which I would not have done were I a Mexican female, particularly of their social class. Although the sexual mores operating among the Mexican poor did not *ipso facto* apply to me, I was reluctant to take advantage of the prerogative. Occasionally men suggested seeing me at work or in the evening, with the intention of turning the meeting into a social rather than a "professional" occasion. Since they rarely made their intent explicit, I found myself in a bind, for I very much wanted to interview them. As a consequence, on a few occasions I found myself in the awkward position of intending a get-together purely for research purposes whereas they did not. Never, however, did I find myself unable to handle the situation and never did I find my life or sexual integrity threatened. One of my most embarrassing experiences involved a doctor who invited me to dinner at his home, but asked me to meet him at his office. Since he was not at work at the designated time I went to his house, thinking that he had gone home early. When I arrived there I realized that his wife expected her husband, not me. I subsequently learned that while he planned to dine with me, he intended to take me out, alone, to a restaurant.

In sum, my nationality and sex, willy-nilly, affected my ability to do research and my research experiences.

Ethical Dilemmas

Field research inherently raises ethical issues, even when the researcher is unaware of them. Most U.S. scholars who address themselves to the ethicacy of U.S.-sponsored investigations concern themselves mainly with issues of funding,[16] disclosure of findings, and of researcher involvement in the domestic affairs of foreign countries.[17] However, researchers inherently involve themselves in other ethical and political issues, even if unintentionally and unknowingly. But independently of researchers' motivations and awareness, the involvements are sociologically, politically, and morally consequential. My research involved me in the following dilemmas, not all of which I realized at the time I did my field work.

First, even though my findings are not classified and are available to all interested parties, not all parties are equally able to make use of the information. Persons in positions of power are best able, given their resources, to utilize the data; they could, if they so chose, use the data to better control poor people. I became particularly aware of this issue when some PRI functionaries admitted to me that they would collaborate with my study because they wanted to learn more than they already knew about people in the areas, in view of the PRI's declining support in the district in the 1970 election. I never returned to meet with these functionaries. To the extent that my findings are used to enhance

---

[16] Project Camelot has been one of the most controversial research studies. See Horowitz (ed.), *The Rise and Fall of Project Camelot.*

[17] The concern with researchers' direct involvement in the domestic affairs of foreign countries usually centers on whether the meliorative attempts are kept within limits acceptable to the established government of the country concerned, *not* whether the involvement is in the best interests of the people being researched. For an example of this status quo ethicacy see Robert Ward, "Common Problems in Field Research," pp. 69-70.

the PRI's support among these or other Mexican poor, or used in general to manipulate the poor, they are used for purposes other than I intend and want.

Secondly, my field work involved me in power relations which facilitated my research. In retrospect, I feel that I got access to the private worlds of people I studied in part because I was assumed to have an outside base of power linked to my nationality. Many Mexicans of low socioeconomic status emulate Americans, largely because of their wealth (an image portrayed in the mass media and by Mexicans who have visited the U.S.). Still others probably cooperated with my study because they felt I, as an American, might help them locate jobs in the U.S., serve as their sponsor so that they could enter the U.S. legally, or help them financially. One semi-illiterate Pentecostal minister, for instance, who believed the stereotype that Jews are wealthy, asked me to help him get money for a "temple" he wanted to build for his congregation once he learned that I was Jewish. He even wrote me in the States, after I left Mexico, requesting financial assistance again. Another minister also wrote me after I left Mexico to help him relocate in this country. Rightly or not, I provided no economic assistance to people in the three areas.

Furthermore, as an extension of the power relation, my status as an American inadvertently caused me to confer status on the people I interviewed, by talking with them, and on local groups, by "noticing" them.[18] Local leaders occasionally used me as an excuse to initiate contact with higher-ranking functionaries. Others insisted that I sit with the officers at group meetings and that we exchange words in English in front of their "followers," which obviously was done to impress them. Too self-conscious at the time to realize the social and political implications of my presence on such occasions, I now recognize that my association with these politicians enhanced their prestige and, in some cases possibly also their political prospects.

Moreover, since *políticos* within the area view prestige and influence as a "limited good" I at times had difficulty maintaining

[18] Similarly, Joseph Gusfield describes in his "Fieldwork Reciprocities in Studying a Social Movement," p. 29, how his research association with the Women's Christian Temperance Union conferred a definite status on the group; and David Colfax notes in his "Pressure Toward Distortion and Involvement in Studying a Civil Rights Organization," p. 143, that a civil rights group he studied found his research interest "status conferring."

contact with more than one group within each community without exacerbating local political tensions. I became regarded as a political asset whom local elites felt they could not equally share. On occasion local elites became offended and jealous of my ties with their political rivals. Although, even when asked, I never disclosed information obtained from one leader to another, even when asked, I felt morally compelled to reveal, upon inquiry, names of persons whom I had contacted. However, perhaps dishonestly, I tried to be discreet about my contacts. To avoid having to account for all my interactions and thereby becoming inadvertently enmeshed in local political tensions, I at times parked the car I used the last months I worked in Mexico at some distance from the home or office of the person with whom I had an appointment.[19]

Third, somewhat independently of the power relationship, my very presence as a researcher at times was politically consequential, even when I did not want or intend it to be. For example, a key informant in the housing development sent a communiqué to the man who headed one of the local groups because she thought I would be interested in observing his reaction to her, and because she thought I would reveal his reaction to her. When the head of the group read her letter at one of his meetings he used the opportunity to make fun of her and challenge her credibility as a local leader in front of his followers. Although I never discussed what transpired at the meeting with her, the incident does reveal the way in which field work indirectly involves researchers in political and ethical dilemmas.

Finally, my field research unfortunately involved me in an exploiting relationship, as does all field work. Persons collaborating with me received little in exchange for their assistance or time. Since I interviewed some people who did either piecework or were self-employed, my presence raised economic as well as moral issues. I distracted them from their means of livelihood. Moreover, those *políticos* who benefited from my prestige I would have preferred not to help; even though I liked them personally, I disliked the way their work helped extend and reinforce

[19] I first used public transportation to get to and from the areas where I worked, and traveled by foot within the areas. Reluctantly I bought a car when, after six months, my feet became so sore that I could barely walk and pursue my research. Since a car is a status symbol in Mexico, people in the three areas, unfortunately, were very impressed by my purchase.

the legitimacy of the inegalitarian regime. Had I deliberately involved myself in local affairs I would have resolved the ethical dilemma of reciprocity, but, as a foreigner, I would in the process have involved myself in the internal affairs of a foreign country and thereby raised still another ethical issue.

On the basis of my experiences I feel that social scientists must take into account not only intellectual and feasibility considerations when planning their research, but also the tacit ethical and political issues their work raises. Many research strategies are politically consequential even when the researchers believe they are politically detached.

Questionnaire Administered to Sample of Residents

1. What is your age?_____

2. What is your marital status?
   _____Single
   _____Married
   _____Separated
   _____Widowed
   _____Divorced
   _____Free Union
   IF HAVE SPOUSE: How old is your spouse?_____

3. How many people live with you?_____
   a. IF HAVE SPOUSE: Aside from your spouse and your children, how many relatives live with you?_____
   b. IF NO SPOUSE: Aside from your children, how many relatives live with you?_____

4. How many children do you have?_____
   a. More than 15 years old_____
   b. Less than 15 years old_____

5. Have you always lived in Mexico City? No_____ Yes_____
   (If yes, skip to question 9.)

	Town	Province
a. Where were you born?	_____	_____
b. Where did you live when you were 15?	_____	_____
c. Where did you live before moving to Mexico City?	_____	_____
d. How old were you when you came to Mexico City?	_____	_____

6. What was your main reason for migrating to Mexico City?_____

7. When you came to the city
   a. Did you receive aid from anyone in terms of housing?
      Yes_____   No_____
   b. Did you receive assistance in finding work? Yes_____ No_____
      IF YES: Who helped you? (relationship)_____

8. a. Do you belong to a group together with other people from your town of origin? Yes_____ No_____ (If no, skip to 9.)

   b. What type of activities do you do?

   c. How frequently do you meet?

9. IF HAVE SPOUSE: Has your spouse always lived in the city? Yes_____ No_____ (If no, skip to 10.)

	Town	*Province*
a. Where did your spouse live before coming to the city?	_____	_____
b. How old was your spouse when he/she came to Mexico City?	_____	_____

10. How frequently do you go to the provinces?

   _____Daily   _____Few times per year

   _____Weekly   _____Rarely

   _____Monthly   _____Never

11. a. Do you have close relatives or friends who live in the provinces? Yes_____ No_____ (If no, skip to 12.)

   b. How frequently do you see them?

      _____Daily   _____Few times per year

      _____Weekly   _____Rarely

      _____Monthly   _____Never

12. Since when have you lived in this *colonia* (*unidad*)?_____

13. a. In how many other places have you lived in the city?_____

   b. Where did you live before—in this *colonia* (*unidad*) or in another (which?)? And before that, where did you live? And before that?

      1. _____

      2. _____

      3. _____

   c. Why did you move from (1) to (2)? And why did you move from (2) to (3)?

      (1) to (2):_____

      (2) to (3):_____

14. Do you have relatives who live in the city? Yes_____ No_____ (If no, skip to 15.)

   a. How many families of relatives?_____

   b. Your three closest relatives: What type of work do they do? (IF RELATIVES ARE FEMALE ASK: How do their spouses earn a living?) And in what *colonia* do they live? And how frequently do you see them?

	Relative	Type of Work	Where Live	Frequency of Contact
1.				
2.				
3.				

c. How many relatives do you have in this *colonia* (*unidad*)?_____

d. IF LIVE IN VECINDAD ASK: And how many families in your *vecindad* are relatives?_____

15. And do you have *compadres* in the city? Yes_____ No_____
(If no, skip to 16.)

a. How many *compadres* in the city?_____

b. Your three closest *compadres*, what type of work do they do? (IF MENTION COMADRES ASK: How do their spouses earn their living?) Where do they live? How frequently do you see them?

	Sex	Type of Work	Where Live	Frequency of Contact
1.				
2.				
3.				

c. How many *compadres* do you have in your *colonia* (*unidad*)?_

d. IF LIVE IN VECINDAD ASK: And how many *compadres* do you have in your *vecindad*?_____

16. And do you have any friends? Yes_____ No_____ (If no, skip to 17.)

a. How many friends?_____

b. Your three closest friends, what type of work do they do? (IF FRIENDS ARE WOMEN ASK: How do their spouses earn their living? Where do they live? How frequently do you see them?)

	Sex	Type of Work	Where Live	Frequency of Contact
1.				
2.				
3.				

c. How many friends do you have in your *colonia* (*unidad*)?_____

d IF LIVE IN VECINDAD ASK: And how many friends do you have in your *vecindad*?_____

17. Is this place

_____rented? IF SO: How much do you pay monthly?_____

_____property of your family?

_____are you in the process of buying the place? IF SO: How much do you pay monthly?_____

_____other; what?_____

18. How many bedrooms do you have in your place?_____

19. a. Do you know people who formerly lived here but no longer do?
       Yes_____ No_____ (If no, skip to 20.)
    b. Why did they leave?

20. When you first moved here what were you most concerned about?

21. a. Are you basically content or discontent living in this *colonia*
       (*unidad*)?
       _____content
       _____neither content nor discontent
       _____discontent
    b. What is it that you especially like about living here?
    c. What is it that you dislike most about living here?
    d. ASK PEOPLE IN UNIDAD: Are there problems with the way the
       unidad is administered?
       _____No
       _____Yes; what?_____
    e. Would you like to live in another part of the city, the provinces,
       or would you always like to live here?
       _____in other part of the city
       _____in the provinces
       _____always here (If always, skip to 22.)
    f. Where would you like to live?
    g. Why would you like to live there?
    h. Are you thinking of moving there? Yes_____ No_____
       (If no, skip to 22.)
       1. When are you thinking of moving?
       2. Why haven't you moved yet?

22. a. Do you think the people in the city are
       _____very friendly
       _____more or less friendly
       _____unfriendly?
    b. And in this *colonia* (*unidad*), are they
       _____very friendly
       _____more or less friendly
       _____unfriendly?
    c. And the people in the province, are they
       _____very friendly
       _____more or less friendly
       _____unfriendly?

23. Do you think you can confide in the majority of people?
    a. In the city?   Yes_____ No_____
    b. In this *colonia* (*unidad*)?   _____ _____
    c. In the provinces?   _____ _____

24. Do you think
 _____that the unions help the worker or
 _____that the leaders of the unions don't defend the interests
 of the workers?

25. Do you work now? Yes_____ No_____ (If no, skip to 26.)
 a. How many occupations do you now have?
 b. What is the name of your main one?
 c. Since when are you doing that?
 d. What position do you hold?
 e. What is the name of the business where you work?
 f. 1. How many people work with you?
  2. How many of them are relatives?
 g. Do you consider your work permanent or temporary?
  _____permanent
  _____temporary
 h. How did you find your job? Did someone help you find it?
 i. Where do you work?
  _____in your home
  _____in other part of the *colonia* (*unidad*)
  _____in another *colonia* (which?_____) or
  _____in the State of Mexico
 j. Are you content, discontent, or indifferent about your work?
  _____content
  _____neither content nor discontent
  _____discontent
 k. Would you like to change jobs? Yes_____ No_____ (If no,
 skip to "l".)
  1. What kind of work would you like to have?
  2. Are you thinking of getting such a job?
   Yes_____ When?_____
   No_____
 l. What was your last job?
 m. IF MIGRANT: What type of work did you generally do in the
 provinces?

26. IF RESPONDENT IS PRESENTLY NOT WORKING:
 a. What was your last job?
 b. How long were you doing that?
 c. What was your position?
 d. What was the place where you worked called?
 e. 1. About how many people worked with you?_____
  2. How many of them were relatives?_____
 f. How did you get that job? Did someone help you find it?
 Who?_____ What is his/her relation to you?

g. Where do you work?
    _____in your home
    _____in other part of the *colonia* (*unidad*),
    _____in other part of the city (in what *colonia*?_____)
        or
    _____in the State of Mexico

h. What is the main reason why you presently are not working?

i. Since when aren't you working?

j. What type of work would you like?

k. What type of work do you realistically think you can obtain?

l. When do you think you can get the job?

m. What type of work did you do before your last job?

n. Why did you leave that job?

o. IF MIGRATED ASK: What type of work did you generally do in the provinces?

27. WITH RESPECT TO SPOUSE'S OCCUPATION: Does your spouse presently work? Yes_____ No_____ (If no, skip to 28.)

a. How many occupations does your spouse now have?

b. What is his/her main occupation?

c. Since when is he/she doing that?

d. What is the title of his/her job?

e. What is the name of the place where he/she works?

f. 1. How many people, more or less, work in the business?
   2. How many of them are relatives?

g. Does he/she consider the work permanent or temporary?
    _____permanent
    _____temporary

h. How did he/she obtain this work? Who, if anyone helped him/her obtain the job?

i. Where does your spouse work?
    _____at home
    _____in another part of the *colonia* (*unidad*)
    _____in other *colonia*? (which?_____) or
    _____in the State of Mexico

j. Would your spouse like to change jobs? Yes_____ No_____ (If no, skip to "k.")
   1. What type of work would he/she like to obtain?
   2. Does he/she expect to be able to get such a job?
      _____Yes; when?_____
      _____No

k. What type of work did your spouse have before his/her present job?

l. Why did he/she leave the job?

m. IF SPOUSE MIGRATED: What type of work did your spouse generally do in the provinces?

28. ASK ONLY IF SPOUSE IS NOT PRESENTLY WORKING:

a. What type of work did your spouse last do?

b. How long did he/she do that?

c. What was his/her title?

d. What was the name of the place where he/she worked?

e. Do you know how many people, more or less, worked in the business?

f. How did your spouse get the job? Through someone he/she knew?

g. Where did your spouse work?

_____at home

_____in another part of the *colonia* (*unidad*)

_____in another *colonia* (which?_____), or

_____in the State of Mexico

h. What is the main reason why your spouse is not now working?

i. Since when is he/she not working?

j. What type of work, if any, would your spouse like to obtain?

k. Realistically, what type of work does he/she think he/she can obtain?

l. Before his/her last job, what type of work did he/she do?

m. IF SPOUSE MIGRATED, ASK: What type of work did your spouse generally do in the provinces?

ASK EVERYONE:

29. a. Are you basically satisfied or dissatisfied with the present economic situation of your family?

_____satisfied

_____neither satisfied nor dissatisfied

_____dissatisfied

b. Why?

30. In your opinion, is the economic situation of the country higher, about the same as, or lower than it was 5 years ago?

_____higher

_____about the same as

_____lower

31. To live as you would like, how much money would your family need?

32. Could you tell me approximately what your family income is per month?

    _____less than $500 (pesos)
    _____$500 to $749
    _____$750 to $999
    _____$1000 to $1499
    _____$1500 to $1999
    _____$2000 to $2999
    _____$3000 to $4999
    _____$5000 or more

33. How many people contribute money to help support the family?

34. Is the economic situation of your family better, equal, or worse than it was 5 years ago?

    _____better
    _____equal
    _____worse

35. IF MIGRANT: Do you think your economic situation here in the city is better, about the same as, or worse than it used to be in the provinces?

    _____better
    _____about the same as
    _____worse

36. a. Do you think your father did better than you, about the same as you, or worse?

    _____better
    _____about the same
    _____worse

  b. Why do you say that?

37. a. Do you think your children will do better economically than you, about the same, or worse?

    _____better
    _____about the same
    _____worse

  b. Why do you say that?

38. How would you define your socioeconomic level? Your socioeconomic class?

    _____poor
    _____humble
    _____lower class
    _____middle class
    _____upper middle class
    _____upperclass
    _____other

39. What type of work did your father do most of his life?

40. a. What type of work would you like your sons to do?
    b. Realistically, what type of work do you think they actually will do?

41. Was anyone in your family ever a *bracero*?   Yes_____ No_____
    (If no, skip to 42.)
    a. Who?
    b. How long?
    c. When?

42. a. Many people in Mexico have debts. Do you as well?
        _____Yes
        _____No (Skip to 42e.)
    b. How much do you owe for the following items?
        _____furniture, appliances
        _____your home
        _____medicine and doctors
        _____what other debts do you have?
    c. To which of the following do you owe money?
        _____relatives
        _____*compadres*
        _____friends
        _____union
        _____shop owner
        _____bank; (which?_____)
        _____money lender
        _____informal loan association
        _____other person or group; which?_____
    d. Do you have more, equal, or fewer debts than you did a year ago?
        _____more
        _____equal
        _____fewer
    e. In general, do you think it is good to buy things on credit?
        _____Yes; why?_____
        _____No; why?_____

43. a. Which of the following items does your family have? Of the items you have, since when have you had them—more, or less than 5 years?
    Less than 5   More than 5   Does not have
    _____   _____   _____radio
    _____   _____   _____television
    _____   _____   _____refrigerator
    _____   _____   _____sewing machine

Less than 5   More than 5   Does not have

_____	_____	_____bicycle
_____	_____	_____car
_____	_____	_____wristwatch
_____	_____	_____beds; how many?_____
_____	_____	_____forks; how many?_____

b. Of those which you don't have, which would you like to obtain?

_____radio   _____car

_____television   _____wristwatch

_____refrigerator   _____beds; how many?_____

_____sewing machine   _____forks: how many?_____

_____bicycle

c. Of those things that you want, which are you thinking of buying within the next year or two? Will you pay for them in cash or pay in installments?

Will not buy   Cash   Installments

_____	_____	_____	radio
_____	_____	_____	television
_____	_____	_____	refrigerator
_____	_____	_____	sewing machine
_____	_____	_____	bicycle
_____	_____	_____	car
_____	_____	_____	wristwatch
_____	_____	_____	beds; how many?_____
_____	_____	_____	forks; how many?_____

44. a. Where do you buy most of your furniture—in this *colonia* (*unidad*), or somewhere else?

_____this *colonia* (*unidad*)

_____other; which?_____

b. In what shop?_____

c. Why do you buy there?

_____can buy on installments

_____know someone there

_____goods are inexpensive

_____large selection

_____closest place

_____other reason; which?_____

45. a. Where do you buy most of your food? In this *colonia* (*unidad*), or somewhere else?

_____this *colonia* (*unidad*)

_____other; which?_____

b. Do you mainly buy
_____in a market?
_____in a supermarket?
_____in a shop in the *colonia* (*unidad*)?
_____from street vendors?

c. Why do you buy there?
_____can buy on credit
_____know someone who works there
_____inexpensive
_____large selection
_____is the closest place
_____other reason; what?_____

46. a. Do you have savings? Yes_____ No_____ (Skip to 47.)
    b. More or less how much savings do you have?_____
    c. Where do you keep your savings? in
       _____a bank; which?_____
       _____a savings association
       _____at work
       _____some other association
       _____or somewhere else

47. In order to secure a good position, what is most important?
    _____have good education
    _____work hard
    _____be influential
    _____be from a wealthy family
    _____luck
    _____or something else; what?_____

48. a. Do you think there has been a lot, some, or no social progress
       in Mexico—for example, in terms of education, worker's rights,
       etc.?
       _____much
       _____some
       _____none
    b. And you personally, how much do you feel you have benefited
       from this social progress—much, little, or not at all?
       _____much
       _____a little
       _____not at all

49. a. Do you think social security is good or not?
       _____good; why?_____
       _____bad; why?_____

b. What benefits does social security offer?

c. Have you received benefits from social security?

    _____yes; which?_____

    _____no

50. Generally, when you or someone else in your family is sick, where do you go?

    _____hospital; which?_____

    _____clinic; which?_____

    _____private doctor

    _____herb doctor

    _____someone who is not a doctor

    _____other; what?_____

51. What was the last year of school that your father completed? And your mother?

Father		Mother		
Some	Finished	Some	Finished	
____	_____	____	_____	primary
____	_____	____	_____	secondary
____	_____	____	_____	preparatory
____	_____	____	_____	commercial
____	_____	____	_____	normal (teaching)
____	_____	____	_____	university
____	_____	____	_____	other; what?_____

52. And you, how much schooling have you had? And your spouse?

Respondent		Spouse		
Some	Finished	Some	Finished	
____	_____	____	_____	primary
____	_____	____	_____	secondary
____	_____	____	_____	preparatory
____	_____	____	_____	commercial
____	_____	____	_____	normal (teaching)
____	_____	____	_____	university
____	_____	____	_____	other; what?_____

53. Which of the following statements expresses your feelings?

    _____spent too much time in school

    _____spent sufficient time in school

    _____spent insufficient time in school

54. a. How much schooling would you like your sons to have?

    Some   Finish

    _____   _____ primary

Some	*Finish*	
———	———	secondary
———	———	preparatory
———	———	commercial
———	———	normal (teaching)
———	———	university
———	———	other; which?———

b. Realistically, what do you think they can obtain?

Some	*Finish*	
———	———	primary
———	———	secondary
———	———	preparatory
———	———	commercial
———	———	normal (teaching)
———	———	university
———	———	other; which?———

55. In terms of religion, would you tell me what your religion is?
———Protestant
———Catholic
———other; which?———

56. a. How frequently do you attend religious services?
———daily
———weekly
———monthly
———only on special occasions, e.g., weddings, baptisms, etc.
———rarely
———never
b. IF CATHOLIC, ASK: How frequently do you confess?———

57. a. Which church do you attend?———
b. Where is it located?
———in this *colonia* (**unidad**)
———other; which?———
c. Do you belong to any religious groups? Which?———

58. Did you celebrate the Day of the Dead last November?
———Yes; how did you celebrate it?———
———No; why not?———

59. a. For what purposes do you use herbs?
b. More or less how frequently do you use them?
———daily
———weekly
———monthly
———rarely

60. a. Do you think the Church in Mexico has too much influence,
       too little influence, or just the right amount?
       _____too much
       _____sufficient or
       _____insufficient
    b. Why do you think that?

61. a. Do you read a newspaper? Yes_____ No_____ (Skip to 62.)
    b. How frequently?
       _____daily
       _____weekly
       _____monthly
       _____only on special occasions
       _____rarely
    c. What newspaper do you read most frequently?

62. a. Do you generally read magazines? IF YES: Which?_____
    b. And comics? IF YES: Which?_____

63. a. Do you go to the movies? Yes_____ No_____ (Skip to 64.)
    b. More or less how many times do you go per month?
    c. Where do you generally go—in this *colonia* or in some other?
       _____this *colonia*
       _____other; which?_____
    d. What type of movies do you generally see?
       _____Mexican
       _____American
       _____other; which?_____

64. a. How many hours per day do you listen to the radio?_____
    b. What are the names of your favorite programs?
       1._____ 2._____

65. a. Do you watch television? Yes_____ No_____ (If no, skip to
       66.)
    b. How frequently do you watch it?
       _____daily
       _____weekly
       _____monthly
       _____special occasions
       _____rarely
       _____never
    c. What are your 2 favorite programs?
       1._____ 2._____

66. Do you always speak Spanish or do you sometimes speak a dialect?
    _____always Spanish
    _____dialect at times

67. How many times per week do you eat the following foods?

_____tortillas

_____bread

_____beans

_____milk

_____meat

68. Do you belong to any groups or organizations, for example, to a union, a sports club, a group to develop or defend the interests of people in your community, or some other group? IF YES, ASK:
    a. What are the names of the groups?
    b. Where do they meet—in this *colonia* (*unidad*) or elsewhere?
    c. What type of activities do they sponsor?
    d. Have you ever held a post in the group?
    e. How frequently do you participate?

				Frequency of
Name	Location	Activities	Post	Participation
1.____	____	____	____	____
2.____	____	____	____	____
3.____	____	____	____	____

69. Did you belong in the past to any groups or organizations to which you presently do not belong? IF YES, ASK:
    a. What were the names of the groups?
    b. Where did they meet—in this area or elsewhere?
    c. What type of activities did they sponsor?
    d. Did you hold a position in any of the groups?
    e. How frequently did you participate?

				Frequency of
Name	Location	Activities	Post	Participation
1.____	____	____	____	____
2.____	____	____	____	____
3.____	____	____	____	____

    f. Why do you no longer belong?

70. a. When there is a problem here in the *colonia* (*unidad*), which of the following people generally has most influence?

_____owners of businesses

_____priests

_____owners of factories

_____government functionaries

_____politicians

_____teachers

    b. What are the names of the 3 most important persons in the *colonia* (*unidad*)?
    1._____ 2._____ 3._____

71. How has the *colonia* (*unidad*) changed in the last few years?
    WITH RESPECT TO EACH CHANGE, ASK:
    a. Was the change good or not?
    b. Who was responsible for the change?

Change	Good/Bad	Who Was Responsible
1.____	_____	_____
2.____	_____	_____
3.____	_____	_____

72. What would you like to see changed in the area in the future?
    WITH RESPECT TO EACH CHANGE, ASK:
    a. Do you think the change will come about?
    b. Who will bring about the change—the government, the people, or who?

Change Want	Will/Will Not Occur	Who Will Be Responsible
1._____	_____	_____
2._____	_____	_____
3._____	_____	_____

73. a. Do you feel people like yourself ought to have benefits from the government?
       _____No; why?_____
       _____Yes; which benefits?_____
    b. Do you actually have benefits from the government?
       _____No
       _____Yes; which?_____
    c. In the future, do you think you will receive more or less benefits from the government?
       _____more
       _____less

74. a. What news interests you most? News of
       _____the *colonia* (*unidad*)
       _____the city
       _____the country
       _____other countries
       _____none
    b. Do you read about political and governmental affairs in the newspaper?
       _____daily
       _____weekly
       _____occasionally
       _____never
    c. With what people do you talk politics?

_____relatives
_____friends
_____fellow workers
_____members of groups to which belong; which
        groups?_____
_____none

75. a. Are you very proud, somewhat proud, or not very proud of
       being Mexican?
       _____very proud
       _____somewhat proud
       _____not very proud
    b. In general, what is it that makes you feel proud of being
       Mexican?

76. In your opinion who are the 3 greatest heroes of this country?
    1._____ 2._____ 3._____

77. a. Suppose you had a question that you wanted to take care of in
       some government office here in the city. Do you think that you
       would be treated better, equal to, or worse than other people?
       _____better
       _____equal to
       _____worse
    b. Have you ever had any dealings with some office of the gov-
       ernment?
       _____Yes
       _____No (Skip to 78.)
    c. How do you feel you were treated?
       _____better than other people
       _____equal to others
       _____worse than others
    d. What was the issue?

78. a. If you had a problem with the police—for example, if you
       were accused of some minor crime—do you think you would
       be treated better, equal to, or worse than others?
       _____better
       _____equal to
       _____worse
    b. Have you had any dealings with the police? Yes_____ No_____
       (If no, skip to 79.)
    c. Do you feel you were treated better, equal to, or worse than
       others?
       _____better
       _____equal to
       _____worse
    d. What was the issue?

79. What are the names of the political parties in Mexico?

    1._____   3._____   5._____

    2._____   4._____   6._____

80. a. Where is the closest PRI office?

    b. IF KNOW LOCATION, ASK: How frequently do you go there?

81. a. Do you belong to a political party? Yes_____ No_____

    b. To which party do you belong?

    c. IF BELONG TO PRI: To which sector?

    d. Since when do you belong?

    e. Have you ever held a post in the party?

        _____yes; presently

        _____yes; previously

        _____no; never

82. Have you ever voted in a national election? IF YES: in which election did you first vote?

83. Could you tell me for whom you voted in the last two elections?

    1964:_____

    1958:_____

84. a. How much influence do you feel people like yourself have on the government? Do you have a lot of influence, little, or no influence?

        _____much

        _____some

        _____none

    b. Do you think people like yourself will have more, equal, or less influence on the government in the future than you now have?

        _____more

        _____equal

        _____less

85. a. Do you think Mexico is influenced a lot, somewhat, or not at all by the U.S.?

        _____a lot

        _____somewhat

        _____not at all (Skip to 86.)

    b. In what way is it influenced by the U.S.?

    c. Do you think the influence is good or not?

        _____good

        _____bad

86. a. What is the name of the president and the two previous presidents?

    1._____

    2._____

    3._____

    b. Who is the local PRI leader?

    c. And the Congressman of the district, do you know his name?

    d. And the President of the U.S.?

    e. And the leader of the Soviet Union?

87. What are the ideals of the Mexican Revolution?

88. Do you think the goals

    _____never will be realized

    _____have already been realized

    _____are presently being realized

    _____have not yet been realized, but will be?

OBSERVATIONS:

1. Respondent wore

    _____shoes

    _____sandals

    _____barefoot

2. Type of dress

    _____all indigenous

    _____some indigenous

    _____none indigenous

Abegglen, James. *The Japanese Factory: Aspects of Its Social Organization*. Glencoe, Ill.: The Free Press, 1960.

Adelman, Irma, and Morris, Cynthia. *An Anatomy of Patterns of Income Distribution in Developing Nations*. Washington, D.C.: Agency for International Development, Department of State, 1971.

Aguilar, M., and Alonso y Carmona, Fernando. *México: riqueza y miseria*. Mexico, D.F.: Editorial Nuestro Tiempo, 1967.

Aiken, Michael, and Hage, Jerald. "Organizational Interdependence and Intra-organizational Structure." *American Sociological Review* 33 (December 1968), 912-31.

Alavi, Hamza. "The State in Post-colonial Societies: Pakistan and Bangladesh." *New Left Review* 74 (1972).

Alcazar, Marco Antonio. *Las agrupaciones patronales en México*. Mexico: El Colegio de México, Jornadas 66, 1970.

Almond, Gabriel, and Coleman, James (eds.). *The Politics of the Developing Areas*. Princeton: Princeton University Press, 1960.

Almond, Gabriel, and Verba, Sidney. *The Civic Culture*. Princeton: Princeton University Press, 1965.

Amaro Victoria, Nelson. "Mass and Class in the Origins of the Cuban Revolution." In *Masses in Latin America*, edited by Irving Horowitz. New York: Oxford University Press, 1965.

Ames, Barry. "Bases of Support for Mexico's Dominant Party." *American Political Science Review* (March 1970), 153-67.

Anderson, Bö, and Cockcroft, James. "Control and Co-optation in Mexican Politics." In *Latin American Radicalism*, edited by Irving Horowitz, Josué de Castro, and John Gerassi. New York: Vintage Books, 1969.

Antoine, Charles. *Church and Power in Brazil*, translated by Peter Nelson. London: Sheed and Ward, 1973.

Anuario Estadístico, 1964. Mexico, D.F.: Universidad Nacional Autonoma de México, 1966.

Ashby, Joe. *Organized Labor and the Mexican Revolution under Lázaro Cárdenas*. Chapel Hill: University of North Carolina Press, 1963.

Balán, Jorge. "Are Farmers' Sons Handicapped in the City?" *Rural Sociology* 33 (1969), 3-29.

―――. "Migrant-Native Socio-economic Differences in Latin American Cities: A Structural Analysis." *Latin American Research Review* 4 (Winter 1969).

Balán, Jorge; Browning, Harley; and Jelin, Elizabeth. *Men in a Developing Society; Social and Geographical Mobility in Monterrey, Mexico.* Austin: University of Texas Press, 1973.

Balassa, Bela. "La industrialización y el comercio exterior: análisis y proposiciones." In *Crecimiento o desarrollo económico?*, edited by Miguel Wionczek et al. Mexico, D.F.: SEP/SETENTAS, 1971.

Banco de México, S.A., *La distribución del ingreso en México.* Mexico, D.F.: Fondo de Cultura Económica, 1973.

Banco Nacional Hipotecario Urbano y de Obras Públicas. *Estudios, no. 6: el problema de la habitación en la Ciudad de México.* Mexico, D.F., 1952.

Banfield, Edward. *The Unheavenly City.* Boston: Little, Brown, 1968.

Barkin, David. "Schooling and Social Distance in Mexico." *Politics and Society* 7 (1975).

―――. (ed.). *Los beneficiarios del desarrollo regional.* Mexico, D.F.: SEP/SETENTAS, 1972.

Barkin, David, and Manitzas, Nita (eds.). *Cuba: The Logic of the Revolution.* Andover, Mass.: Warner Modular Publications, 1973.

Barraclough, Solon, and Arthur Domike. "Agrarian Structure in Seven Latin American Countries." In *Agrarian Problems and Peasant Movements in Latin America*, edited by Rodolfo Stavenhagen. Garden City, New York: Doubleday, 1970.

Beals, Ralph, Jr. "Bureaucracy and Change in the Mexican Catholic Church, 1926-50." Berkeley: Ph.D. dissertation, University of California, 1966.

Beilin, Harry. "The Pattern of Postponability and Its Relation to Social Class Mobility." *The Journal of Social Psychology* 44 (1956), 33-48.

Bell, Daniel. *The Coming of Post-industrial Society: A Venture in Social Forecasting.* New York: Basic Books, 1973.

Bendix, Reinhard. "Bureaucracy and the Problem of Power." In *Reader in Bureaucracy*, edited by Robert Merton et al. New York: The Free Press, 1952.

Bennett, John, and Ishino, Iwao. *Paternalism in the Japanese Economy*. Minneapolis: University of Minnesota Press, 1963.

Beyer, Glenn. *The Urban Explosion in Latin America: A Continent in Process of Urbanization*. Ithaca: Cornell University Press, 1967.

Blau, Peter, and Duncan, Otis Dudley. *The American Occupational Structure*. New York: John Wiley, 1967.

Bonachea, Rolando, and Valdés, Nelson (eds.). *Cuba in Revolution*. Garden City: Anchor Books, 1972.

Bowles, Samuel. "Unequal Education and the Reproduction of the Social Division of Labor." *Review of Radical Political Economics* 3 (Fall/Winter 1971).

Brandenburg, Frank. *The Making of Modern Mexico*. Englewood Cliffs, N.J.: Prentice-Hall, 1964.

Breese, Gerald. *Urbanization in Newly Developing Countries*. Englewood Cliffs, N.J.: Prentice-Hall, 1966.

Bronfenbrenner, Urie. "Socialization and Social Class through Time and Space." In *Class, Status and Power*, edited by Reinhard Bendix and Seymour M. Lipset. New York: The Free Press, 1966.

Brown, Jane Cowan. "Patterns of Intra-urban Settlement in Mexico City: An Examination of the Turner Theory." Ithaca: Cornell University, Latin American Studies Program Dissertation Series, 40, 1972.

Browning, Harley. "Urbanization in Mexico." Berkeley: Ph.D. dissertation, University of California, 1962.

Browning, Harley, and Feindt, Waltraut. "Diferencias entre la población nativa y la migrante en Monterrey." *Demografía y economía* 2 (1968), 183-204.

Bruneau, Thomas. *The Political Transformation of the Brazilian Catholic Church*. London: Cambridge University Press, 1974.

Bukharin, Nikolai. *Imperialism and World Economy*. New York: Monthly Review Press, 1973.

Burgess, Ernest. *The City*. Chicago: University of Chicago Press, 1925.

Butterworth, Douglas. "Grass-roots Political Organization in Cuba: A Case of the Committees for the Defense of the Revolution." *Latin American Urban Research* 4 (1974), 183-203.

―――. "A Study of the Urbanization Process Among Mixtec Migrants from Tilaltongo in Mexico City." *America Indígena* 22 (July 1962), 257-74.

Cabezas, Betty, and Durán, Fernando. "Orientaciones teorícas y operacionales de la marginalidad." Santiago, Chile: DESAL, 1970.

Cacho, Raul. "La vivienda." In *México, cincuenta años de revolución, II, La vida social*. Mexico, D.F.: Fondo de Cultura Económica, 1963.

Cain, Glen. *The Challenge of Dual and Radical Theories of the Labor Market to Orthodox Theory*. Madison: Institute for Poverty Research, University of Wisconsin, 1975.

Cardoso, Fernando, and Reyna, José Luis. "Industrialization, Occupational Structure, and Social Stratification in Latin America." In *Constructive Change in Latin America*, edited by Cole Blasier. Pittsburgh: University of Pittsburgh Press, 1968.

Carnoy, Martin. "Rates of Return to Schooling in Latin America." *Journal of Human Resources* 2 (1967), 359-74.

"Carta pastoral del episcopado Mexicano sobre el desarrollo e integración del país." Mexico, 1968.

Castells, Manuel. *La question urbaine*. Paris: François Maspero, 1972.

Castells, Manuel et al. *Revista Latinoamericana de estudios urbano regionales* 3 (April 1973), 9-112.

Ceceña, José Luis. *El capitalismo monopolista y la economía Mexicana*. Mexico, D.F.: Cuadernos Americanos, 1963.

Centro de Estudios Económicos y Demográficos. *Dinámica de la población de México*. Mexico, D.F.: El Colegio de México, 1970.

Chaplin, David. "Industrial Labor Recruitment in Peru." In *Workers and Managers in Latin America*, edited by Stanley Davis and Louis Goodman. Lexington, Mass.: D.C. Heath, 1972.

Chinoy, Eli. *Automobile Workers and the American Dream*. Boston: Beacon Press, 1965.

Cinta, Ricardo. "Burguesía nacional y desarrollo." In *El perfil de México en 1980—III*. Mexico, D.F.: Siglo XXI, 1972.

Cline, Howard. *Mexico: Revolution to Evolution: 1940-1960*. London: Oxford University Press, 1962.

Cockcroft, James. "Coercion and Ideology in Mexican Politics." In *Dependency and Underdevelopment: Latin America's Political Economy*, edited by Cockcroft, André Gunder Frank, and Dale Johnson. Garden City, New York: Doubleday, 1972.

Cohen, Michael. *Urban Policy and Political Conflict in Africa.* Chicago: University of Chicago Press, 1974.

Colfax, David. "Pressure Toward Distortion and Involvement in Studying a Civil Rights Organization." *Human Organization* 25 (Summer 1966), 140-49.

Collier, David. *Squatters and Oligarchs: Authoritarian Rule and Policy Change in Peru.* Baltimore: The Johns Hopkins Press, 1976.

Constitución Política de los Estados Unidos Mexicanos. Mexico, D.F.: Edicíon del Senado de la Republica, 1966.

Córdova, Arnaldo. *La política de masas del Cardenismo.* Mexico, D.F.: Era, 1974.

Cornelius, Wayne. "The Impact of Governmental Performance on Political Attitudes and Behavior: The Case of the Migrant Poor in Mexico City." *Latin American Urban Research* 3 (1973), 213-51.

————. "Urbanization and Political Demand-making: A Study of Political Participation Among the Migrant Poor." *American Political Science Review* 68 (December 1974).

————. "Urbanization as an Agent in Latin American Political Instability: The Case of Mexico." *American Political Science Review* (September 1969), 833-57.

————. *Politics and the Migrant Poor in Mexico City.* Stanford: Stanford University Press, 1975.

Crain, Robert. "School Integration and Occupational Achievement of Negroes." *American Journal of Sociology* 75 (1970), 593-606.

Cumberland, Charles. *Mexico: The Struggle for Modernity.* New York: Oxford University Press, 1968.

Dahl, Robert. "A Critique of Ruling Elite Model." *American Political Science Review* 52 (June 1958), 463-69.

————. *Who Governs? Democracy and Power in an American City.* New Haven: Yale University Press, 1961.

Dahrendorf, Ralph. *Class and Class Conflict in Industrial Society.* Stanford: Stanford University Press, 1959.

Davis, Stanley. "Authority and Control in Mexican Enterprise." In *Workers and Managers in Latin America,* edited by Stanley Davis and Louis Goodman. Lexington, Mass.: D.C. Heath, 1972.

Davis, Stanley. "Social Change in Mexican Enterprise." Cambridge: Unpublished manuscript, Harvard University Graduate School of Business Administration, 1967.

————. "United States vs. Latin America: Business and Culture." In *Workers and Managers in Latin America*, edited by Davis and Louis Goodman. Lexington, Mass.: D.C. Heath, 1972.

Delhumeau, Antonio. *México: Realidad política de sus partidos: Una investigación psicosocial acerca de los partidos políticos Mexicanos*. Mexico, D.F.: Instituto Mexicano de Estudios Políticos, 1970.

Derossi, Flavia. "Familism in Industry." In *Workers and Managers in Latin America*, edited by Stanley Davis and Louis Goodman. Lexington, Mass.: D.C. Heath, 1972.

————. *The Mexican Entrepreneur*. Paris: OECD, 1971.

Deutsch, Karl. "Social Mobilization and Political Development." In *Development and Social Change*, edited by Jason Finkle and Richard Gable. New York: John Wiley, 1966.

Dietz, Henry. "Urban Squatter Settlements in Peru: A Case History and Analysis." *Journal of Inter-American Studies* 2 (July 1969), 353-70.

Dill, William. "The Impact of Environment on Organizational Development." In *Concepts and Issues in Administrative Behavior*, edited by Sidney Mailick and Edward Van Ness. Englewood Cliffs, N.J.: Prentice-Hall, 1962, pp. 94-109.

Doeringer, Peter, and Piore, Michael. *Internal Labor Markets and Manpower Analysis*. Lexington, Mass.: Heath Lexington Books, 1971.

Domhoff, G. William. *Who Rules America?* Englewood Cliffs, N.J.: Prentice-Hall, 1967.

Domínguez, Jorge. "The Performance of the Cuban Revolution." Paper presented at the American Society for International Law, Washington, D.C., April 1973.

Durand, John, and Pelaez, Cesar. "Patterns of Urbanization in Latin America." *Milbank Memorial Fund Quarterly* 47.2 (1965), 166-96.

Durkheim, Emile. *The Division of Labor in Society*, translated by George Simpson. Glencoe, Ill.: The Free Press, 1947.

Eckstein, Salomon. *El marco macroeconómico del problema agrario*. Mexico, D.F.: Centro de Investigaciones Agraria, 1968.

Economic Commission for Latin America (ECLA). *Economic Survey of Latin America, 1970*. New York: United Nations, 1972.

——. *Economic Bulletin for Latin America* 18, New York: United Nations, 1974.

Edel, Mathew. *Food Supply*. New York: Frederick Praeger, 1969.

Edwards, Ric. "Religion in the Revolution?—A Look at Golconda." *North American Committee on Latin America*, Newsletter III, No. 10 (February 1970).

Einaudi, Luigi et al. *The Changing Catholic Church*. Santa Monica: The Rand Corporation, 1969.

Elling, R. H., and Halbsky, S. "Organizational Differentiation and Support: A Conceptual Framework." *Administrative Science Quarterly* 6 (September 1961), 185-209.

Epstein, David. *Brasilia, Plan and Reality: A Study of Planned and Spontaneous Urban Settlement*. Berkeley and Los Angeles: University of California Press, 1973.

Evan, William. "The Organization-Set: Toward a Theory of Interorganizational Relations." In *Approaches to Organizational Design*, edited by James Thompson. Pittsburgh: University of Pittsburgh Press, 1966.

Evans, Peter. "The Latin American Entrepreneur: Style, Scale and Rationality." In *Workers and Managers in Latin America*, edited by Stanley Davis and Louis Goodman. Lexington, Mass.: D.C. Heath, 1972.

Fagen, Richard, and Tuohy, William. *Politics and Privilege in a Mexican City*. Stanford: Stanford University Press, 1972.

Fava, Sylvia Fleis. "Contrasts in Neighboring: New York City and a Suburban Community." In *The Suburban Community*, edited by William Dobriner. New York: Putnam, 1958.

Fiszman, Joseph. "Education and Social Mobility in People's Poland." Paper presented at the American Association for the Advancement of Slavic Studies, 1971.

Form, William. "Occupational and Social Integration of Automobile Workers in Four Countries: A Comparative Study." In *Comparative Perspectives on Industrial Society*, edited by William Faunce and William Form. Boston: Little, Brown, 1969.

Foster, George. "The Dyadic Contract: A Model for the Social Structure of a Mexican Peasant Village." In *Peasant Society:*

A Reader, edited by Jack Potter, May Diaz, and George Foster. Boston: Little, Brown, 1967.

――――. "Peasant Society and the Image of the Limited Good." In *Peasant Society: A Reader*, edited by Jack Potter, May Diaz, and George Foster. Boston: Little, Brown, 1967.

Fried, Robert. "Urbanization and Italian Politics." *Journal of Politics* 29 (1967), 509-30.

Fromm, Erich, and Maccoby, Michael. *Social Character in a Mexican Village*. Englewood Cliffs, N.J.: Prentice-Hall, 1971.

Fuentes, Carlos. "The Other Mexico: Critique of the Pyramid." *New York Review of Books* 20 (September 1973).

――――. *The Death of Artemio Cruz*, translated by Sam Hileman. New York: Farrar, Straus and Giroux, 1964.

"El futuro de tepito: Un asilo." *Excelsior*, October 25, 1971.

Galindo Muñez, Arturo. "Desarrollo e integración de la industria del calzado en México." Mexico, D.F.: Tesis para Licenciado en Economía, Escuela Nacional de Economía, 1969.

Gans, Herbert. *People and Plans*. New York: Basic Books, 1968.

――――. *The Urban Villagers*. New York: The Free Press, 1962.

Germani, Gino. "Inquiry into the Social Effects of Urbanization in a Working Class Sector of Buenos Aires." In *Urbanization in Latin America*, edited by Philip Hauser. New York: International Documents Service, 1961.

――――. "Social and Political Consequences of Mobility." In *Social Structure and Mobility in Economic Development*, edited by Neil Smelser and Seymour M. Lipset. Chicago: Aldine, 1966.

Gillin, John. "The Middle Segments and Their Values," In *Latin American Politics*, edited by Robert Tomasek. Garden City, New York: Doubleday, 1966, 24-40.

Glaser, Barney, and Strauss, Anselm. "Awareness Contexts and Social Interaction." *American Sociological Review* 29 (1964), 669-79.

Glazer, Nathan, and Moynihan, Daniel. *Beyond the Melting Pot: The Negroes, Puerto Ricans, Jews, Italians and Irish of New York City*. Cambridge: M.I.T. Press and Harvard University Press, 1963.

Goldrich, Daniel. "Toward the Comparative Study of Politicization in Latin America." In *Contemporary Cultures and Societies in Latin America*, edited by Dwight Heath and Richard Adams. New York: Random House, 1965.

Goldthorpe, J. H. "Social Stratification in Industrial Society." In *Class, Status and Power*, edited by Reinhard Bendix and Seymour M. Lipset. New York: Free Press, 1966.

González Casanova, Pablo. *Democracy in Mexico*. New York: Oxford University Press, 1970.

González Cosío, Arturo. "Clases y estratos sociales." In *México: Cincuenta años de revolución, II*. Mexico, D.F.: Fondo de Cultura Económica, 1961.

Gordon, David. *Theories of Poverty and Underdevelopment*. Lexington, Mass.: D.C. Heath, 1972.

————, Edwards, Richard, and Reich, Michael. "Labor Market Segmentation in American Capitalism." Paper presented at the Conference on Labor Market Segmentation, Cambridge, Mass. 1973.

Guetzkow, Harold. "Relations among Organizations." In *Studies on Behavior in Organizations*, edited by Raymond Bower. Athens: University of Georgia Press, 1966.

Gusfield, Joseph. "Fieldwork Reciprocities in Studying a Social Movement." *Human Organization* 14 (Fall 1955).

Hagen, Everett. *On the Theory of Social Change: How Economic Growth Begins*. Homewood, Ill.: Dorsey Press, 1962.

Hansen, Roger. *The Politics of Mexican Development*. Baltimore: The Johns Hopkins Press, 1971.

Hardoy, Jorge. "Spatial Structure and Society in Revolutionary Cuba." In *Cuba: The Logic of the Revolution*, edited by David Barkin and Nina Manitzas. Andover, Mass. Warner Modular Publications, 1973.

Harth Deneke, Jorge Alberto. "The Colonias Proletarias of Mexico City: Low Income Settlements on the Urban Fringe." Cambridge: M.A. thesis, Department of City Planning, Massachusetts Institute of Technology, 1966.

Hobsbawm, Eric. "Peasants and Rural Migrants in Politics." In *The Politics of Conformity in Latin America*, edited by Claudio Véliz. London: Oxford University Press, 1967.

Horowitz, Irving (ed.). *The Rise and Fall of Project Camelot: Studies in the Relationship between Social Sciences and Practical Politics*. Cambridge: M.I.T. Press, 1969.

Hoselitz, Bert. "The City, the Factory and Economic Growth." In *Comparative Perspectives on Industrial Society*, edited by William Faunce and William Form. Boston: Little, Brown, 1969.

Hoselitz, Bert. "Economic Growth and Development: Noneconomic Factors in Economic Development." *Political Development and Social Change*, edited by Jason Finkle and Richard Gable. New York: John Wiley, 1966.

Hunter, Floyd. *Community Power Structure: A Study of Decision Makers.* Chapel Hill: University of North Carolina Press, 1953.

Huntington, Samuel. *Political Order in Changing Societies.* New Haven: Yale University Press, 1968.

Hutchinson, Bertram et al. *Mobilidade e trabalho; um estudo na cidade do São Paulo.* Rio de Janeiro, 1960.

Inkeles, Alex. "The Modernization of Man." In *Modernization: The Dynamics of Growth*, edited by Myron Weiner. New York: Basic Books, 1966.

———, and Bauer, R. *Soviet Citizen: Daily Life in a Totalitarian Society.* Cambridge: Harvard University Press, 1969.

Instituto Mexicano de Seguro Social. *Investigación de vivienda en 11 ciudades del país.* Mexico, D.F.: Editorial Rabasa, 1967.

Instituto Nacional de la Vivienda. *Colonias proletarias: Problemas y soluciones.* Mexico, D.F.: 1958.

———. *Herradura de tugurios: Problemas y soluciones.* Mexico, D.F.: 1958.

Isbister, John. "Urban Employment and Wages in a Developing Economy: The Case of Mexico." *Economic Development and Cultural Change* 20 (October 1970), 22-46.

Iturriaga, José. *La estructura social y cultural de México.* Mexico, D.F.: Fondo de Cultura Económica, 1951.

Jackson, Harold. "Intra-Urban Migration of Mexico City's Poor." Boulder: Unpublished dissertation, 1973.

Jencks, Christopher et al. *Inequality: A Reassessment of the Effect of Family and Schooling in America.* New York: Basic Books, 1972.

Johnson, Kenneth. *Mexican Democracy: A Critical View.* Boston: Houghton Mifflin, 1971.

Kahl, Joseph. *The Measurement of Modernism.* Austin: University of Texas Press, 1968.

Kazin, Phyllis. "Socio-cultural Aspects of Development: A Case Study of an Introduction of a Textile Factory into a Community in Southern Mexico." Cambridge: Ph.D. dissertation, Harvard University, 1972.

Kemper, Robert. "Family and Household Organization among Tzintzuntzan Migrants in Mexico City." *Latin American Urban Research* 4 (1974), 347-57.

Kindleberger, C. P. *American Business Abroad.* New Haven: Yale University Press, 1969.

Kornhauser, William. *The Politics of Mass Society.* Glencoe, Ill.: The Free Press, 1959.

Lamartine Yates, Paul. *El desarrollo regional de México.* Mexico, D.F.: Banco de México, 1962.

Leacock, Eleanor (ed.). *The Culture of Poverty: A Critique.* New York: Simon and Schuster, 1971.

Leeds, Anthony. "Brazilian Careers and Social Structure: A Case History and Model." In *Contemporary Cultures and Societies of Latin America,* edited by Dwight Heath and Richard Adams. New York: Random House, 1965.

————. "Housing-Settlement Types, Arrangements for Living, Proletarianization and the Social Structure of the City." *Latin American Urban Research* 4 (1974), 67-99.

————. "The Significant Variables Determining the Character of Squatter Settlements." *America Latina* 12 (July-September 1969).

Lenin, V. I. *Imperialism: The Highest Stage of Capitalism.* New York: International Publishers, 1972.

Lenski, Gerhard. *The Religious Factor.* New York: Doubleday, 1961.

Lerner, Daniel. *The Passing of Traditional Society.* Glencoe, Ill.: The Free Press, 1958.

Levine, Sol, and White, Paul. "Exchange as a Conceptual Framework for the Study of Inter-organizational Relationships." *Administrative Science Quarterly* 5 (March 1961), 583-601.

Lewis, Oscar. *The Children of Sanchez: Autobiography of a Mexican Family.* New York: Random House, 1961.

————. *Five Families: Mexican Case Studies in the Culture of Poverty.* New York: Random House, 1959.

————. *La Vida: A Puerto Rican Family in the Culture of Poverty.* New York: Random House, 1966.

————. *Life in a Mexican Village: Tepoztlan Restudied.* Urbana: University of Illinois Press, 1963.

————. "Urbanization without Breakdown: A Case Study." In

Contemporary Cultures and Societies in Latin America, edited by Dwight Heath and Richard Adams. New York: Random House, 1965.

Liebman, Arthur et al. *Latin American University Students: A Six Nation Study.* Cambridge: Harvard University Press, 1972.

Lieuwen, Edwin. *Mexican Militarism.* Albuquerque: University of New Mexico Press, 1968.

Light, Ivan. *Ethnic Enterprise in America.* Berkeley: University of California Press, 1972.

Linz, Juan. "An Authoritarian Regime: Spain." In *Cleavages, Ideologies and Party Systems, Contributions to Comparative Political Sociology,* edited by E. Allardt and Y. Littunen. Helsinki: Transactions of the Westermarck Society, 1964.

Lipset, Seymour M. *Political Man.* Garden City, New York: Doubleday, 1960.

Lipset, Seymour M., and Bendix, Reinhard. *Social Mobility in Industrial Society.* Berkeley: University of California Press, 1967.

Litwak, Eugene, and Hylton, Lydia. "Interorganizational Analysis: A Hypothesis on Coordinating Agencies." *Administrative Science Quarterly* 6 (March 1962), 395-426.

Lomnitz, Larissa. "The Social and Economic Organization of a Mexican Shantytown." *Latin American Urban Research* 4 (1974), 135-55.

Loyo Brambila, Aurora, and Pozas Horcasitas, Ricardo. "Notes on the Mechanisms of Control Exercised by the Mexican State over the Organized Sector of the Working Class, A Case Study: The Political Crisis of 1958." Paper presented at the Center for Inter-American Relations, New York, April 1975.

Lozoya, Jorge. *El ejército Mexicano (1911-1965).* Mexico: El Colegio de México, Jornadas 65, 1970.

Lysgaard, Sverred. "The Deferred Gratification Pattern: A Preliminary Study." *American Sociological Review* 18 (1953).

Mabry, Donald. *Mexico's Acción Nacional: A Catholic Alternative to Revolution.* Syracuse: Syracuse University Press, 1973.

Maccoby, Michael. "Love and Authority." In *Peasant Society, A Reader,* edited by Jack Potter, May Diaz, and George Foster. Boston: Little, Brown, 1967.

MacEwen, Allison. "Marginalidad y movilidad en una villa miseria," *Revista Latinoamericana de sociología* 7 (1971), pp. 37-53.

Marshall, T. H. *Class, Citizenship and Social Development.* Garden City, N.Y.: Doubleday, 1965.

Marx, Karl. *Capital.* New York: International Publishers, 1967.

——. "The Eighteenth Brumaire of Louis Bonaparte." In *Marx and Engels: Basic Writings on Politics and Philosophy,* edited by Lewis Feuer. Garden City, N.Y.: Doubleday, 1959.

——, and Engels, Friedrich. "The German Ideology." In *Marx and Engels: Basic Writings on Politics and Philosophy,* edited by Lewis Feuer. Garden City, N.Y.: Doubleday, 1959.

——. "Manifesto of the Communist Party." In *Marx and Engels: Basic Writings on Politics and Philosophy,* edited by Lewis Feuer. Garden City, N.Y.: Doubleday, 1959.

Mattelart, Armand, and Garretón, Manuel. *Integración nacional y marginalidad: Un ensayo de regionalización social de Chile.* Santiago, Chile: Editorial del Pacifico, 1965.

Matza, David. "The Disreputable Poor." In *Class, Status and Power,* edited by Reinhard Bendix and Seymour M. Lipset. New York: The Free Press, 1966.

McClelland, David. *The Achieving Society.* New York: Van Nostrand, 1961.

Mecham, J. Lloyd. *Church and State in Latin America: A History of Politico-Ecclesiastical Relations,* revised edition. Chapel Hill; University of North Carolina Press, 1966.

Medin, Tzvi. *Ideología y praxis política de Lázaro Cárdenas.* Mexico, D.F.: Siglo XXI, 1972.

Medina, Luis et al. *La vida política en México, 1970-74.* Mexico: El Colegio de México, 1974.

Merton, Robert. *Social Theory and Social Structure.* Glencoe, Ill.: The Free Press, 1961.

Meyer, Lorenzo. *México y los Estados Unidos en el conflicto petrolero, 1917-1942.* Mexico, D.F.: El Colegio de México, 1968.

——. "The Origins of Mexico's Authoritarian State, Political Control in the Old and New Regimes." Paper presented at the Center for Inter-American Relations, New York, June 1975.

——, et al. *La política exterior de México: Realidad y perspectivas.* Mexico, D.F.: El Colegio de México, 1974.

Michels, Robert. *Political Parties: A Sociological Study of the Oligarchical Tendencies of Modern Democracy,* translated by Eden and Cedar Paul. New York: The Free Press, 1962.

Michl, Sara. "Urban Squatter Organization as a National Government Tool: The Case of Lima, Peru." *Latin American Urban Research* 3 (1973).

Miliband, Ralph. "Poulantzas and the Capitalist State." *New Left Review* 82 (November-December 1973).

Miller, S. M. "Comparative Social Mobility." *Current Sociology* 9 (1960), 1-89.

Miller, S. M.; Reissman, Frank; and Segull, Arthur. "Poverty and Self-indulgence: A Critique of the Non-deferred Gratification Pattern." In *Poverty in America: A Book of Readings*, edited by Louis Ferman, Joyce Kornbluh, and Alan Haber. Ann Arbor: University of Michigan Press, 1968.

Miller, Walter. "Lower Class Culture as a Generating Milieu of Gang Delinquency." *Journal of Social Issues* 14 (1958), 5-19.

Mills, C. Wright. *The Power Elite*. New York: Oxford University Press, 1956.

——. *The Sociological Imagination*. New York: Oxford University Press, 1959.

Mintz, Sidney, and Wolf, Eric. "An Analysis of Ritual Co-parenthood (Compadrazgo)." In *Peasant Society, A Reader*, edited by Jack Potter, May Diaz, and George Foster. Boston: Little, Brown, 1967.

Montes de Oca, Elena. "State, Agrarian Reform and Peasant Organizations in Mexico." Paper presented at the Center for Inter-American Relations, April 1975.

Moore, Barrington, Jr. *Social Origins of Dictatorship and Democracy*. Boston: Beacon Press, 1966.

Moore, Wilbert, and Feldman, Arnold (eds.). *Labor Commitment and Social Change in Developing Areas*. New York: Social Science Research Council, 1960.

Moreno Sanchez, Manuel. *La crisis política de México*. Mexico, D.F.: Editorial Extemporáneos, 1970.

Morse, Richard. "Internal Migrants and the Urban Ethos in Latin America." Paper presented at the Seventh World Congress of Sociology, Varna, Bulgaria, September 1970.

——. "Recent Research on Latin American Urbanization: A Selective Survey with Commentary." *Latin American Research Review* 1 (1965), 35-74.

——. "Trends and Issues in Latin American Urban Research, 1965-1970." *Latin American Research Review* 6 (Spring and Summer 1971), 3-52, 19-75.

Mosk, Sanford. *Industrial Revolution in Mexico.* Berkeley and Los Angeles: University of California Press, 1954.

Mueller, Marnie. "Changing Patterns of Agricultural Output and Productivity in the Private and Land Reform Sectors in Mexico 1940-1960." *Economic Development and Cultural Change* 18 (January 1970), 252-65.

Murray, Robin. "The Internationalization of Capital and the Nation State." *New Left Review* 67 (May-June 1971).

Myers, Charles. *Education and National Development in Mexico.* Princeton: Industrial Relations Section, Princeton University, 1965.

Nash, Manning. *Machine Age Maya.* Chicago: University of Chicago Press, 1967.

Navarrete, Ifigenia. "La distribución del ingreso en México: tendencias y perspectivas." In *El perfil de México en 1980, I.* Mexico City, D.F.: Siglo XXI, 1970.

Navarrete, Jorge. "Desequilibrio y dependencia: las relaciones económicas internacionales en los años sesenta." In *Crecimiento o desarrolo económico?*, edited by Miguel Wionczek et al. Mexico, D.F.: SEP/SETENTAS, 1971.

Nelson, Joan. *Migrants, Urban Poverty and Instability in Developing Nations.* Cambridge: Center for International Affairs, Harvard University, 1969.

El nero. 1971-72. Bi-weekly newspaper, Mexico, D.F.

Newfarmer, Richard. "Structural Sources of Multinational Corporate Power in Recipient Economies." Paper presented at CONCCCYT/CIDE Symposium on the Effects of Multinational Corporations, Queretaro, Mexico, 1975.

Niebuhr, N. R. *Social Sources of Denominationalism.* New York: Living Age Books, 1962.

Nun, José. *Latin America: The Hegemonic Crisis and the Military Coup.* Berkeley: Institute of International Studies, University of California, 1969.

Obregón, Alvaro. "What's Ahead for Business in Mexico." *System* (October 1921).

Offe, Claus. "The Theory of the Capitalist State and the Problem of Policy Formation." Paper presented at the VIII World Congress of Sociology, Toronto, 1974.

Oldman, Oliver et al. *Financing Urban Development in Mexico City.* Cambridge: Harvard University Press, 1967.

Ortiz Reyes, Maria de Lourdes. *Manifestaciones demográficas a nivel familiar.* Mexico, D.F.: Facultad de Ciencias Políticas y Sociales, Universidad Nacional Autónoma Mexicana, 1969.

Padgett, L. Vincent. *The Mexican Political System.* Boston: Houghton Mifflin, 1966.

Parsons, Talcott. *The Social System.* New York: The Free Press, 1951.

————. *Societies: Evolutionary and Comparative Perspectives.* Englewood Cliffs, N.J.: Prentice-Hall, 1966.

Parsons, Talcott, and Smelser, Neil. *Economy and Society: A Study in the Integration of Economic and Social Theory.* New York: The Free Press, 1965.

Patch, Richard. "Life in a Callejón: A Study of Urban Disorganization." *American University Field Staff Reports,* West Coast South American Series 8 (1961).

Paz, Octavio. *The Labyrinth of Solitude.* New York: Grove Press, 1961.

Peattie, Lisa. *The View from the Barrio.* Ann Arbor: University of Michigan Press, 1968.

Perlman, Janice. "The Fate of Migrants in Rio's Favelas." Cambridge: Ph.D. dissertation, Massachusetts Institute of Technology, 1971.

Perry, Clarence. "The Neighborhood Unit." In *Regional Survey of New York and Its Environs.* New York: Committee on Regional Plan of New York and Its Environs, 1929, 22-140.

Petras, James, and Zeitlin, Maurice. "Miners and Agrarian Radicalism." In *Latin America: Revolution or Reform?,* edited by James Petras and Maurice Zeitlin. Greenwich, Conn.: Fawcett, 1968.

Piore, Michael. "The Dual Labor Market: Theory and Implications." In *Problems in Political Economy: An Urban Perspective,* edited by David Gordon. Lexington, Mass.: D.C. Heath, 1971.

————. "Notes for a Theory of Labor Market Stratification." Working Paper No. 95. Cambridge: Massachusetts Institute of Technology, 1972.

Piven, Frances, and Cloward, Richard. *Regulating the Poor: The Functions of Public Welfare.* New York: Vintage Books, 1972.

Policies and Institutions for the Promotion of Exports of Manufacturers, A Selected Case Study, Mexico. Washington, D.C.: Pan American Union, 1967.

Polsby, Nelson. *Community Power and Political Theory.* New Haven: Yale University Press, 1963.

————. "How to Study Community Power: the Pluralist Alternative." In *The Structure of Community Power,* edited by Michael Aiken and Paul Mott. New York: Random House, 1970.

Portes, Alejandro. "Political Primitivism, Differential Socialization, and Lower-Class Leftist Radicalism." *American Sociological Review* 36 (October 1971), 820-35.

————. "Urbanization and Politics in Latin America." *Social Science Quarterly* 52 (1971), 697-720.

————. "The Urban Slum in Chile: Types and Correlates." *Land Economics* 47 (August 1971), 235-48.

Poulantzas, Nicos. *Political Power and Social Class.* London: New Left Books, 1973.

Powell, Sandra. "Political Participation in the Barriadas: A Case Study," *Comparative Political Studies* 2 (1969), 195-215.

Pratt, Raymond. "Parties, Neighborhood Associations, and the Politicization of the Urban Poor in Latin America." *Midwest Journal of Political Science* 15 (August 1971).

Purcell, Susan, and Purcell, John. "Community Power and Benefits from the Nation: The Case of Mexico." *Latin American Urban Research* 3 (1973).

————. "Machine Politics and Socio-Economic Change in Mexico." In *Contemporary Mexico: Papers of the IV International Congress of Mexican History,* edited by James Wilkie, Michael Meyer, and Edna Monzón de Wilkie. Berkeley and Mexico City: University of California Press and El Colegio de México, 1975.

Quijano, Aníbal. "La constitución del 'mundo' de la marginalidad urbana," *Revista Latinoamericana de estudios urbano regionales* 2 (July 1972), 89-106.

Quirk, Robert. *The Mexican Revolution and the Catholic Church, 1910-1929.* Bloomington: Indiana University Press, 1973.

Ramírez Rodríguez, Armando. *Chin-Chin, el teporocho.* México, D.F.: Organización Editorial Novaro, 1972.

Ramos, Samuel. *Profile of Man and Culture in Mexico.* New York: McGraw-Hill, 1962.

Randall, Laura. "Labor Migration and Mexican Economic Development." *Social and Economic Studies* 11 (March 1962).

Randall, Laura. "The Process of Economic Development in Mexico from 1940 to 1959." New York: Ph.D. dissertation, Columbia University, 1962.

Ray, Talton. *The Politics of the Barrios of Venezuela.* Berkeley and Los Angeles: University of California Press, 1969.

Redfield, Robert. "The Folk Society." *American Journal of Sociology* 52 (1947), 293-308.

Redfield, Robert, and Rojas, Alfonso Villa. *Chan Kom.* Chicago: University of Chicago Press, 1967.

Reid, William. "Interagency Coordination in Delinquency Prevention and Control." *Social Service Review* 38 (December 1964), 418-28.

Reyna, José Luis. "Control político, estabilidad y desarrollo en México." In *Cuadernos del Centro de Estudios Sociológicos.* México, D.F.: El Colegio de México, 1974.

———. "An Empirical Analysis of Political Mobilization: The Case of Mexico." Ithaca: Cornell University, Latin American Studies Program Dissertation Series, No. 26, 1971.

———. "Occupational Mobility: The Mexican Case." In *Workers and Managers in Latin America*, edited by Stanley Davis and Louis Goodman. Lexington, Mass.: D. C. Heath, 1972.

Reynolds, Clark. *The Mexican Economy: Twentieth Century Structure and Growth.* New Haven: Yale University Press, 1970.

Richmond, Patricia. "Mexico: A Case Study of One-Party Politics." Berkeley: Ph.D. dissertation, University of California, 1965.

Ridgeway, V. F. "Administration of Manufacturer-Dealer Systems." *Administrative Science Quarterly* 1 (June 1957), 463-83.

Roberts, Bryan. "The Interrelationships of City and Provinces in Peru and Guatemala." *Latin American Urban Research* 4 (1974).

———. *Organizing Strangers: Poor Families in Guatemala City.* Austin: University of Texas Press, 1973.

Rogler, Lloyd. "Slum Neighborhoods in Latin America," *Journal of Inter-American Studies* 9 (1967), 507-28.

Rogoff, Natalie. *Recent Trends in Occupational Mobility.* Glencoe, Ill.: The Free Press, 1953.

Ronfeldt, David. *The Mexican Army and Political Order Since 1940.* Santa Monica: The Rand Corporation, 1973.

Ross, Stanley (ed.). *Is the Mexican Revolution Dead?* New York: Alfred A. Knopf, 1966.

Ruddle, Kenneth, and Barrows, Kathleen. *The Statistical Abstract of Latin America, 1972.* Los Angeles: Latin American Center, University of California, 1974.

Salmen, Lawrence. "The Casas de Cômodos of Rio de Janiero: A Study of the Occupations and Accommodations of Inner-city Slums and a Comparison of their Characteristics with Favelas." Ann Arbor: University Microfilm, 1971.

Schmitter, Philippe. *Interest Conflict and Political Change in Brazil.* Stanford: Stanford University Press, 1971.

————. "Paths to Political Development in Latin America." In *Changing Latin America: New Interpretations of Its Politics and Society,* edited by Douglas Chalmers. New York: Academy of Political Science, Columbia University, 1972.

————. "The 'Portugalization' of Brazil?" In *Authoritarian Brazil: Origins, Policies, and Future,* edited by Alfred Stepan. New Haven: Yale University Press, 1973.

Schnore, Leo. "On the Spatial Structure of Cities in the Two Americas." In *The Study of Urbanization,* edited by Philip Hauser and Leo Schnore. New York: John Wiley, 1967.

Schulze, Robert, and Blumberg, Leonard. "The Determination of Local Power Elites." In *The Structure of Community Power,* edited by Michael Aiken and Paul Mott. New York: Random House, 1970.

Scott, Robert. *Mexican Government in Transition,* revised edition. Urbana: University of Illinois Press, 1964.

————. "Mexico: The Established Revolution." In *Political Culture and Political Development,* edited by Lucian Pye and Sidney Verba. Princeton: Princeton University Press, 1965.

Selznick, Philip. *TVA and the Grass Roots.* New York: Harper and Row, 1966.

Sepúlveda, Bernardo et al. *Las empresas transnacionales en México.* Mexico, D.F.: El Colegio de México, 1974.

Shafer, Robert. *Mexican Business Organization: History and Analysis.* Syracuse: Syracuse University Press, 1973.

Sills, David. *The Volunteers.* New York: The Free Press, 1957.

Silvert, Kalman. "The Costs of Anti-nationalism: Argentina." In *Nationalism and Development,* edited by Kalman Silvert. New York: Vintage Books, 1967.

Silvert, Kalman, and Silvert, Frieda. "Fate, Chance, and Faith: Some Ideas Suggested by a Recent Trip to Cuba." *American Universities Field Staff*, North American Series No. 2, September 1974.

Simpson, Eyler. *The Ejido: Mexico's Way Out.* Chapel Hill: University of North Carolina Press, 1937.

Singer, Morris. *Growth, Equality and the Mexican Experience.* Austin: University of Texas Press, 1969.

Sjoberg, Gideon. "Rural-urban Balance and Models of Economic Development." In *Social Structure and Mobility in Economic Development*, edited by Neil Smelser and Seymour Lipset. Chicago: Aldine, 1966.

Smith, Peter. "La movilidad política en el México contemporáneo." *Foro internacional* 15 (January-March 1975), 379-413.

Soares, Glaucio Ary Dillon. "The New Industrialization and the Brazilian Political System." In *Latin America: Reform or Revolution?*, edited by James Petras and Maurice Zeitlin. Greenwich, Conn.: Fawcett, 1968.

Sociedad de Arquitectos Mexicanos y del Colegio Nacional de Arquitectos de México. *La vivienda popular en México.* Mexico, D.F.: 1960.

Soláun, Mauricio; Cepeda, Fernando; and Bagley, Bruce. "Urban Reform in Colombia: The Impact of the 'Politics of Games' on Public Policy." *Latin American Urban Research* 3 (1973), 97-130.

Solís, Leopoldo. "Mexican Economic Policy in the Post-war Period: The Views of Mexican Economists." *American Economic Review* 10 (June 1971), 28-46.

Stavenhagen, Rodolfo. "Social Aspects of Mexican Agrarian Structure." In *Agrarian Problems and Peasant Movements in Latin America*, edited by Rodolfo Stavenhagen. Garden City, N.Y.: Doubleday, 1970.

Stein, Stanley. "The Brazilian Cotton Textile Industry, 1850-1950." In *Economic Growth: Brazil, India, Japan*, edited by Simon Kuznets, Wilbert Moore, and J. Spengler. Durham, N.C.: Duke University Press, 1955.

Stern, Claudio, and Kahl, Joseph. "Stratification Since the Revolution." In *Comparative Perspectives on Stratification: Mexico, Great Britain, Japan*, edited by Joseph Kahl. Boston: Little, Brown, 1968.

Stevens, Evelyn. *Protest and Response in Mexico*. Cambridge: M.I.T. Press, 1974.

Stokes, Charles. "A Theory of Slums." *Land Economics* 38 (1962) 187-97.

Tannenbaum, Frank. *The Struggle for Peace and Bread*. New York: Alfred Knopf, 1950.

Tax, Sol. *Penny Capitalism*. Chicago: University of Chicago Press, 1963.

Thernstrom, Stephen. *Poverty and Progress: Social Mobility in a Nineteenth Century City*. Cambridge: Harvard University Press, 1964.

Thiesen, Gerald. "The Case of Camilo Torres Restrepo." *Journal of Church and State* 16 (Spring 1974).

Thompson, James. "Organizations and Output Transactions." *American Journal of Sociology* 68 (November 1962), 309-24.

Thompson, James, and McEwen, William. "Organizational Goals and Environment: Goal-setting as an Interaction Process." *American Sociological Review* 23 (February 1958), 23-31.

Tönnies, Ferdinand. *Community and Society*. New York: Harper and Row, 1963.

Trejo Reyes, Saúl. *Industrialización y empleo en México*. Mexico, D.F.: Fondo de Cultura Económica, 1973.

Trimberger, Ellen Kay. *Bureaucratic Revolution from Above: A Comparative Study of the Modernization of Japan and Turkey*. New Brunswick, N.J.: Transaction Books, 1975.

Troncoso, Moises, and Burnett, Ben. *The Rise of the Latin American Labor Movement*. New Haven: College and University Press, 1960.

Turk, Herman. "Interorganizational Networks in Urban Society: Initial Perspectives and Comparative Research." *American Sociological Review* 35 (February 1970), 1-18.

Turner, Frederick. "The Compatibility of Church and State in Mexico." *Journal of Inter-American Studies* 9 (October 1967).

Turner, John. "Housing Priorities, Settlement Patterns and Urban Development in Modernizing Countries." *Journal of the American Institute of Planners* 34 (November 1968), 354-63.

Ugalde, Antonio. *Power and Conflict in a Mexican Community*. Albuquerque: University of New Mexico Press, 1970.

Unikel, Luis. "El proceso de urbanización en México." *Demografía y Economía* 2 (1968), 139-82.

United Nations Industrial Development Organization. *Small-Scale Industry in Latin America*. New York: United Nations, 1969.

United States, Department of Agriculture. *Changes in Agriculture in 26 Developing Countries: 1948 to 1963*. Washington, D.C.: Department of Agriculture, Economic Research Service, November 1965.

Valencia, Enrique. *La merced: Estudio ecológico y social de una zona de la Ciudad de México*. Mexico, D.F.: Instituto Nacional de Anthropología e Historia, Serie Investigaciones 11, 1965.

Valentine, Charles. *Culture and Poverty*. Chicago: University of Chicago Press, 1968.

Vallier, Ivan. *Catholicism, Social Control and Modernization in Latin America*. Englewood Cliffs, N.J.: Prentice-Hall, 1970.

Vaupel, James, and Curhan, Joan. *The World's Multinational Enterprises: A Sourcebook of Tables*. Boston: Division of Research, Harvard Business School, 1973.

Vekemans, Roger, and Guisti, Jorge. "Marginality and Ideology in Latin American Development." *Studies in Comparative International Development* 5 (1969-70).

Verba, Sidney, and Nie, Norman. *Participation in America*. New York: Harper and Row, 1972.

Vernon, Raymond. *The Dilemma of Mexico's Development*. Cambridge: Harvard University Press, 1963.

————. *Sovereignty at Bay: The Multi-national Spread of U.S. Enterprises*. New York: Basic Books, 1971.

———— (ed.). *Public Policy and Private Enterprise in Mexico*. Cambridge: Harvard University Press, 1964.

La villa. 1964-1966. Weekly newspaper. Mexico, D.F.

Villarreal, René. "External Disequilibrium, Economic Growth without Development: The Import Substitution Model, the Mexican Experience (1929-1974)." Paper presented at the Center for Inter-American Relations, New York, March 1975.

Wagley, Charles. "From Caste to Class in North Brazil." *Comparative Perspectives on Race Relations*, edited by Melvin Tumin. Boston: Little, Brown, 1969.

Wallerstein, Immanuel. "The Rise and Future Demise of the World Capitalist System: Concepts for Comparative Analysis." *Comparative Studies in Society and History* 16 (September 1974), 387-415.

Ward, Robert. "Common Problems in Field Research." In *Studying Politics Abroad: Field Research in the Developing Areas*, edited by Robert Ward. Boston: Little, Brown, 1964.

Warren, Bill. "Imperialism and Capitalist Industrialization." *New Left Review* 81 (September-October 1973).

Weber, Max. *The Protestant Ethic and the Spirit of Capitalism.* New York: Charles Scribner's Sons, 1958.

Wechstein, R. S. "Evaluating Land Reform." *Economic Development and Cultural Change* 18 (April 1970), 391-409.

Weffort, Francisco. "State and Mass in Brasil." In *Masses in Latin America*, edited by Irving Horowitz. New York: Oxford University Press, 1970.

Weiskoff, Richard. "Income Distribution and Economic Growth in Puerto Rico, Argentina, and Mexico." New Haven: Yale University Growth Center, Papers No. 162, 197.

Whetten, Nathan, and Burnight, Robert. "Internal Migration in Mexico." *Rural Sociology* 21 (June 1956).

Whiteford, Andrew. *Two Cities of Latin America.* Garden City, New York: Doubleday, 1964.

Whyte, William. *Street Corner Society.* Chicago: University of Chicago Press, 1969.

Wilkie, James. *The Mexican Revolution: Federal Expenditures and Social Change Since 1910.* Berkeley: University of California Press, 1967.

Willems, Emileo. "Culture Change and the Rise of Protestantism in Brazil and Chile." In *The Protestant Ethic and Modernization*, edited by S. N. Eisenstadt. New York: Basic Books, 1968.

Williams, Lawrence; Whyte, William; and Green, Charles. "Do Cultural Differences Affect Workers' Attitudes?" In *Workers and Managers in Latin America*, edited by Stanley Davis and Louis Goodman. Lexington, Mass.: D. C. Heath, 1972.

Wilson, Bryan. "An Analysis of Sect Development." *American Sociological Review* 24 (1959), 3-15.

Wilson, Charles. "Social Organization of Mexican Factories." New York: Ph.D. dissertation, Columbia University, 1969.

Wirth, Louis. "Urbanism as a Way of Life." *American Journal of Sociology* 44 (July 1938), 1-24.

Wolfinger, Raymond. "Reputation and Reality in the Study of 'Community Power.'" In *The Structure of Community Power*, edited by Michael Aiken and Paul Mott. New York: Random House, 1970.

Yinger, J. Milton. *Religion in the Struggle for Power*. Durham, N.C.: Duke University Press, 1946.

Zeitlin, Maurice. *Revolutionary Politics and the Cuban Working Class*. New York: Harper and Row, 1970.

Library of Congress Cataloging in Publication Data

Eckstein, Susan, 1942–
    The poverty of revolution.

    Bibliography: p.
    Includes index.
    1. Poor—Mexico. 2. Slums—Mexico. 3. Squatters—
Mexico. 4. Housing—Mexico. I. Title.
HV4051.A5E4   362.5'0972   76-3253
ISBN 0-691-09367-9

DATE DUE